A STUDENT PERSONNEL PROGRAM
for
HIGHER EDUCATION

A STUDENT PERSONNEL PROGRAM
for
HIGHER EDUCATION

BY

ESTHER McD. LLOYD-JONES, Ph.D.

Associate Professor of Education, Associate Director of Student Personnel, in Charge of the Guidance Laboratory, Teachers College, Columbia University; Past President of the American College Personnel Association

AND

MARGARET RUTH SMITH, Ph.D.

Director of Personnel for Women, Northwest Missouri State Teachers College; Formerly Social Director, Martha Cook Building, University of Michigan

First Edition

McGRAW-HILL BOOK COMPANY, Inc.
NEW YORK AND LONDON
1938

COPYRIGHT, 1938, BY THE
MCGRAW-HILL BOOK COMPANY, INC.

PRINTED IN THE UNITED STATES OF AMERICA

All rights reserved. This book, or parts thereof, may not be reproduced in any form without permission of the publishers.

THE MAPLE PRESS COMPANY, YORK, PA.

PREFACE

This book attempts to outline a total personnel program, to show its purpose in the total program of higher education, and to show the various aspects of the personnel program in relation to each other.

We do not here argue elaborately the question as to whether, if education included a good personnel program, we might mistake the total result merely for a good system of higher education. In fact, we think this is what very desirably would happen. We do believe, however, that, if the program of personnel work herein outlined were to be intelligently applied, the character of higher education would inevitably be altered.

Two other questions with which many thoughtful people are concerned, we hope find answer here. The first is whether or not personnel work encourages the "coddling" of students—whether or not personnel work, by its very nature, tends to paternalism.

To some extent all advances in civilization might be considered to have "softening" effects on the individual. Ruthlessness is minimized by civilization; intelligent planning based on prognostication is increasingly evoked in an attempt to avoid wasteful consequences. We have tried to make it clear that the personnel program we advocate is not "softly" paternalistic—although it does concern itself with the genuine welfare of each student. Nor are we concerned in saving individuals from the consequences of their own experimentation and of their own mistakes, unless the consequences promise ultimately to be too wasteful of energy and human values.

The second question concerns the pretension which some people feel that the personnel program makes that "it will develop the student." It should be clear here that the personnel program includes no suggestion of black magic, no hocus-pocus that will reveal all and solve all problems. It should, on the other hand, be evident that the authors are vitally concerned with developing social, healthful, intellectually stimulating environments within the frame of higher education in which the sound development of students will most surely take place. To be sure, the quality of the environment must continuously be tested out by studying whether or not, in each individual student, desirable development *is* taking place, and studying how further environmental modification might be made in order to improve the opportunities offered students to advance their own development.

We do not in any sense disclaim the importance of individual counseling in the personnel program. Very often it is the direct influence of some really great personality that provides the leverage for desirable personality change. But we do maintain that the personnel program is in no way limited to the more or less direct and individual dynamics that counseling affords. Very important in the personnel program are all the efforts to provide individuals and groups with the services and the settings conducive to the development so highly desired in individuals of college caliber.

We have used a number of titles in a somewhat parallel sense throughout the book: director of personnel, dean of students, vice-president, dean of men, dean of women. All these titles are being used in different institutions as though the duties involved were synonomous. It would be convenient if we could agree upon some one title that would designate clearly the person in each institution who was responsible for the direction of the personnel program. Since the executive heads of all our colleges and universities, however, are not unanimously called "president," perhaps we need not mourn too greatly over the fact that the heads of the personnel programs in various institutions throughout the country will probably not answer conveniently to some one title.

We have usually, in this book, referred to the person who heads the personnel program as "he." This pronoun is used in the well-known generic sense. It must be confessed, however, that there was unquestionably in the minds of the authors as they wrote a subconscious realization that the biases and mores of our time would probably operate to have men (not in a generic sense) appointed to the most important positions in this field, especially as it became increasingly apparent how important these positions may be. We cannot refrain from urging, however, that presidents consider carefully the desirability of using these positions to bring more influentially into the field of higher education outstanding women, well-trained and richly endowed with the human qualities so important in anyone to whom is entrusted the direction of the sort of program herein described.

This book does not pretend to deal exhaustively with every phase of the personnel program. There is much amplification of every aspect that could profitably be made. The authors know of books now in process which will deal with each aspect of the personnel program. The selected bibliographies presented at the end of each chapter indicate that attention has already been given to all parts of the program. There is evidence in these bibliographies, however, of unevenness. Some fields need development far more than others; the knowledge of some of the aspects of personnel work seems unnecessarily limited, while scholarship continues to be turned generously to certain fields that have already yielded rich rewards.

It has been the purpose of the authors in this book to discuss an aspect of higher education which might well receive more attention. It is our hope that college administrative officers will find here suggestions for educational programs; that college instructors may find new encouragement for the personnel work so many of them are already carrying on; that each personnel specialist will see more clearly the part his particular specialty should play in the whole personnel program; and that those in charge of student personnel programs will find their imaginations quickened and their thinking clarified in surveying anew the personnel programs which it is their responsibility to direct in the interest of the young men and women students in our colleges and universities.

ESTHER McD. LLOYD-JONES,
MARGARET RUTH SMITH.

NEW YORK,
July, 1938.

CONTENTS

PREFACE......................... v

PART I
PHILOSOPHY AND ORGANIZATION OF THE STUDENT PERSONNEL PROGRAM

CHAPTER I
RELATION OF THE STUDENT PERSONNEL PROGRAM TO HIGHER EDUCATION................. 3

CHAPTER II
WHAT IS "THE STUDENT PERSONNEL PROGRAM"?..... 16

CHAPTER III
THE SCOPE AND ORGANIZATION OF THE STUDENT PERSONNEL PROGRAM.................... 26

PART II
FUNCTIONS OF THE STUDENT PERSONNEL PROGRAM

CHAPTER IV
SELECTING AND ADMITTING STUDENTS (SELECTION AND ADMISSIONS).................... 51

CHAPTER V
HELPING STUDENTS TO BELONG TO COLLEGE (ORIENTATION) 70

CHAPTER VI
HELPING STUDENTS TO LEARN SOCIAL WISDOM AND SKILL (THE SOCIAL PROGRAM)............... 92

CHAPTER VII
GIVING STUDENTS INDIVIDUALIZED HELP (COUNSELING).. 102

CHAPTER VIII
More about Giving Students Individualized Help (Discipline).................119

CHAPTER IX
Helping Students to Make and to Realize Educational and Vocational Plans (Educational and Vocational Guidance)................129

CHAPTER X
Helping Students Financially and Helping Them to Help Themselves (Financial Aid).........147

CHAPTER XI
Facilitating and Directing the Organized Extraclass Life of Students (Extracurricular Activities)..165

CHAPTER XII
Educating Students through Housing Environment (Housing)..................190

CHAPTER XIII
Educating Students to Live Healthfully (Health)..209

CHAPTER XIV
Helping Students to Discover Values (Religion)...220

CHAPTER XV
Helping Alumni to Get Jobs (Placement).........235

CHAPTER XVI
Keeping Account of Educational Assets and Liabilities, Efforts and Results (Student Personnel Records).....................247

CHAPTER XVII
Administering the Personnel Office (Office Administration)....................265

CHAPTER XVIII
Studying the Objectives, Processes, and Results of the Personnel Program (Research and Evaluation)......................278

Appendix.........................291

Index............................313

PART I
PHILOSOPHY AND ORGANIZATION OF THE STUDENT PERSONNEL PROGRAM

Chapter I

RELATION OF THE STUDENT PERSONNEL PROGRAM TO HIGHER EDUCATION

The failure of those writing in the personnel field to relate student personnel work to some understood philosophy of higher education has automatically deprived many educators in the latter field of an interest in, and appreciation of, what a student personnel program is and how it can contribute to the development of youth in our colleges and universities. One reason for this failure is that at present there are no generally accepted philosophies of higher education. The problem of a proper collegiate education for the youth of this country has stimulated the flow of a great many words during the past 10 years. But those attempting to formulate a statement of the philosophy and function of higher education are by no means, as yet, in agreement. Most of those writing about student personnel work during this same period have apparently tried to avoid involvement in the general confusion by ignoring the problem of its relation to the total task of higher education. There is in much of the discussion of personnel work a tacit assumption of an underlying philosophy, but this is entirely too indefinite for those who are not already sympathetic with the personnel point of view.

From the standpoint of the present authors, it seems eminently worth while to attempt to establish a point of view with regard to higher education so that the student personnel program herein proposed may be viewed in relation to that point of view.

If one selects statements from the writings of those who are concerned with the larger purposes of higher education, it becomes clear how sharply conflicting their points of view are. Flexner, for instance, has said that "secondary education involves a responsibility of an intimate kind for the student, for the subject-matter he studies, even for the way in which he works, lives, and conducts himself—for his manner, his morals, and his mind," but that "the university has no such complicated concern."[1]

Hutchins maintains that "the university is intellectual. It is wholly and completely so."[2] "In general education we may wisely leave experience to life and set about our job of intellectual training."[3] "The three worst words in education are 'character,' 'personality,' and 'facts.'"[4]

From quite a different point of view we have men like Wriston of Brown proclaiming: "College is an experience both individual and social; it is intellectual, physical, emotional, spiritual. It is a time for the maturation of personality."[5] And Lowell of Harvard points out: "Aristotle remarked that man is by nature a social animal; and it is in order to develop his powers as a social being that American Colleges exist. The object of the undergraduate department is not to produce hermits, each imprisoned in the cell of his own intellectual pursuits, but men fitted to take their places in the community and live in contact with their fellow-men."[6]

This confliction of ideas is not confined to the present time for the whole history of higher education shows a succession of varying points of view. Duffus summarizes certain of the major steps in the progression that has taken place in the patterns of collegiate education:

[1] FLEXNER, ABRAHAM, *Universities: American, English, German*, pp. 28–29, Oxford University Press, New York, 1930.

[2] HUTCHINS, ROBERT MAYNARD, *The Higher Learning in America*, p. 118, Yale University Press, New Haven, 1936.

[3] *Ibid.*, p. 70.

[4] HUTCHINS, ROBERT MAYNARD, *No Friendly Voice*, p. 29, University of Chicago Press, Chicago, 1936.

[5] WRISTON, HENRY MERRITT, "The Integrity of the College," *School and Society*, 43 (1102): 183–193, Feb. 8, 1936.

[6] LOWELL, A. LAWRENCE, in W. H. Cowley, "The College Guarantees Satisfaction," *Educational Record*, 16 (1): 27–48, January, 1935.

The old pattern of college education broke down as new subjects forced their way into the curriculum; the result of this breakdown was a period of educational anarchy in which it became almost impossible for educators to agree on the content or objectives of a college course, and in which educational standards were threatened because no one could define them; the next step was an attempt to reduce education to mathematical units; this attempt failed because it was found that units, hours, and credits did not and could not measure the student's achievement or present worth; and the current tendency is toward the evaluation of the individual student and the use of that evaluation as a basis for his further education . . . In almost every college worthy of the name some effort is being made to break down mass education, to furnish individual guidance, to take advantage of the individual student's tastes, enthusiasms and abilities, to put less emphasis upon enforced classroom exercises and more upon self-propelled activities, and, in short, to set the student free to educate himself and test him by his success in doing so.[1]

The idea which Duffus believes is challenging the attention of higher education today is not new. On the contrary, it is deeply embedded in the thinking of some of the world's major social philosophers. The psychology of individual differences from which many personnel activities have grown is but a recognition by science and education of an age-old philosophical insight. Plato in his *Republic* presented many concepts which are theses of the modern theory of differential education. In 1695 John Locke said in *Some Thoughts Concerning Education:*

He, therefore, that is about children, should well study their natures and aptitudes, and see, by often trials, what turn they easily take, and what becomes them; observe what their native stock is, how it may be improved, and what it is fit for: He should consider, what they want; whether they be capable of having it wrought into them by industry, and incorporated there by practice; and whether it be worthwhile to endeavor it. For in many cases, all that we can do, or should aim at, is to make the

[1] DUFFUS, R. L., *Democracy Enters College*, pp. 234–235, Charles Scribner's Sons, New York, 1936.

best of what nature has given; to prevent the vices and faults to which such a constitution is most inclined, and give it all the advantages it is capable of. Everyone's natural genius should be carried as far as it could, but to attempt the putting another upon him, will be but labor in vain; and what is so plaister'd on will at best fit but untowardly, and have always hanging to it the ungracefulness of constraint and affectation.

Speaking at the N.E.A. meetings in 1892, in Saratoga, N. Y., Charles W. Eliot, then President of Harvard University, made this statement:[1]

Democratic society does not undertake to fly in the face of nature by asserting that all children are . . . alike and should be treated alike. . . . Every child is a unique personality. It follows, of course, that uniform programmes and uniform methods of instruction, applied simultaneously to large numbers of children, must be unwise and injurious. . . . It is for the interest of society . . . that every individual child's peculiar gifts and powers should be developed and trained to the highest degree. . . . We all know that children, like adults, are not alike, but infinitely different; that the object of education, as of life, is to bring out the innate power, and develop to the highest possible degree the natural and acquired capacities of each individual.

In 1902 Dewey told us that "personality and character is more than subject matter," that "we must take our stand with the child and our departure from him," and that "it is he and not subject matter which determines quality and quantity of learning."[2]

But while we have been told these truths many times by outstanding thinkers and although Duffus believes higher education is beginning to apply them to itself, nevertheless it is our opinion that colleges and universities have not yet done very well at representing them in practice. If higher

---

[1] ELIOT, CHARLES W., "Undesirable and Desirable Uniformity in Schools," p. 83, and "Shortening and Enriching the Grammar School Course," p. 621, *Proceedings of National Education Association*, 1892.

[2] DEWEY, JOHN, *The Child and the Curriculum*, pp. 13–14, University of Chicago Press, Chicago, 1902.

education were to make full use of programs of personnel work to individualize education and to take practical cognizance of each individual student's needs, capacities, abilities, and possibilities, we should have moved much closer to an ideal of education that has much to commend it.

A survey of literature and practice leads one to the conclusion that there are two major cleavage lines in the philosophies of those who work in the field of higher education at the present time: (1) The first of these lines tends to divide:

(a) those who interpret "preparation for life" predominantly in a vocational, professional, utilitarian sense

from

(b) those who interpret "preparation for life" from a broader standpoint as including properly one's ability to function successfully in nonvocational activities and relationships; those who believe that there is an "art of living" which is as important as the "business of earning a living."

We live in an era that tends to gauge successful living in terms of one's ability to earn money. To some extent one's money-earning ability is an indication of one's value to society, but even the most vocationally minded must admit that it is only a rough measure. Certainly no one would be content to name as his list of most valuable members of society those with the top incomes in this country. It is probably true that those who have, throughout history, made the most valuable contributions to society have never had commensurate economic reward. The truly great of history have never seemed to be animated primarily by economic concern. Certainly few women would concede that their "life" consisted most importantly of money-earning activities. Nor are those men who are the best money earners always the best husbands and fathers. Other things being equal, it is certainly desirable for each to be able to contribute vocationally in such a way as to be able to secure economic rewards sufficient to permit him to command what he needs for comfortable living. But "life" is usually, after all, a much bigger thing for most people than their vocational or professional activities, and any really adequate higher education must recognize this fact. Each student in higher education, in addition to learning more or less directly how to *do* something for society that will have economic rewards for the doer, must also learn to *be* someone who can contribute to society other values than purely economic ones.

The student personnel program in higher education must find its role with respect to these opposed points of view. There are some personnel workers who tend to think of themselves only in relation to the vocational interests and aims of students and who limit their efforts to helping students work out their occupational plans and secure placement in jobs. Educational guidance for these personnel workers finds its exclusive objective in eventual occupational adjustment. Personnel work, for those who think in terms of such a utilitarian philosophy of higher education, consists exclusively, or certainly most importantly, of educational and vocational guidance and of job-placement activities. The other aspects of the personnel program, consisting of social education, housing, health, religion, discipline, etc., lie outside the field of interest and effort of these personnel workers.

If the personnel program is to be adequate to what we see as its role in higher education, however, it must be fully as concerned with the art of living as it is with the more utilitarian aspects of education. It must concern itself with the student as he is at present, with the sort of design for living that he is working out for himself *right now*, just as fully as it must concern itself with the eventual vocational adjustment which the student will be able to make.

The comparative emphasis that is given to the art of living versus the business of earning a living varies greatly in the various institutions of higher education: professional schools are much more concerned, of course, with technical proficiency, while liberal arts colleges are usually more concerned with the less professional aspects of culture. There seems to the authors, however, to be a tendency for professional schools to recognize increasingly the importance of the "nonprofessional" aspects of professional education at the same time that liberal arts colleges are including in their educational programs more consideration for the vocational futures of their students.

Personnel programs in every institution of higher education, whether it be primarily a technical or a professional or a "cultural" institution, cannot escape responsibility for considering *all* aspects of the student. No student can be understood adequately, nor can he be educated most successfully, nor can he live most effectively on the basis of any one or a few aspects of his personality alone. All personnel work with students must take into account, not only present and potential professional knowledge and skill and abstract verbal intelligence, but also physical health, social knowledge and skill, ability to make and keep friends, artistic appreciation, practical managerial ability, emotional stability, and all the other personal attributes that so thoroughly condition the kind of life that anyone will be able to live and the total contribution which he will be able to make to society.

(2) The second of the two major cleavage lines separates

(a) those who tend to think of education primarily in terms of *a body of culture* to be transmitted

from

(b) those who think of education as *a process* that goes on in those who are to be modified by, and who are (incidentally) to transmit, that culture.

The student personnel program in higher education must find its role with respect to these opposed points of view also. Those educators who tend to think of education primarily in terms of a body of culture to be transmitted are usually themselves scholars, intent on increasing the body of scholarship itself. They, rather naturally, tend to exalt intellectuality as something that can profitably be separated from the other aspects of the individual. In attempting to deal with intellect without regard for other aspects of the organism, they introduce a dualism which is entirely contrary to the findings of psychology, biology, and psychiatry.

Certain personnel workers, misled by the philosophy of the 2(a) group above, have tended to think of themselves as concerned rather exclusively with facilitating the intellectual objectives of the college. These personnel workers have spent a great deal of their time and effort in analyzing intellectual abilities of students, with little or no concern for them as total personalities. These personnel workers typically test and retest students, they spend years of their lives studying relationships between I.Q.'s and class marks; they find their high calling in making more and better tests of "intellectual intelligence" (as Thorndike calls it); they live to make more, and more authoritative, pronouncements in the field of educational guidance and study habits, usually without criticism for the curriculum or the current educational method. They accept uncritically the dualism which the academic scholars, to whom we have already alluded, have been content to maintain in the face of overwhelming counter evidence.

On the other hand, there are an increasing number of personnel workers, well-grounded in psychology, the biological sciences, and educational philosophy, who, while they by no means underestimate the importance of intelligence, are as thoroughly cognizant of the importance of the emotional, social, and physical aspects of the student as they are of the purely intellectual. These personnel workers consider it comparable to tilting at windmills to argue elaborately against continuing to accept in our educational practice a dualism which sets intelligence over against the other attributes of the individual.

In our opinion, the student personnel program must take its stand with those who conceive of the student not only as an intellect, but also as a total organism whose learnings, even at eighteen years of age, are importantly conditioned by the way he acts and feels, as well as by the words he reads and hears and by his logical thought. The student personnel program must be built on a recognition of the essential interrelation between thought, feeling, and action.

We would certainly minimize in no way the responsibility that the college or university has for maintaining and enriching the culture which is the most precious heritage we have from the experience, scholarship, research and creative imagination of past generations. We do maintain, however, that the transmission and enrichment of that culture can be accomplished more fully if the total nature of the present agents (college students) in all their countless varieties is taken into account by every means that science and experience afford. We also maintain that individuals do (and should) possess, and are (and should be) possessed by, their physical bodies, social drives, emotions, interests, and aesthetic tastes as fully as they possess, and are possessed by, their minds. Day-by-day living in college should be such as to bring all of these aspects into an increasingly effective balance. Personnel workers should certainly be among those who maintain that the agents for the transmission and enrichment of culture are important and worth while, not only because they are agents, but also in and of themselves; that living should not all be in terms of the future but that it is worth while for each "present" to be as full and immediately rewarding as possible; that only thus are all of society's interests best served.

Concretely, this means that, if the student personnel program is to serve higher education well, it must include within its scope a concern not only for educational guidance, intelligence testing, the selection and admission of students, etc., but also health programs, social programs, counseling, religious programs, housing programs, extracurricular activities, etc. It furthermore means, if we are to implement our theories effectively, that these various programs, set up to serve the various aspects of the student, must all be well coordinated so that they will not function separately but rather with a common viewpoint and in relation to each other.

Is it too ambitious for higher education to set itself all of the following objectives and to attempt to maintain a careful balance of all:

1. To preserve and transmit cultural information on an advanced level (certainly there is a very valuable portion of our hard-won racial heritage that can be preserved only through the agency of the kind of minds that go to college).

2. To stimulate and discipline the habits of thinking of a large group of our best minds.

3. To enrich culture through the creation of new elements and the unique combination of old elements.

4. To increase each student's understanding of the economic and social structure and needs of the world, to increase his interest in effectively contributing his efforts to meet these needs, and, more or less directly, to increase his knowledge and skill in some technical or professional field.

5. To arrange controllable forces and situations during college years so as to encourage social growth, aesthetic appreciations, spiritual insight, and physical, mental, and emotional health, and moral conduct in each student.

6. So to individualize method as to contribute most effectively to *each* student's self-realization, high purpose and wise planning for the immediate and more distant future, in relation to his present status and to the greatest extent possible within the limits of time allotted to the period of such higher education.

The emphasis placed on each of these six objectives of higher education will always vary from institution to institution. The personnel program in each institution must adapt itself to the objectives of that particular institution. The personnel program must, as an integral part of the whole educational program of any institution, implement the objectives of the institution to which it belongs with all the skills and wisdom that can be brought to bear from the various sciences upon which personnel work draws.

It is our belief, however, that, if the personnel program is wisely conceived and well directed and executed, the objectives of the institution will gradually be modified. Educational shortages will be revealed, while at the same time methods for remedying them will be available. Instructors, better trained in understanding subject matter than in understanding adolescents, will find interpreters at hand. Instructors will find skilled assistants to help them answer the questions which Kent so shrewdly asks:

1. Do those taught actually master what we think they do?
2. Does what is mastered have the meanings for students that we claim it to have?
3. What is the effect upon individuals of the studies they pursue and of the other procedures to which they are subjected in their experience called education?[1]

Engaged in the personnel program will be trained individuals to supervise and render educationally most profitable those experiences outside the classroom which constitute an important part of the total learnings during college years. Active in the personnel program will be those who are especially competent to influence and control the conditions under which students live while in college, the conditions that indirectly determine the way students will be disposed to behave and determine the attitudes they will acquire.

[1] KENT, RAYMOND A., "Implications of the Youth Problem," *Occupations*, 15: 694–704, May, 1937,

The personnel program should not be thought of as a "fifth wheel" of education. It is an integral part of higher education, bringing to bear the findings of psychology, biology, and sociology to help higher education actually realize its objectives by adapting them to the needs, capacities, abilities, and potentialities of each student.

Higher education finds prepared to its hand, in the personnel program, tools and methods for understanding individuals so that education can be effectively individualized and, consequently, students may become increasingly self-directing and successful in making and realizing worthwhile plans for themselves and for society.

BIBLIOGRAPHY

American Council on Education Studies, "The Student Personnel Point of View," vol. 1, ser. 2, no. 3, 14 pp.

BERTOCCI, PETER A.: "We Send Them to College—to Be Confused," *Journal of Higher Education*, 8: 343–350, October, 1937.

BREWER, JOHN M.: *Education as Guidance*, The Macmillan Company, New York, 1932, ix + 668 pp.

COLLIGAN, EUGENE A.: "Training Teachers for Guidance," *Report of Third Educational Conference under Auspices of Committee on Personnel Methods on Educational Testing of American Council on Education, Commission on Relation of School and College of Progressive Education Association, Cooperative Test Service, and Educational Records Bureau*, New York, Nov. 1, 2, 1934, pp. 150–162.

COWLEY, W. H.: "The College Guarantees Satisfaction," *Educational Record*, 16: 27–48, January, 1935.

DEWEY, JOHN: *The Child and the Curriculum*, University of Chicago Press, Chicago, 1902, 40 pp.

———: *Human Nature and Conduct*, Henry Holt & Company, New York, 1922, vii + 336 pp.

DUFFUS, R. L.: *Democracy Enters College*, Charles Scribner's Sons, New York, 1936, ix + 244 pp.

ELIOT, CHARLES W.: "Undesirable and Desirable Uniformity in Schools," *Proceedings of National Education Association*, 1892, pp. 82–95.

———: "Shortening and Enriching the Grammar School Course," *Proceedings of National Education Association*, 1892, pp. 617–625.

FLEXNER, ABRAHAM: *Universities: American, English, German*, Oxford University Press, New York, 1930, x + 381 pp.

GIDEONSE, HARRY DAVID: *The Higher Learning in a Democracy; a Reply to President Hutchins' Critique of the University* Farrar & Rinehart Inc., New York, 1937, 34 pp.

GRAY, WILLIAM S. (Ed.): "General Education: Its Nature, Scope and Essential Elements," in *Proceedings of the Institute for Administrative Officers of Higher Institutions*, vol. VI, University of Chicago Press, Chicago, 1934, 184 pp.

HAWKES, HERBERT E.: "Values in Personnel Work," in W. S. Gray (Ed.), *Provision for the Individual in College Education*, pp., 21–27, University of Chicago Press, Chicago, 1932.

HUTCHINS, ROBERT MAYNARD: *The Higher Learning in America*, Yale University Press, New Haven, 1936, 119 pp.

———: *No Friendly Voice*, University of Chicago Press, Chicago, 1936, viii + 197 pp.

JESSUP, WALTER ALBERT: "The Integrity of the American College from the Standpoint of Administration," *School and Society*, 43: 177–183, Feb. 8, 1936.

KALLEN, HORACE M.: *College Prolongs Infancy*, Réynal & Hitchcock, Inc., New York, 1932, 28 pp.

KENT, RAYMOND A.: "Implications of the Youth Problem," *Occupations*, 15: 694–704, May, 1937.

LOCKE, JOHN: *Some Thoughts Concerning Education* (with introduction and notes by R. H. Quick), Cambridge University Press, London, 1913, 40 pp.

Republic of Plato, An Ideal Commonwealth, translated by Benjamin Jowett, M. A., rev. ed., John Wiley & Sons, Inc., New York, 1901, xciv + 329 pp.

REYNOLDS, ROLLO G.: "The Teacher's Part in Guidance." *Teachers College Record*, 37: 691–697, May, 1936.

WOOD, BEN D.: "Criteria of Individualized Education," *Occupations*, 14: 781–786, May, 1936.

———: "Neglected Functions of the Guidance Officer," *Report of the Ninth Annual Meeting, New York State Association of Deans, Bulletin* 5: 10–13, Nov. 8–9, 1935.

WRISTON, HENRY MERRITT: "The Integrity of the College," *School and Society*, 43: 183–193, Feb. 8, 1936.

———: *Nature of a Liberal College*, Lawrence College Press, Appleton, Wis., 1937, 117 pp.

CHAPTER II

WHAT IS "THE STUDENT PERSONNEL PROGRAM"?

Certainly one of the difficulties that the personnel movement in education has faced is a verbal one. Terminology in this field has proven a bête noire. "Guidance," "vocational guidance," "educational guidance," "counseling," "placement," "personnel work," "personnel point of view," "personnel research," "personnel administration," all have been used in any number of senses, to the great confusion of all concerned.

General educational administrators are not the only ones who are pretty thoroughly bewildered about it; one has only to attempt an organizational study among the personnel officers on almost any campus, one has only to be familiar with the situation as regards national organizations of personnel workers, to recognize that those who are themselves engaged in the personnel field are many of them afflicted with a myopia that has not yet been satisfactorily corrected. There are a number of reasons for this confusion in terminology, and technicians in the personnel field, generalists in the personnel field, and general educators have all contributed to it.

The various specialized kinds of personnel work require the services of highly trained technicians, specialists who are highly, but, on the whole, narrowly, trained. These men and women tend to be impatient over what seems to them "agonizing over words." These "tree doctors" are often uninterested in the forest. Many of these personnel experts have believed, because of ignorance of the importance of other specialties, that their own especial undertaking must certainly include the whole and must, indeed, be IT about which there was arising such general interest. One of the drives of such scientifically trained people is to break into print as often as possible. This group has done its fair share to build the Tower of Babel which has arisen in that general area often designated as student personnel work.

The personnel specialists are not, however, the only ones responsible for the confusion of terminology in this field. Many others, not technically trained, who for years have had general charge of the forest, have thought, as they saw the "tree doctors" receive such interested attention, that they certainly comprehended the whole and deserved as much recognition as the specialists. They have attempted to take over possessively and somewhat indiscriminately as many as possible of the terms used in the field.

Teachers, genuinely interested in students, imbued with what they now were hearing described as a "personnel point of view" have wondered why this "thing" publicized as new and remarkable was anything different from what they had long been doing with such satisfying results. We have, therefore, found a further confusion in an attempted complete identification of good teaching as "personnel work."

One college president recently told a group of educators that in his college they "had not gone in for any personnel work but they had a thoroughly fine plan of counseling." One can only guess what his description of personnel work would be. Another college president, who early established and has always loyally supported an efficient placement office in his institution, makes a complete identification of placement activities and personnel work. By a convenient psychological mechanism he totally disregards any references to personnel work that do not assume this identification.

It is not enough to clarify the relationship of the personnel field to higher education in general; it is also important to bring about a clearer understanding of the nature of the student personnel program itself. Philosophers have frequently pointed out how dependent thinking is on words. The whole matter of terminology in this field is important.[1]

The student personnel program has as many separately distinguishable aspects as has the curriculum. When one speaks of the curriculum he may describe the general, underlying philosophy of both its content and its method. But there are always, at the college level, specialized divisions of the curriculum which require highly trained, competent scholars to carry them forward. The total curriculum requires coordination and direction and administrative facilitation. In just the same way, the total student personnel program has a certain philosophy which animates it. The student personnel program includes highly specialized aspects (such as those described in Part II of this book) which require highly trained, competent people to carry them forward. And the total student personnel program requires coordination and direction and administrative facilitation.

If one attempted to discuss the curriculum with a college president who thought of the curriculum only as the study of Greek, who completely ignored the fact that art and science and many other considerations properly belonged within the topic under discussion, the confusion would certainly be great. Even though (to carry the analogy further) a teacher of mathematics who had never studied anthropology were able to win the complete admiration of a professor of anthropology for his fine, student-centered philosophy of teaching, still the professor of anthropology would be apt to challenge sharply the mathematics professor's expressed ambition to take over the anthropology classes in that institution. And, to carry the analogy still

[1] COWLEY, W. H., "The Nature of Student Personnel Work," *Educational Record*, 18: 198–226, April, 1936; LLOYD-JONES, ESTHER, "What Is This Thing Called Personnel Work," *Teachers College Record*, 38: 477–484, March, 1937; *Occupations*, 15: 718–723, May, 1937, "What Do We Mean by Guidance and Personnel in Education?" *School and Society*, 46: 261–266, August, 1937.

farther, the dean of instruction might have an admirable educational philosophy, he might be very skillful in administering and coordinating the instructional program of the institution, he might be very successful in developing the instructional staff, but certainly this would not justify him if he wished to claim expertness in every subject-matter field included within the curriculum.

The personnel aspect of the educational program is not a simple, unitary thing any more than is the curriculum. There seem to be three fairly distinguishable aspects to it. There is, first, what may be described as the personnel point of view. The personnel point of view regards sensitively the welfare of the student; it regards the individual differences from student to student; it considers the individual to be quite as dynamic and important an element in the learning process as is the stored-up culture of the race. This is, in reality, nothing but a philosophical point of view that has been stated over and over again by philosophers for many generations (see pages 5-6 of Chap. I), but one that is, as yet, by no means adequately represented in educational method. No claim is made that it is unique or new, but the claim is made that it could profitably animate the whole educational process far more than it does. This particular philosophical point of view, which coincides with what we shall designate as the personnel point of view, may well further modify the curricular program, methods of instruction, and the extracurricular program of the institution in order to place emphasis upon the individual student and his all-round development rather than upon his intellectual training alone. It would compel attention to Kent's provocative questions (see page 13). It would underlie all the aspects of the total program of student personnel work.[1]

---

[1] Some aspects of personnel work itself, though rooted originally in such a philosophy, have been known to forget their genesis and to become as mechanized and impersonal as any part of the curriculum ever was, as though robots instead of persons were being dealt with.

There are, second, within the student personnel program, a good many services, which, though closely related to the curricular program of the institution in many important ways, still are readily seen to be separate from it. These services include: the selecting and admitting of students to college; orienting the student to his new environment; studying the student by means of all tested diagnostic instruments to help him discover his abilities, aptitudes, and objectives; counseling with the student to sensitize him to the various choices open to him (choices which will condition his growth and development along many various lines) and to help him clarify his purposes as he makes his successive choices; coordinating and administering a program of financial aid and part-time work and assisting the student who needs it to obtain such help; determining the physical and mental health status of each student, providing appropriate remedial health measures, supervising the health of students, and controlling environmental health factors; setting up and administering a system of cumulative personnel records that give a continuous audit of the personal assets and possible points of weakness of each student for use in his educational program; providing a housing program for the maximum of social and educational values for students; supervising, evaluating, and developing the social life, interests, and extracurricular activities of students; administering student discipline to the end that the individual will be strengthened and the welfare of the group preserved; articulating college and postcollege experiences through counseling, and through placement; carrying on studies designed to evaluate and improve the personnel services; assembling and making available information to be used in the improvement of instruction and the more effective individualization of the curriculum.[1] These, taken all together, comprise a second

[1] American Council on Education, "The Student Personnel Point of View," *American Council on Education Studies*, series I, vol. I, no. 3, June, 1937.

aspect of the total program of student personnel work—the personnel services.

There is, in addition to the personnel point of view and the personnel services, a third aspect to the personnel program. This has to do with the supervision or direction of all the personnel services and is directly concerned with all college- or university-student relationships aside from formal instruction and routine business relationships. It has a direct responsibility for "bringing to bear upon each student all of those influences, of whatever nature, which will assist him through his own efforts to develop in body, mind, and character to the limit of his individual capacity for growth, and to help him apply his powers, so developed, most effectively to the work of the world."[1] This third aspect, of course, is the administrative aspect of student personnel work. The one in charge of the program of student personnel work should be an administrator; his is the responsibility for supervising and facilitating the various parts of the program of personnel work with the instructional program and with the business concerns of the institution.[2]

We might represent the student personnel program diagrammatically in some such fashion as this:

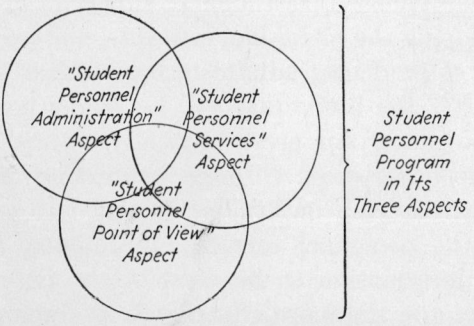

[1] CLOTHIER, ROBERT, "College Personnel Principles and Functions," (report of Committee on Principles and Functions), *Personnel Journal*, 10: 9–17, June, 1931.
[2] LLOYD-JONES, ESTHER, "Student Personnel Administration," *Journal of Higher Education*, 5: 141–147, March, 1934.

A STUDENT PERSONNEL PROGRAM

When we find our discussion about student personnel work confused, it may well be that there is unconscious exclusion of a legitimate aspect of the whole in the premises of the parties to the discussion, or that there may be a disconcerting jumping about from one to another of the aspects without a clear understanding of this fact.[1]

A diagrammatic representation of the relationship of the instructional program, the business administration, and the personnel program might take some such form as the following:

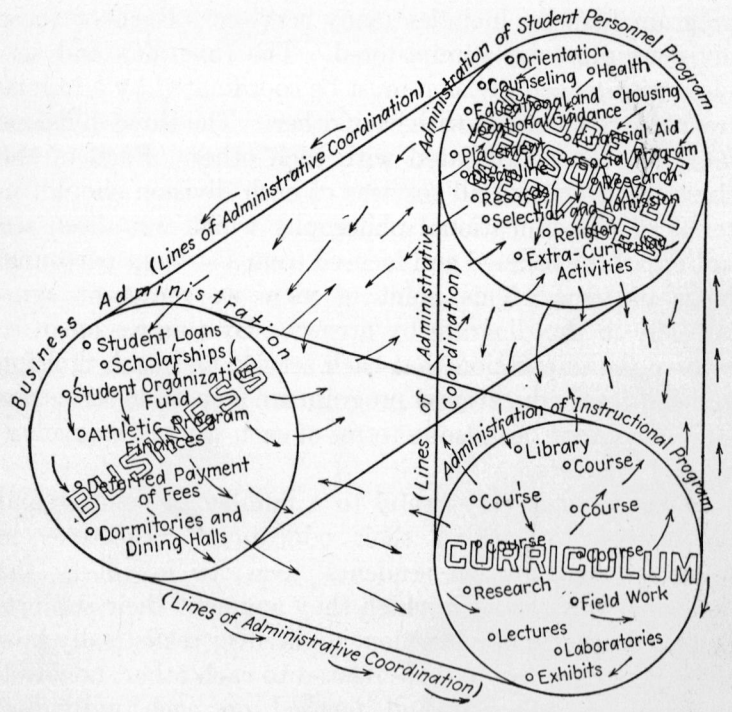

[1] Some of those thoughtfully concerned with the development of the student personnel program in higher education would add a fourth aspect: student personnel research. It seems to us unnecessary to do this, since evaluation is—or should—be involved in each activity and should not be laboriously introduced as something separate and important in and of itself. See chapter on Research and Evaluation (Chap. XVIII).

This diagram attempts to represent symbolically three divisions of the college or university organization: the business program, the student personnel program, and the instructional program. Each of these programs includes certain functions or services. The instructional program, for example, is made up of the library and its services and facilities, the many courses of instruction, laboratories, lectures, exhibits, field work, research, etc. The business division includes many functions and services, some of which (those included in the diagram) are closely related to the student personnel program. The student personnel program likewise includes many services. Each of these divisions must be administered. The functions and services within each division must be coordinated by administrative arrangements with each other. The three divisions must also be coordinated with each other. Each of the three divisions and all services of each division should, in terms of the educational philosophy which was discussed in Chap. I, be imbued and focused from a student personnel point of view. This point of view we represent symbolically in the diagram by arrows. By this we mean to convey the impression that each service and each division and the total educational program are focused in terms not only of content but also in terms of each student's developmental interests.

It has proved very useful to a number of colleges and universities to rethink their educational objectives in terms of outcomes in students' lives; to inventory the personnel services with which they augment their subject-matter programs of education; to discover realistically how these personnel services are related to each other, how well they are coordinated and focused on each individual student; and how the personnel services of the institution are related to the business and curricular programs of the institution. If there is a dean of men, does he administer the total student personnel program? Or is he, in reality, the director of housing for men, the director of the social program for men, the disciplinarian of the institution? Is there a counseling program? Who is involved in it, and who directs and coordinates it? Is there anyone to whom all the personnel services head up, who is actively engaged in improving the standards for the various services, in coordinating their efforts, in seeing from a vantage point how they impinge on each student; who is actively concerned to coordinate the student personnel program with the instructional program and the business administration of the institution?

The situation in most institutions at the present time is a pretty ragged one. There are a surprisingly large number of personnel services in most institutions, but little philosophy or organization. The heads of most of the services report directly to a president who is already burdened by so many administrative problems that he is able to do little but receive their reports. The head of each service regards himself as an independent entity instead of as a member of a total program related to many other personnel services, all of which are also important, and to the total educational program of the institution.

It is probably true that there are now a respectable number of individuals, trained expertly in certain of the personnel services, who are capable of taking charge of one or more of the personnel services which a college wishes to provide for its students. It is also probably true that there are not yet many individuals thoroughly grounded in a broad understanding of education and administration, familiar with the theory and principles of the various personnel services, competent to administer a program of student personnel work. Such individuals must be available in larger numbers before colleges and universities can have the sort of student personnel programs that contribute most to the development of students.

Colleges and universities will not and should not all balance their program of student personnel services in the same way: some will wish to make much of their social programs, for example, while others—especially professional schools—will want to put a great deal of emphasis on placement. But, increasingly, colleges and universities will want to strengthen their programs of student personnel work, will emphasize more strongly the personnel aspect of their educational philosophy, and will make more satisfactory provision for the supervision and coordination of the total student personnel program within itself and for its more satisfactory coordination with the total educational program of the institution.

BIBLIOGRAPHY

CLOTHIER, ROBERT C.: "College Personnel Principles and Functions" (report of Committee on Principles and Functions), *Personnel Journal,* 10: 9–17, June, 1931.

COWLEY, W. H.: "The College Guarantees Satisfaction," *Educational Record,* 16: 27–48, January, 1935.

———: "The Nature of Student Personnel Work," *Educational Record,* 18: 198–226, April, 1936.

LLOYD-JONES, ESTHER: "Personnel Administration," *Journal of Higher Education,* 5: 141–147, March, 1934.

———: "What Is This Thing Called Personnel Work?" *Teachers College Record,* 38: 477–484, March, 1937; *Occupations,* 15: 718–723, May, 1937.

MILLER, J. HILLIS: "Personnel Work—Adjunct or Education Itself?" *Report of Thirteenth Annual Meeting of the American College Personnel Association,* February, 1936, pp. 59–64.

Chapter III

THE SCOPE AND ORGANIZATION OF THE STUDENT PERSONNEL PROGRAM

Almost every writer in the field of student personnel work has emphasized the acceleration of interest in this field since 1920. Activity has increased by leaps and bounds. The number of published articles and books, the reports of research, and the increase in the number of personnel officers in colleges and universities are ample evidence of this fact. Cowley's *Personnel Bibliographical Index*, a publication of 1932, containing 2,138 titles, the *Partial List of Research Projects of the U.S. Office of Education*, giving the titles of 196 researches in the field of student personnel work which were under way during 1932 in institutions of higher learning, and the 582 investigations relating to guidance and personnel reported in 10 educational and psychological journals over a period of 10 years are all evidence that the personnel aspect of education is receiving important attention.[1]

It has long been thought desirable to obtain a sort of panoramic view of the recognition afforded personnel functions in institutions of higher education and to find out the way in which these functions are typically staffed at the present time. Experience has proved that it is impossible to get true organizational pictures of institutions without detailed and prolonged study. In one university where Lloyd-Jones attempted to survey the personnel work being done and to discover by whom it was performed, it was evident that those participating in the program had no clear ideas as to who was performing which personnel

[1] STRANG, RUTH M., "Developments in Student Personnel Research," *Teachers College Record*, 35 (2): 120–134, November, 1933.

functions or as to how those doing the various kinds of personnel work were related to each other and to other administrative officers of the institution. Although a great deal of thought had been spent on the student personnel program in that institution, even those most involved in the program still did not understand what the program as a whole was supposed to be, nor the roles which each member of the administrative and teaching staff was expected to play in it. It required months of study by an experienced and impartial outside agency before the situation was thoroughly clarified.

Perhaps this state of confused organization is not to be wondered at in colleges and universities. These are institutions where organization per se is typically not accorded much attention and where tenure of office acts constantly to distort organizational plan. In institutions of higher education, functions are often draped loosely, more in terms of local history, personal aggressions, and venerability than in terms of organizational plan and meaningful titles.

Since it was of questionable value to attempt to secure accurate reports of personnel organization from local personnel officers on various campuses (or even from college presidents), a compromise plan was adopted in order to attempt to secure some kind of picture of the personnel programs in colleges and universities today. Lloyd-Jones examined in detail the lists of faculty and administrative staff and their titles in recent catalogue announcements of 521 colleges and universities.[1] The 521 college and university catalogues analyzed were from those institutions listed in the reference book *American Universities and Colleges*, edited by John Henry McCracken and published by the American Council on Education in 1932. The functions which have been said by the American College Personnel Association to belong to a complete

[1] Prepared with the assistance of the United States Works Progress Administration for the City of New York, Project 65-97-295, Sub-project 7.

student personnel program[1] were the criteria used in scanning the lists of administrative officers and faculty titles. Obviously, it was impossible to discover in each of the 521 institutions who was actually performing each of the personnel functions that belong to a personnel program. A compromise was made by selecting from the many thousands of administrative and academic titles listed by these colleges and universities those titles which frequently imply the performance of at least some of the personnel functions. Deans of colleges, for example, often devote a great deal of their time to the educational counseling of students, to student discipline, to the administration of financial aid for students, etc., so that it was obviously necessary to list deans of colleges wherever one was discovered. Since secretaries to presidents are known frequently to carry responsibility for all sorts of personnel functions from assignment of housing to part-time employment, these titles are also included in the list. Although deans of women and of men are usually assigned specifically to perform certain personnel services for students and/or to administer the personnel program, a few instances are known to the authors where the person who holds this title does not even attempt to contribute anything to the personnel program, not even as much as many of the teaching faculty whose academic titles do not imply responsibility for student personnel work. All titles of deans of women and deans of men, however, were included in the list.

On the basis, then, of titles which frequently imply performances of one or more of the functions conceded to belong to the student personnel program, the following list of 6,850 persons was compiled (see pages 29–34). This number is probably as fair an indication as can be obtained at the present time of the tremendous number of people in

[1] CLOTHIER, ROBERT C., "College Personnel Principles and Functions" (report of the Committee on Principles and Functions), *Personnel Journal*, June, 1931, pp. 9–17.

higher education who are probably engaged in student personnel programs.

6,850 COLLEGE PERSONNEL OFFICERS, CLASSIFIED AS TO TITLE AND LISTED IN ORDER OF FREQUENCY OF MENTION IN 521 COLLEGE CATALOGUES

Dean	1394
Registrar	522
Director	495
Secretary	350
Secretary to President	316
Dean of Women	298
Secretary to the Dean	294
Y. W. C. A. Secretary	192
Y. M. C. A. Secretary	168
Dean of Men	151
Assistant Dean	141
Assistant Registrar	116
Head of Residence Hall	108
Hostess	75
Secretary to Registrar	67
Assistant to Dean	63
Assistant to Registrar	62
Director of Placement and Appointments	61
Executive Secretary	59
Assistant Director	58
Assistant Secretary	57
Director of Dormitory	56
Recorder	51
Office Secretaries	47
Chaplain	45
Secretary to Director	42
Assistant Dean of Women	38
Assistant to Secretary	36
Associate Dean	35
Dean of Students	34
Placement Secretary	31
Director of Admissions	31
Assistant to President	30
Proctor	29
Secretary to Dean of Women	28
Student Advisors	25
Matron	25
Personnel Advisors	25
Freshmen Advisors	24
Assistant to Dean of Women	23
Secretary-Registrar	21
Registrar's Assistants	20

6,850 COLLEGE PERSONNEL OFFICERS, CLASSIFIED AS TO TITLE AND LISTED IN ORDER OF FREQUENCY OF MENTION IN 521 COLLEGE CATALOGUES.—
(Continued)

Rectors	17
Assistant Dean of Men	16
Upper Class Advisors	16
Social Director	16
Director of Personnel and Student Activities	14
Assistant Director of Admissions	13
Secretary to Dean of Men	13
Dean of Freshmen	11
Secretary to Director of Admissions	11
Advisor to Women	11
Bureau of Appointments	10
Dean-Secretary	8
Administration Assistant	8
Student Secretary	8
Associate Director	8
Placement Office Assistant	8
Bureau of Vocational Information	8
Master of House	8
President's Office Assistants	7
Dean-Registrar	7
Assistant to Dean of Men	7
House Mother	7
Bureau of Educational Service	7
Bureau of Placement	7
Assistant Secretary to President	5
Assistant Secretary to Dean	5
Secretary to Dean of Students	5
Assistant to Director	5
Personnel Counselors	5
Vocational Counselor	5
Vocational Secretary and Assistants	5
Commandant	5
Director of Religious Activities	5
Administrator	4
Provost	4
Student Employment and Self-Help Bureau	4
Secretary to Dean-Registrar	3
Dean of Religious Education	3
Dean of Studies	3
Associate Registrar	3
Assistant Recording Secretary	3
Assistant to Executive Secretary	3
Director of Student Relations	3
Assistant to Director of Student Relations	3
Advisor to Men	3

PHILOSOPHY AND ORGANIZATION

6,850 COLLEGE PERSONNEL OFFICERS, CLASSIFIED AS TO TITLE AND LISTED IN ORDER OF FREQUENCY OF MENTION IN 521 COLLEGE CATALOGUES.—
(Continued)

Student Counselor	3
Advisor of Vocational Guidance	3
Director of Personal Guidance	3
Mental Hygiene Counselor	3
Prefect	3
Housemistress	3
Assistant in Dean's Office	3
Assistant Dean-Secretary	2
Associate Dean of Women	2
Dean of Discipline	2
Dean of Instruction	2
Assistant Dean of Freshmen	2
Dean and Counselor of Upper Classmen	2
Director of Student Health	2
Superintendent of Nurses	2
Advisor to Foreign Students	2
Consultant on Careers	2
Assistant Chaplain	2
Assistant Supervisor of Dormitories	2
Pastors	2
Warden	2
Regent	2
Procurator	2
Secretary of Residence Halls	2
Preceptress of Residence Hall	2
Secretary to Social Director	2
Assistant Director of Placement Office	2
Bureau of Employment	2
Bureau of Personnel	2
Bureau of Recommendation for Teachers	2
Assistant Dean and Hostess	1
Executive Secretary to Dean	1
Administration Secretary	1
Dean of Men and Registrar	1
Supervisor of Men	1
Assistant Dean of Students	1
Assistant Dean of Discipline	1
Assistant Dean of Residence	1
Dean of Student Affairs	1
Dean of Chapel	1
Dean of Special Students	1
Junior Dean	1
Supervisor of Student Activities	1
Registrar and Dean of Women	1
Assistant Secretary to Registrar	1

A STUDENT PERSONNEL PROGRAM

6,850 COLLEGE PERSONNEL OFFICERS, CLASSIFIED AS TO TITLE AND LISTED IN ORDER OF FREQUENCY OF MENTION IN 521 COLLEGE CATALOGUES.—
(Continued)

Registrar and Appointment Secretary	1
Registrar and Director of Appointments	1
Registrar and Director of Promotions	1
Recording Secretary	1
Secretary Student Selections	1
Director of Registration	1
Credential Secretary	1
Associate Secretary	1
Director of Information Service	1
Executive Director	1
Director of Student Union	1
Supervisor of Training School	1
Assistant Superintendent of Nurses	1
Director of Educational Guidance	1
Director of Personal Relations	1
Secretary to Director Personnel and Student Activities	1
Assistant Consultant on Careers	1
Consultant on Vocational Education	1
Professor of Personnel Study	1
Professor of Personnel Study and Vocational Guidance	1
Assistant to Rector	1
Superintendent of Military Academy	1
Military Executive	1
Secretary to Procurator	1
Secretary of Dormitory	1
Host	1
Assistant Hostess	1
Chaperon of Hall	1
Director of Activities for Women	1
Director of Activities for Students	1
Bureau of Guidance and Records	1
Bureau of Placement (teachers)	1
Religious Conference	1
Appointment Bureau (teachers)	1

COMMITTEES, LISTED IN ORDER OF FREQUENCY

Admissions	124
Religion	49
Advisory Counsel	38
Discipline	37
Placement (including self-help)	35
Registration	32
Vocational Guidance	25
Student Welfare	23
Appointments	23
Social	21

COMMITTEES, LISTED IN ORDER OF FREQUENCY.—(*Continued*)

Executive	19
Student Employment	15
Placement (teachers)	15
Personnel	13
Student Activities	10
Recommendations (teachers)	10
Faculty and Class Advisors	8
Student Aid	8
Religious Activities	8
Religious Life	8
Student Affairs	7
Student Organizations	7
Appointment (teachers)	7
Faculty-student Relations	6
Religious Interests	6
Student Councilors	5
Extension	5
Guidance	5
Student Life and Interests	5
Credentials	4
Eligibility	4
Freshmen	4
Foreign Students	4
Fraternities	4
Chapel	4
Recommendations	4
Students' Advisors	3
Extension and Personnel	3
Board and Lodging Houses	3
Personnel Work	3
Enrollment	2
Entrance and Classification	2
Group Councilors for Freshmen	2
Student Conduct	2
Courtesy	2
Rules and Regulations	2
Personnel Service	2
Student Direction	2
Student Guidance	2
Chaplain's Advisory	2
Entrance and Advanced Standing	1
Re-admission and Probation	1
Management	1
Professional Advisement	1
Extra-campus Opportunities	1
Summer Activities	1
Graduate	1
Exchange Students	1

COMMITTEES, LISTED IN ORDER OF FREQUENCY.—(*Continued*)

Residential Life	1
Dormitory Life	1
Dormitory Counselors	1
Dormitory for Men	1
Heads of Houses	1
Self-survey	1
Advanced Standards	1
Promotion of Honesty in Student Work	1
Industrial Method and Guidance	1
Vocational Council	1
Men's Council	1
Women's Council	1
Personnel Guidance	1
Personnel Research	1
Student Government and Personnel	1
Student Finance and Assistance	1
Religion and Social Welfare	1
Church Relations	1
Religious Counselors	1

These 6,850 officers have 216 different titles. Moreover, more than six hundred persons (611) were members of 77 different committees dealing with personnel functions. There was an average of 13 people with titles which implied personnel responsibilities in each of the 521 colleges or universities. From these figures, we see that the field of student personnel work cannot be dismissed casually, but that it is playing a very important role in higher education.

At the same time, an extensive examination of the titles of the 6,850 persons so engaged and of the committee titles of the 661 committee members astounds one with the overlapping and the confusion of nomenclature and duties implied. It is evident from any analysis that the definition and organization of duties in this field are anything but clear. Great interest and activity are evident— but not much order, again no doubt due to organizational inertia, to the personalities and whims of those concerned, but even more to the lack of knowledge of what actually constitutes a good student personnel program.

Many persons responsible for personnel programs assume that they have in their institutions clearly defined patterns of personnel duties comparable to those in other colleges or universities. But on the whole, this is not true, for an examination of the duties of individuals holding the same title in different institutions also shows great diversity. As Strang points out, it is more satisfactory to describe personnel work in terms of unit functions than in terms of personnel officers because the functions performed by an officer having a certain official title vary enormously in different institutions, *e.g.*, the personnel director, the vocational counselor, the dean of women, and the psychologist all tend in various institutions to perform the same functions.[1]

Clearly, there is a growing active interest in personnel work, and as evident as this interest is the need for a widespread knowledge of the elements of a good student personnel program. What constitutes a good student personnel program in higher education? How can the stage be set to insure a good student personnel program?

Each college or university, although offering in many instances the same degrees, will not and cannot offer the same services. Just as individuals vary in their range of abilities and interests, so collegiate institutions do (and should) vary in their offerings. Jessup supports this fact:

In the Carnegie Foundation ten-year study of 30,000 high-school and college students in Pennsylvania there has been found wide variability among institutions as well as students. . . . Some colleges are very much more successful than others in dealing with students of the same or similar ability.[2]

The success of each institution will be largely determined by its ability to *find its job*, to undertake only as much of a program as it can carry out honestly, to select students who can profit by its resources, to leave to other agencies everything else. There can be no standard degree, no standard

[1] STRANG, RUTH, *Personal Development and Guidance in College and Secondary School*, p. 31, Harper & Brothers, New York, 1934.

[2] JESSUP, WALTER ALBERT, "The Integrity of the American College from the Standpoint of Administration," *School and Society*, 43 (1102): 178, Feb. 1, 1936.

college, no standard student personnel program. But at the same time, there is no institution which does not have some nucleus for a personnel program that could be developed consciously to the point where it would make valuable contributions to the educational power of the institution. On every campus there is some one or a few who consciously or unconsciously have the student personnel point of view. This individual or these persons could be utilized as the basis for a functioning program.

Fundamentally the development of a student personnel program in any institution will be determined by: (1) the objectives and educational program of the institution; (2) the present and future needs of the students; (3) the knowledge, skills, judgment, and vision of the faculty and administrative staff; (4) the financial resources for personnel services; and (5) the physical facilities available in the institution. But merely determining once, the needs of the students or the objectives of the institution, does not suffice, for these needs and objectives change from time to time and are seen with progressively greater clarity and understanding. The personnel program should be continually modified in terms of needs, as they are more clearly revealed, and should function in relation to these needs.

The personnel services that should be set up for each institution to meet its needs, as determined after careful study, will tend in each institution to arrange themselves into constellations of services. For example, it is probable that few institutions will employ an expert for every one of the personnel services that, taken altogether, constitute the student personnel program. Many institutions might, for example, employ one person to administer the placement program, both full-time and part-time placement, to head up the program of financial aid to students, and perhaps to contribute largely to the program of vocational guidance of the college. Similarly, the housing program and the social program might be combined under one person's direction. Some of the same colleges may find it wise to employ two or three specialists to work on the health program. In very small institutions it might even be possible for a well-trained director of personnel to carry much of the total program himself with expert assistance at only a few points. On the other hand, there will be an increasing number of institutions that will find it profitable to increase the numbers of experts that they already are employing on each aspect of the program. Each institution should combine and staff the various personnel functions in terms of its special needs and of the emphases it wishes to make.

The wisest organizational plan, in our opinion, will include provision for a great deal of facilitation and extension of the program via the instructional staff of the institution. Here again, institutions will differ in the extent to which they will be able or will wish to enlist the interest and the effort of the faculty. Institutions, where the majority of the faculty have subscribed to the idea that students are necessary evils but unfortunate distractions to a well-ordered educational system, will do well to be realistic about the kind and amount of contribution that can be expected from the faculty. In other colleges, however, individual faculty members are already doing such excellent personnel work that any program that did not make important provision for continuing and extending their contribution would be overlooking a valuable source of strength.

No matter how many services the institution wishes to provide for its personnel program, no matter how these services are combined into constellations, no matter which ones are emphasized, no matter how adequately or inadequately it is possible to staff the various services, no matter the extent to which it is possible for the instructional staff to participate in the personnel program, the program must be headed up by some one person. This person should be not only an educator, broadly and thoroughly trained in the philosophy and method of personnel work, but he should also be an administrator with the ability to organize and operate a program.

At the present time we find all too frequently a hodgepodge of personnel services, all related directly to the president, with little or no coordination, and with little appreciation of the fact that these services, taken all together, constitute one important aspect of the total educational program of the institution. Under these conditions it is inevitable that much of the potential contribution of the personnel services is dissipated. There is no one to see them as a whole and to speak for them as a whole in administrative councils, as the dean of the college speaks for the various teaching departments and the instructional program as a whole.

The more excellent the specialists whom a president may have been able to bring in to carry on the various aspects of a personnel program, the more necessary is a strong, wise coordinator. We have seen unfortunate results in some institutions where a number of high-powered specialists, unsupervised and uncoordinated, all let forth their unrestrained, uncoordinated efforts on a helpless student body.

It should be the responsibility of the director of the student personnel program, whether he be called a dean or a vice-president or a director of personnel, to define functions, to see that the various services are competently staffed, and to coordinate the various services with each other and with the program of instruction. He should see to it that duties and definitions are frequently reviewed and kept clearly defined; that the program as a whole never lapses into complacency but is consistently improved in the interest of students and of a more adequate educational plan. His should be the ultimate responsibility for persuading teachers and administrative officers to the necessity, philosophy, and methodology of the personnel program.

It is probably true that no program will function satisfactorily unless all the faculty and staff acquire a personnel point of view and come to feel a responsibility and a desire to participate actively in the personnel program. The responsibility for initiating and carrying out a personnel program can never rest with a central personnel staff alone, although theirs must be the ultimate responsibility for the program. Teachers, from our point of view, have a dual responsibility: to the welfare of the individual as well as to the culture and learning of the race. Admittedly, most college professors are much better in their particular field of academic subject matter than they are in understanding the physical, emotional, and social needs of students and what to do about them. Professors can, however, be given valuable help by personnel experts trained in these fields.

Ideally every instructor is a link in the personnel organization, though we cannot overlook the fact that he must depend upon specialists or experts to perform certain services for which he is untrained. He cannot treat his students when they are ill, but he can take cognizance that they are ill; he cannot administer loans or scholarships, but he can recognize the need for financial aid; he cannot direct the intelligence-testing program, but he can utilize the results to his and the student's advantage, and he can see that the student with more complicated problems be brought to the attention of the expert when solution is beyond the instructor's knowledge or training.

Decentralized responsibility, or the incorporation of every faculty member into some phase of the student personnel program through a division of labor or the development of a point of view, is both unavoidable and desirable in organizing and establishing a plan for student personnel work. It is not our proposal that the personnel staff be set up completely separate from the instructional staff. On the contrary, it is important that as many members of the personnel staff as is possible should teach some classes and hold regular faculty appointments. This arrangement has two important advantages: it gives members of the personnel staff a natural contact with students, and it affords an opportunity for personnel and instructional staffs to contribute jointly to faculty discussion and decisions on college affairs.

We are acquainted with some situations in which all members of the personnel staff are attached organizationally to the president's office, with personnel titles but no academic status, with no opportunity for contacts with students in classes, with no opportunity to meet with the faculty in regular faculty meetings. In certain institutions, even the chief personnel officers do not have professorial rank. This, in our opinion, is a very unfortunate arrangement; it severely handicaps the personnel program; it effectually hinders the personnel point of view from finding consistent expression in faculty councils; and it makes much more difficult effective coordination of personnel and instructional programs into a total educational plan for the institution.

There are only two ways by which the college can have a personnel staff that is thoroughly integrated with the instructional staff: by appointing to special positions as counselors on the personnel staff those members of the faculty who are especially gifted and interested in counseling, and by appointing to the personnel staff men and women of such caliber and professional training that the college honors itself in giving them professorial rank and seats in its faculty.

Certainly it is not our idea that every member of the instructional staff is qualified for every personnel service. Rather, the authors of this book advocate both a staff of personnel experts and the utilization in the actual program of as many faculty members as possible, as well as the desirability of persuading all faculty members to the personnel point of view. Again it may be said that the plan of a special staff of experts with the participation of many of the teaching faculty necessitates centralized control and direction of the program and also careful coordination. Without coordination and direction the program cannot function to its greatest efficiency, and without coordination and direction the philosophy of such a program is too easily lost.

It may be useful to describe and criticize various typical ways in which institutions are attempting to build programs of personnel work.

There is the institution, for example, which believes the only effective personnel program is the one that depends exclusively on the teaching staff without the use of experts specifically trained in personnel work. The authors are familiar with an institution where such a plan is in operation. An individualized curriculum is worked out for each student which involves 24 hours of every one of his days. Every member of the faculty in this institution is a teacher of subject matter but is also required to be a counselor. The faculty are all selected with these dual duties in mind. Each member of the staff is asked to be flexible, imaginative, progressive, and genuinely interested in people, at the same time that he is expected to be an outstanding scholar. The program in this particular institution is centralized by means of complete records centered in what is called a "curriculum-guidance office." These records are freely available to all staff members. The records show each student's curricular work and all of his significant experiences, in so far as known, outside as well as in the classroom. Only two of the faculty have any special personnel functions, the health counselor and the social director, and they are expected to work with and through the other faculty members.

The weaknesses of such a setup are evident. It is extremely difficult to maintain a functioning personnel program where every one of the staff has a full time load of instruction as well as heavy personnel responsibilities. Then, too, it seems to be the exceptional person who is equally gifted as scholar, teacher, and counselor, even though he may have been employed with many elaborate criteria clearly in mind. Either counseling or scholarship may easily descend to a secondary consideration where there are not well-established foci of initiative and enthusiasm in the administrative plan to balance them. Moreover, as the institution grows larger, it becomes more difficult to coordinate the counseling each student is receiving. The chief needs in this college at present are for better coordination and direction of the counseling program and for more supplementation of the faculty counseling efforts by experts.

Another institution has attempted much the same personnel plan, that of using the entire staff in the program, with no especially designated personnel officers. It has finally placed a psychiatrist in charge of the program as coordinator. He counsels individually and regularly with the faculty and, in a manner, supervises the handling of each student, but the faculty are still expected to carry on the personnel program. In carrying on their counseling under the close supervision of the psychiatrist, the faculty members receive expert help with immediate problems; but, more valuable still, those who possess any very considerable amount of natural talent are gradually being developed into excellent counselors. This college is small enough so that this can all be done quite informally. The advantages of this type of organization are that all staff members can fairly safely take responsibility for personnel services because they are themselves constantly receiving guidance, and those who have talent for such work may progressively assume greater responsibility.

This system could not function effectively in a larger institution where a greater degree of formality and organization becomes necessary. Yet each student—in whatever type of institution—should have the right to be known as a whole person by someone on the campus.

In a certain large university the dean of students is in charge of the program for the guidance of students. Faculty advisers for the students are recommended for appointment by this dean of students with the approval of the dean of the college. The dean of students himself also serves as adviser for a group of students in addition to his other duties. Each adviser teaches at least part time and some teach full time, receiving extra compensation for the supplementary service as adviser. Upon the basis of their educational and vocational interests and ambitions, students are classified and assigned to advisers. Advisers are selected with the greatest care on the scores of personality, judgment, temperament, and interest in this type of service.

In this institution, 10 years ago, it was thought a good policy to change advisers frequently, in order to educate an ever increasing number of faculty members in administrative problems and in the character and extent of student interests and problems. Though it was advantageous for the faculty to have as large a leaven as possible of members who had gained a broader view of the student side of the picture, this gain was found to be too much at the expense of student welfare. With advisers serving for only a year or two, no one of them served long enough to reach the stage of most effective service. It was found that any adviser is sure to make many mistakes of both omission and commission during his first year and still too many in his second year; he really begins to reach his true stride only in the third year and is still improving in his fifth year, if he has it in him to become thoroughly successful in this service. Appointments of counselors in this institution are kept on an annual basis, however, with the possibility of discontinuance of reappointment, so that a change may be made if this seems best for all concerned. The counselors of this institution are actually becoming quite specialized and expert. They are well-bulwarked with a staff of personnel experts responsible for admissions, testing, records, placement, etc. The program has the confidence and the interest of the whole faculty because a number of their fellow teachers work in it so actively. This setup represents an interesting attempt to secure the advantages of coordination and direction without running into the error of high centralization, ultimate isolation, and consequent impotence.

In many institutions, it may not be necessary or desirable to develop an organization to the degree outlined in the last situation described above. But in any institution it is desirable to designate special counselors from the regular members of the faculty upon the bases of personality, judgment, and interest in, and aptitude for, counseling. Their teaching load should be reduced, and they should be required to become familiar with principles of individual and adolescent psychology and mental hygiene, as well as with special techniques such as tests, study incentives, and study techniques, measures of emotional or personality traits, and the professional literature in the areas of counseling and general principles of higher education. They should be granted leaves of absence and summers regularly for professional study in the personnel field. Data from all sources should be made available to these individuals so that they may counsel the student effectively and intelligently. These special counselors, together with a personnel staff of experts, all of whose efforts are coordinated by a vice-president or a director of personnel, or a dean of students, should be able to produce an effective and functioning student personnel program.

Without coordination and direction the special staff of student personnel experts and the many teaching faculty taking part in the program may operate as a ship without a rudder. Each participant in the program may function in the plan from the perspective of his own interests and abilities, and he may easily lose sight of the whole program which is established with due recognition of the objectives of the institution and the all-round welfare of the students. It is essential that a coordinator endeavor to supplement the work of any one expert with the work of all others where this is desirable. It is the coordinator who originates the clearly defined duties and prevents too much overlapping. It is he who gives the entire program institutional significance in the light of the philosophy of the college or university. It is he who takes the initiative in policy making and supplies general supervision.

The coordinator should cooperate with other members of the institutional staff in progressively clarifying the instructional purposes of the institution, and he should have the purposes uppermost in his thinking in order to focus them in terms of each individual student and in order to insure that the instructional purposes are served by the experts included in the student personnel program. The coordinator must direct the personnel services, emphasizing their interrelationship with each other and their relationship to the whole program, to the business administration of the institution, and to the curriculum. He has the opportunity to prevent an overemphasis on tests and measurement, on vocational guidance, on placement (if these threaten to become preoccupying), and to reinforce other services such as the social program, the counseling program, or the health program. He should be constantly aware that all of these services and many others have a justifiable place in the student personnel program, and, just as an individual may grow one-sided in his interests, he should know that a student personnel program may overdevelop certain phases of the work to the neglect of others. There are instances, of course, where at times it is necessary to concentrate on one service in order to bring that phase of the work up to a par with other services, but the coordinator should realize when the emphasis should be lessened to prevent lopsidedness in the program. He should stimulate continuous research and revision of the total program instead of periodic and explosive replanning, followed by periods of static and routine administration of unchanging plans.

A duty of the coordinator, moreover, is to see that the contributions of each one who has information and insight concerning a specific student are secured, that this information is verified, supplemented, coordinated, and recorded cumulatively and made to function in its true proportion as a guide for the education of that individual.

Nor should the coordinator lose sight of the fact that there is evidence to show that young people in colleges and universities are still closely tied up with their homes and families. It is his opportunity to integrate and articulate these "pulls" with those of the college life. Another of his many responsibilities, therefore, is that of coordinating the efforts of the college and the home even for these older adolescents. The efforts of many colleges and universities in this direction have not yet proved sufficiently effective.

Education too often develops a monastic, isolated atmosphere. While such a setting no doubt stimulates integration within the smaller group, it may interfere seriously with the coordination of this group with the larger life into which its members must inevitably go. The coordinator of the student personnel program should realize this and attempt to articulate the institution's program with as many outside agencies in the community as possible. He can probably utilize the musical, dramatic, health, social service, recreational, civic, athletic agencies, and placement agencies within the community to the distinct advantage of the program as a whole.

We cannot assume, unfortunately, that all personnel directors or coordinators are going to be burdened within the next few years with an oversupply of expert help. It may be that the coordinator is going to have to do his own directing of extracurricular activities and much of his own counseling. He may himself have to be an expert in one or more phases of the program. He may have to be the director of admissions or director of the social program. He must be adaptable enough, intelligent enough, and well enough trained to be able to supplement the services of those few experts in personnel work who may be available for his staff.

The coordinator of the student personnel program dare not play the part of an administrative autocrat. Dictators in the role of administrators or coordinators of student personnel, not only doom themselves to short tenure, but also greatly jeopardize the success of the work itself. A policy of "putting something over," or of "making someone come to time," of "riding roughshod over the opposition," while temporarily intoxicating enough to make one feel the brilliant, irresistible leader, inevitably spells disaster to the professed purposes of the personnel program and of sound education. Above all, the coordinator must know how to work with his superior officers, his faculty and staff, and the members of the student body.

The job of the vice-president in charge of the student personnel program or of the dean or director of personnel may sound like an impossibly difficult one. Certainly it does not consist of a few easy tasks. It is our contention, however, that, since it is a big job, it must be recognized as such and only those individuals should be appointed to assume administrative responsibility for the personnel program who are well qualified for it.

Those who are naturally gifted by nature for this responsibility must increasingly equip themselves so that they can most competently direct such a program. This part of the task of higher education is only now beginning to receive its due measure of recognition. The contribution of some of our ablest present-day educators, however, will undoubtedly find expression through this field.

Bibliography

"Board of Personnel Administration at Northwestern University," *School and Society*, 44: 91–92, July 18, 1936.

BOUCHER, CHAUNCEY S.: *The Chicago College Plan*, University of Chicago Press, Chicago, 1935, xi + 344 pp.

BRADSHAW, FRANCIS F.: "The Scope and Aim of a Personnel Program," *Educational Record*, 17: 120–128, January, 1936.

GARDNER, DONFRED H.: *The Evaluation of Higher Institutions* V. "Student Personnel Service," University of Chicago Press, Chicago, 1936, xx + 235 pp.

JONES, ARTHUR J.: *Principles of Guidance*, McGraw-Hill Book Company, Inc., New York, 1930, xxiv + 385 pp.

LLOYD-JONES, ESTHER: "Personnel Administration," *Journal of Higher Education*, 5: 141–147, March, 1934.

———: *Student Personnel Work at Northwestern University*, Harper & Brothers, New York, 1929, xx + 253 pp.

MACCRACKEN, JOHN HENRY: *American Universities and Colleges*, Williams & Wilkins Company, Baltimore, 1932, xiv + 1066 pp.

McGrath, Earl J.: "The Dean," *Journal of Higher Education*, 7: 427–432, November, 1936.

Partridge, Florence A.: "The Evolution of Administrative Offices in Liberal Arts Colleges from 1875 to 1933," unpublished manuscript University of Chicago Library, 1934.

Strang, Ruth: "Developments in Student Personnel Research," *Teachers College Record*, 35: 120–134, November, 1933.

———: *Personal Development and Guidance in College and Secondary School*, Harper & Brothers, New York, 1934, vii + 341 pp.

Walters, J. E.: *Individualizing Education*, John Wiley & Sons, Inc., New York, 1935, xiv + 278 pp.

PART II
FUNCTIONS OF THE STUDENT PERSONNEL PROGRAM

Chapter IV
SELECTING AND ADMITTING STUDENTS

Selection and Admissions

One of the important functions of a student personnel program in institutions of higher learning is the selection and admission of students. The increasing number of individuals who desire education beyond the secondary school level has emphasized and made imperative a selective program of admissions. Moreover, there is a wealth of college and university material appearing each year in our high schools and preparatory schools. Among these students are many who do not plan to go to college but who should, while on the other hand there are many who now seek higher education who should to their profit be directed into some other channel of activity. Furthermore, the choice of a college is made by many a student without careful knowledge of what his own needs and interests really are and what the various colleges have to offer him. The careful selection of students who will most profit by college or university training, and the more careful articulation of each student with the college most fitting his needs are basic to the success of both the students and an effective program of higher education.

At the beginning of the present century a definite trend in admission policies had become established in higher education. This trend has since developed into the practice of using an increasing amount of objective evidence as bases for the selection of students.

Before 1875, each institution admitted students on the basis of its own entrance examinations. In the year 1871, the policy of admitting students on the basis of transcripts of high school marks began to gain headway. The College Entrance Examination Board rose rapidly in favor after 1900. A few years later a great deal of work was being done on the predictive value of tests of general intelligence. For a time intelligence tests competed with high-school marks for first place in value to college admission officers. Because the correlation between college marks and each of these two factors was far from perfect, efforts were made to isolate other influences which had a significant relationship with college achievement. The relationship between ratings and personality tests and scholarship was studied. Evidences of scholastic preparation, intellectual ability, and the amassed cumulative achievement of the candidate, have, in general, been given more attention than data concerning special interests, moral and social promise, health, and financial status. The value of a combination of tests and measures in furnishing a basis for selecting students who will succeed in college was recognized and subjected to numerous investigations. The latest development along this line is the use of the case study or a comprehensive cumulative record as an instrument in the selection of students.[1]

We can readily see from this statement by Strang that the trend has been toward a more complete study of the individual prospective student and away from single measures such as previous school records and intelligence ratings considered more or less in isolation. The present practice, then, is no longer to depend upon any single admission criterion.

As a matter of fact, it is possible to distinguish several levels of selective admission practices operating at present in institutions of higher education. These levels may be described as follows:

1. The student wishing admittance to college is seen or studied in terms of his transcripts of school marks and other records of academic preparation, his recommendations, his interview, his intelligence- and achievement-test scores, etc. Several or perhaps only one of these may constitute the basis of the college plan of student selection. Bram-

[1] STRANG, RUTH M., *Personal Development and Guidance in College and Secondary School*, p. 63, Harper & Brothers, New York, 1934.

mell[1] reported in 1933 that 23 per cent of 517 institutions of higher education grant admission on presentation of a high-school diploma; 63 per cent admit students on a basis of a transcript of high-school credits (80 per cent of the Western institutions studied use this method, as against 20 per cent of New England institutions); 26 per cent allow students to gain entrance by passing the College Board examinations and 9 per cent grant entrance to students who pass other examinations such as the New York Regents' examinations; 12 per cent use rank in the high-school graduating class as a method of admission. Brammell found that 36 different kinds of admission requirements are in force in these 517 institutions, that 25 methods are used singly, and that 11 other methods are used in combination. Where marks are employed alone for college entrance, these ordinarily reflect only teacher estimate, amount of texts absorbed, and only little useful evidence of the pupil's present working power for effective college living. Where examinations are the only admission device, we have a combination of information, health and temperament, cleverness and good luck as the basis of selection.

On this first level, the college or university is critically examining the prospective student who is on the outside looking in. For the most part, the sole object of the student is to "get in" to college and that of the college is either to "get him in" or "keep him out." At this first level, the college often says in effect: "Accumulate your 15 units of high-school credit, jump certain hurdles we have set up, pass our entrance examinations; we will then begin to help you decide what you should do."

2. At the second level, an effort is made by the college or university to study and discover series of trends in the educational history of the student. The American Council on Education cumulative record card or one similar to it

[1] BRAMMELL, P. ROY, "Bridging the Chasm between High School and College," *Journal of Higher Education*, 4: 378–379, 1933.

may serve as the basis for an understanding of trends in the student's development. The cumulative record card was used extensively in the Pennsylvania Study,[1] which originated in 1928 under the auspices of the Carnegie Foundation for the Advancement of Teaching. This study grew out of the problem of school-college requirements and admission to college. The "graphic cumulative record" was shaped particularly as a means of solving that problem, and, as Learned points out, it is not a bookkeeping device but a valuable educational instrument. One of the chief purposes of this record card is to display a graphic sequence of measures covering a period of years which enables the reader to appreciate at a glance the quality, the amount, and the consistency of a pupil's intellectual progress. It provides in a variety of fields, not only the teachers' ratings of the pupil, but also standardized test scores that disclose in comparable terms the relative achievement of this pupil in comparison with thousands of others all over the country.

There is conclusive evidence of the need for a sounder method of identifying intellectual ability than those which have been followed under level one described above. The Pennsylvania Study has prepared two charts showing variable standards of grading in Pennsylvania high schools and the inadequacy of high-school grades as guides for college admission purposes. These charts show that many pupils receiving letter grade A in English, for example, were at the 30th percentile of the state-wide group (on whom the Columbia Research Bureau test was standardized), while many pupils receiving letter grade D are at the 96th

[1] Carnegie Foundation for the Advancement of Teaching, New York: *Progress Report* I, New York City, 1929– "Study of the Relations of Secondary and Higher Education in Pennsylvania"; *Progress Report* II, New York City, 1930– "The College and the Freshman"; *Progress Report* III, New York City, 1931– "Proposals for the Treatment of the Secondary Enquiry Group in Senior High School"; *Progress Report* IV, Harrisburg, Pa., 1931– "Case Studies and Special Curricula Proposed for Secondary Pupils Expecting to Enter College."

percentile of this same state-wide group. The same chaotic relations hold with respect to the intelligence test results.

For three years, the Pennsylvania Study has followed 12,000 pupils in their educational careers from grades 7 to 9 by means of the cumulative record card. An emphatic outcome of the study thus far is the recognition of the dependence of all successful education on adequate provision for proved differences in individual interests and capacities. Certain of the centers participating in the secondary school section have an experimental program for students of proved ability. Altoona High School, Elkins Park, and Wayne have formed a group of 150 best pupils out of about 1,000 entering grade 10. These are prepared for college; their class attendance is cut down, conference periods are greatly increased and independent work encouraged. It is the purpose of this plan to anticipate for these pupils much of the secondary work done now in the first college year. Electives usually granted in senior high school are cut down in favor of broad fields such as science, literature, or history. As soon as it is known what colleges these Altoona, Elkins Park, and Wayne pupils hope to enter, the Study solicits the cooperation of these colleges. Since the nature of the proposed curriculum (for the picked pupils) is an attempt in a direction long advocated by many colleges, the chosen colleges are cooperating readily in giving these pupils advanced standing.[1]

This second level may be contrasted with the first level, which interprets the student's readiness for college in the light of single units such as his transcripts, his recommendations, his various test scores, etc. At this second level, an attempt is made to consider the intellectual equipment and accomplishment of the prospective student as it has demonstrated itself over a period of time.

[1] Carnegie Foundation for the Advancement of Teaching, New York: *Progress Report* IV, Harrisburg, Pa., 1931– "Case Studies and Special Curricula Proposed for Secondary Pupils Expecting to Enter College."

3. The third level illustrates another step forward in the philosophy and method of admitting students. Here a more dynamic relationship is established between the prospective student and the college. At this level, the college consciously acknowledges itself as only one factor in the relationship between the student and itself. The student is considering what the college can offer him in the light of his needs and interests, as well as the college determining whether the student is the sort who can profit from its opportunities. The college attempts to interpret to the prospective student for his guidance its attributes, facilities, and general program. The college on this level is genuinely interested, not just in acquiring a student body, but rather in bringing together a carefully selected group of students who will all benefit by the program the college is prepared to develop with and for them.

At this level, also, we may find the high school or preparatory school playing an important role by intelligently and continuously assisting each student to decide the after-high-school plans that are most constructive for him. An expert in personnel on the secondary level who has studied each student, as well as the programs of various college and universities of the country, is directing contacts with these institutions and giving advice. After studying, under the direction of an expert, the possibilities of many institutions, the student is able intelligently to evaluate the colleges, as each college is also able to evaluate those interested in becoming its students.

4. On the fourth level, a number of secondary schools and a number of colleges join together into an organization for a mutually cooperative give-and-take. This fourth level is best illustrated by the experiment being carried on in the state of Ohio. The department of education of this state has issued a manual which is not designed to replace the annual catalogues of individual colleges but rather serves to make the "personality" of each college better known. This manual is made available in every high

school in the state, not only to seniors but to juniors, sophomores, and freshmen in the interest of wise educational guidance.[1] The Committee on Intelligence Tests for Entrance of the Ohio College Association is, in addition, working on "two hundred research problems" which are present in the task of selecting students for college. Toops has been gathering data from tests given to high-school students and giving these data statistical treatment on Hollerith machines. A Hollerith card has been punched for every student entering Ohio State University since 1919, or some 60,000 in all. This system, which provides a perpetual personnel inventory, a sort of statistical control over the educative process, has obvious possibilities. The plans of this committee involve giving intelligence tests every year to all high-school pupils in Ohio in order to secure an average of intelligence indices, both for college admission officers and for high-school guidance; and the development of a uniform entrance blank for all Ohio colleges to be used efficiently by a central college bureau of the state.[2]

It is readily seen that on this level a close relationship exists between all high-school students and all the colleges within the state. Educational guidance is not merely being talked, it is actually functioning. Colleges make known the type of student they seek as well as the opportunities they offer. Furthermore, the duty and the responsibility of the college are not ended when students are refused admission. The central college bureau of the state is providing a referral guidance service that is establishing good will and enhancing the reputation of the colleges concerned. Those refused admission in one college are referred to colleges whose standards they can meet, to

[1] TOOPS, HERBERT A., and H. A. EDGERTON, "Opportunities in Ohio Colleges," in *Guidance Manual* 3, 1931, p. 203, Ohio State Department of Education, Columbus.

[2] "Seventh Annual Report of the Committee on Intelligence Tests for Entrance, 1931-1932," *Ohio College Association Bulletin* 82: 1013-1025.

colleges in which they stand a good chance of making a success of their educational careers.

5. At the fifth level, the relationships between the colleges or universities and the students preparing for higher education are even better developed. The institutions of higher education are reaching down into the secondary level and the secondary school anticipating after-school adjustment in such a fashion that the process of admission to college is well on its way before the student's last year of preparation.

This level of admission practice is well-illustrated by the Progressive Education Association's project for the improvement of secondary education, *i.e.* for freeing it from the rigid "college-preparatory" curriculum necessitated by college-entrance requirements. The Association's commission in the spring of 1932

. . . presented to the principal colleges and universities of the country a proposal for a limited experiment in the relaxation of entrance requirements for only a small number of schools. The purpose of this plan was to permit these few selected schools to engage in progressive methods and curricula and still send a fair proportion of their graduates on to college, and thus to enable both the schools and the colleges to find out whether students prepared in accordance with progressive ideas will do better or worse in college than those students who meet existing requirements.[1]

For an experimental period of 5 years, beginning with the autumn of 1936, 20 selected schools were to work in an admissions arrangement with the colleges, so that students should gain admission on the basis of the following criteria:

1. Recommendation from the principal of the cooperating secondary school to the effect that the student is generally of good intelligence, has well-defined purposes, and has shown ability to work successfully in one or more fields of instruction;

[1] McCONN, MAX, "Freeing the Secondary School for Experimentation," *Progressive Education*, 10: 368, November, 1933.

2. A history of the student's school life and interests, including results of standardized tests in various subjects and in intelligence, given while in high school.

The cooperating colleges are not obliged to admit all such students as meet the new requirements but only to accept students under this plan without regard to course and unit requirements now in force and without discrimination. More than 22 colleges agreed to participate in this plan. The task of selecting the secondary schools was very difficult. Private schools for boys, for girls, public-high schools, demonstration or practice schools, all kinds of schools are represented. Of the 20 chosen, three (Altoona, Elkins Park, and Wayne high schools) were already pledged under the Pennsylvania Study to send to Pennsylvania colleges students prepared under a similar plan of admission (discussed under level 2).

The types of experimentation proposed and undertaken by the schools vary considerably. Nevertheless, there is a fair amount of homogeneity of purpose and general pattern. In most cases, the content subjects are given primary attention, with enrichment of factual material. There is increased interweaving of subjects and encouragement of self-directed study. And finally, and most important, greatly augmented attention is given to individual guidance.

The colleges are heartily receiving the abundant information concerning candidates which the schools furnish. The colleges, as well, on the basis of reports about the students sent ahead to them, have advised the schools concerning the students' senior-year and earlier work. Comprehensive personnel data furnished by the high schools are used by the colleges for purposes of guidance after the entrance of the students.[1]

At this fifth level we begin to get a genuine fusion of college and high-school purposes and efforts in the interest

[1] McConn, Max, "A College Dean Looks at the Eight-year Experiment," *Progressive Education*, 12: 454–457, November, 1935.

of each student—an acting together with respect to him rather than separately or even antagonistically. Each institution is interested in learning the student, each is committed to cooperating with the other, as well as with each student, and even to modifying its own program substantially in the interest of students.

Although the levels just discussed show progress toward making admission to higher education an educational experience for the candidate, yet admissions practice is still based too exclusively on measures of intellectual ability. In only a few instances is it realized that there are many other attributes of the individual which should be constantly inventoried and studied as bases of admission. Cumulative personnel records have been developed which record other data, as well as abstract verbal ability and extent and success of book learning, for the modern educator is becoming aware that colleges are more than classes and laboratories, that some of the most important experiences from the broad educational viewpoint are acquired out of the classroom, in sports, in social experiences, in extracurricular activities, and through personal contact with great personalities.

It is glibly stated that the purpose of selecting students for admission to colleges and universities is to choose those who will most profit by higher education. Any honest educator will admit, however, that it is usually the size of the enrollment of his institution rather than educational principles which finally exerts the controlling influence upon the admissions policy. Kurani[1] found that the number of criteria employed in deciding upon a candidate's admission varies with the demand for entrance to that particular college, that there is a disparity between printed and actual requirements, and that the rough uniformity apparent in the printed requirements gives way to wide

[1] KURANI, HABIB AMIN, *Selecting the College Student in America*, p. 56, Teachers College, Bureau of Publications, Columbia University, New York, 1931.

variation in actual practice. It is necessary for every college or university to make an effective and tolerable compromise in an honest way in terms of principles of selection, the objectives of the institution, and the student body it is able to acquire. This compromise should always, however, progress toward better educational practice.

Although all college administrators who aspire to be true educators pay lip service to the ideal of the careful selection of students, the recruiting of students—in fact, almost sandbagging of students—has become in recent years (because, no doubt, of the depression) an increasing activity in many institutions of higher education. Certainly, in some instances, it involves most unethical practices. A number of colleges have field agents, and their success and, in many cases, their salaries depend upon their ability to drag in victims for the college mill. It is reported that the representative of one prominent college in the Middle West receives $100 for each student who signs upon the dotted line of the application for admission. Needless to add, there is not much consideration given by that college to how well it can meet the needs of students. Even the innocent bystander sometimes experiences the avidity of these college salesmen. One individual who contemplated sending a daughter to college, in order to prevent college salesmen from monopolizing her time, asked a friend to write for catalogues from three higher educational institutions. The friend did and immediately her house was besieged by three "field representatives." To their amazement, the field representatives found their supposed prospect had no college-age youngsters and was, in fact, in the hospital having a baby!

Is the field representatives' function guidance? There is little doubt but that the function of many of these agents is merely high-pressure salesmanship. Current practices related to recruiting involve unwarranted scholarships, grants-in-aid, and a great deal of misrepresentation, particularly regarding other colleges than that college which pays the field representative's salary. In some cases, offers of financial aid far exceed the resources of the college and have caused reduction of faculty salaries. Obviously, these types of recruiting are harmful in that they consider the institution's immediate needs rather than those of the students. They also have an unfavorable effect on the student in developing an exaggerated idea of his self-importance.

The solution to the problems of student recruiting must come in part from the high schools working with college administrators and guidance experts. Some plan must be evolved whereby honest information about colleges can be presented by colleges themselves and whereby high-school students can be, early in high school, aided in the interpretation of that information by a disinterested guidance officer, one who is genuinely concerned with the best interests of the student instead of the best interests of the college.

Ogan of the Committee on College Entrance of the Ohio College Association describes a plan[1] for directing high-school seniors to those colleges which will suit them best, eliminating the multiplicity of blanks which the seniors and their high-school principals usually fill out in the student's attempt to find what he needs, and eliminating the problems of present recruiting practices. This plan is now in operation in 26 Ohio colleges. The principal of each high school gives to every student, who (by his record) is capable of succeeding in college, a Uniform College Information Blank. On the last page of this blank, after the student has filled in the preceding pages, the principal fills in information which checks and supplements that of the student about himself. This blank is intended to secure all information, exclusive of transcript of credits, which any college could want for the use of its admission committee. These blanks

[1] OGAN, R. W., "Toward Better Recruiting of College Students," *Ohio Schools*, 13: 317, December, 1935.

are then sent to the central office of the Ohio College Association, where they are copied on cards and referred to the cooperating colleges. The originals are returned to the high schools whence they came and are used for personnel work there until the students leave for college. Through the information at the office of the Ohio College Association, the representative of a particular college calling at a high school, knows just which students are interested in his college and he interviews those students at once. Moreover, students, who are interested in going to college but who cannot pay for it easily, can be visited by such collegiate representatives and informed of ways of earning tuition at some colleges. A third value, as the colleges see it, comes from the fact that each college, with its particular criteria for prospective students, is able to send its catalogue only to those students likely to come up to its standards.

There is no doubt but that the student should be assisted in selecting his college by educators who will serve as educational counselors rather than by high-powered salesmen or hi-jackers. It has been demonstrated that the evils of the current practices of recruiting can be eliminated, for this has been done in Oregon as well as in Ohio. Bennett[1] outlines the plan operating in Oregon:

In less than two years, a correlated program of high school contacts, uniting the interests of the state institutions of higher education, the State Department of Education, and the high school executives, has succeeded in eliminating the proselyting of high school students and the harassing of high school principals by constant visitation of high-pressure speakers, has reduced the heavy expense of duplication in promotional work, and has effected an unbiased and scientific system of guidance and counseling that reaches every high school student in the state.

In Oregon, there is a state-wide committee, responsible to the chancellor and the Board of Higher Education, to

[1] BENNETT, MARY, "Co-operation for Competition," *Journal of Higher Education*, 7 (8): 422–426, November, 1936.

administer the program of high-school contacts, with personnel representing the six state institutions of higher learning, the State Department of Public Instruction, the High School Principals' Association, and the High School Superintendents' Association. This committee employs a full-time high-school visitor as contact man to present to every high-school student in the state the opportunities offered by the state's educational institutions, information as to the allocation of curriculums among the institutions, and he confers with high-school seniors desiring special assistance. The state-wide committee supervises a program of testing and guidance which is undertaken by experts in this field, who are on the faculties of the University of Oregon, Oregon State College, and the normal schools, working in cooperation with the high-school teachers of the state. The purpose of this program is to ascertain the students who are best qualified for advanced training and the type of work for which they are best fitted.

Another phase of the unified program includes a limited and controlled list of conferences for high-school students to be held on the various campuses, including such events as the high-school press conference, band contest, interscholastic track and field meet, drama tournament, debating league, typing contest, and 4-H club sessions. Some of the events are held on a single campus; others alternate each year. The state-wide committee also supervises the awarding of tuition scholarships to outstanding high-school students in need of financial assistance. The number of scholarships granted by each state institution is limited to 2 per cent of the total enrollment for the previous year.

A central division of information directs the program of publications to inform high-school students of the work and opportunities offered by the various institutions. A small leaflet giving entrance requirements, board and room costs, and other general regulations for all six institutions in the state system is sent to all high-school seniors early in the spring. An attractive booklet showing curricular allocations and pictures of campus buildings and scenes is also sent to these seniors once each year near the end of the school term. The complete catalogues of the different institutions are available upon request. The catalogues, however, are uniform in their general plan, are edited under a single policy, and the catalogue for each institution contains certain information which is common to all the catalogues, *e.g.*, an outline of curricular offerings of the six institutions in the state system.

A decided advantage of this plan is that instead of requests coming to every high-school principal from all the colleges and universities in the state for his list of seniors, the mailing list is compiled in the office of the state superintendent of public instruction from cards furnished by the high-school contacts committee; these cards request the name and address of the student, the field of work in which he is interested, and the institution which he desires to attend. After a complete mailing list is made up and forwarded to the central mailing office, which serves all the institutions in the system, the cards are segregated and sent to the institution named by the students. In this way no student is interviewed by more than one institution.

Not only has Oregon done away with recruiting, but it has developed a system of guidance and counseling for its high-school students interested in and capable of higher education. At the same time, the state has reduced the promotional expenses of its higher educational institutions and is operating a dignified, educationally respectable, and efficiently controlled system which reaches every high-school student in the state.

A good system of admissions is perfectly possible of being achieved. It would have these characteristics: It would offer precollege guidance in cooperation with high schools and other colleges for the purpose of directing the prospective student to the college best suited to the individual student's needs. It would conscientiously discover the objectives of the institution and make them well known. These objectives would be clearly reflected in the admission procedures of the college. It would not base its admission exclusively on the criterion of abstract verbal ability but would take into consideration all the other aspects of the individual as well. It would provide for an appraisal of student personality, health, character, interests, and needs, as well as intellectual ability and achievement, and consider honestly how its total program can meet all his needs. It would reach back into the high school and preparatory school, and participate with other institutions in experimental work for the improvement of admission policies and procedures.

Many institutions now have officers known as directors of admissions; some colleges have a committee on admissions with a secretary who acts as director. In other institutions, the director of personnel is the director of admissions. If one individual is responsible for admission procedure, he should have an advisory committee which will help shoulder the responsibility for policy making, difficult decisions, etc. In all instances, the duty of the admission officer by no means consists of sitting in his office figuring out means and standard deviations. His task is not primarily research but rather educational guidance carefully articulated with the educational program of the institution he represents and, frequently, evaluated in terms of the policies agreed upon.

The director of admissions should be trained in those personnel techniques that implement an enlightened philosophy of admissions and selection. He must be trained in the use of cumulative records, how to interview, how to use tests and measurements, statistics and research techniques, and administration and office organization. He must understand adolescent psychology and know something of parent counseling. He should know what sort of handbooks and manuals are really helpful to students. He should know how to effect articulation with all main sources of student supply and how to cooperate with other colleges and associations of colleges in order that a referral service may operate. He must have a personnel point of view, and he must know the aims and objectives of his college. If he is trained in public speaking and speaks well before an audience, all the better. It is desirable that he have taught at some time in secondary schools, and the more he knows about secondary schools and their problems, the more successful he will be. He should know what other colleges are doing in educational guidance. He should familiarize himself with the problems of placement (for positions) and should realize the interrelation of admissions and selection with placement. He should be a member of the college student financial-aid committee and should help form its policies. He should be consulted in the assigning of counselors to freshmen, for he knows the students before they come to the college. It is often wise to make him a freshman counselor, for he should have been able to lay a foundation of friendliness for individual guidance before the students register as freshmen. In any case, he should be available and easily accessible the first month of the school year, since in many instances he is the only person the freshmen know and a familiar face is a godsend to a poor bewildered new student.

Bibliography

AIKIN, WILFORD M.: "Toward School-college Cooperation," *Progressive Education*, 12: 435–440, November, 1935.

BARR, A. S., and LOIS DOUGLAS: "The Pre-training Selection of Teachers," *Journal of Educational Research*, 28: 92–117, October, 1934.

BENNETT, MARY: "Co-operation for Competition," *Journal of Higher Education*, 7 (8): 422–426, November, 1936.

BIXLER, ROY W.: "Rating the College Entrant," *Journal of Higher Education*, 3: 361–365, October, 1932.

BOEHMER, FLORENCE E.: "Possible Guidance Function of the College Field or Promotional Agent," *American College Personnel Association Yearbook*, 1936, pp. 7–11.

BRAMMELL, P. ROY: "Bridging the Chasm between High School and College," *Journal of Higher Education*, 4: 378–379, October, 1933.

BRIGHAM, CARL C.: "Admission Units and Freshmen Placement," in *Educational Measurement and Guidance, Report of Second Conference*, American Council on Education, 1933, pp. 49–67.

BRUMBAUGH, A. J.: "An Outline of a Personnel Program for the Small College," Paper (in manuscript) presented to the Commission on Institutions of Higher Education, the North Central Association of Colleges and Secondary Schools, Apr. 23, 1936.

CAMPBELL, D. S.: "Selection, Admission and Guidance of Students," in *American Educational Research Association Report*, 1936, pp. 57–61.

Carnegie Foundation for the Advancement of Teaching, *Study of the Relations of Secondary and Higher Education in Pennsylvania, Progress Report* I, The Foundation, New York, 1929.

Carnegie Foundation for the Advancement of Teaching, "The College and the Freshman," in *Study of the Relations of Secondary and Higher Education in Pennsylvania, Progress Report* II, The Foundation, New York, 1930, 48 pp.

Carnegie Foundation for the Advancement of Teaching, "Proposals for Treatment of the Secondary Enquiry Group in Senior High School," *Study of the Relations of Secondary and Higher Education in Pennsylvania, Progress Report* III, The Foundation, New York, 1931, 20 pp.

Carnegie Foundation for the Advancement of Teaching, "Case Studies and Special Curricula Proposed for Secondary Pupils Expecting to Enter College," *Study of the Relations of Secondary and Higher Education in Pennsylvania, Progress Report* IV, The Foundation, New York, 1931, 34 pp.

COWLEY, W. H.: "The Recruiting Problem," *Journal of Higher Education*, 7: 395–396, October, 1936.

COXE, WARREN W., and PHILIP A. COWEN: "Applicants Refused Admission by Colleges and Professional Schools in New York State," *University of State of New York Bulletin*, 1042, Apr. 16, 1934.

GARDNER, DONFRED H.: *The Evaluation of Higher Institutions*, V. "Student Personnel Service," University of Chicago Press, Chicago, 1936, xx + 235 pp.

GRAY, WILLIAM S. (Ed.): "Provision for the Individual in College Education," in *Proceedings of the Institute for Administrative Officers of Higher Institutions*, vol. IV, pp. 31–67, University of Chicago Press, Chicago, 1932.

HAWKES, HERBERT E.: "The Co-operative Test Service," *Educational Record*, 12: 30–38, January, 1931.

KURANI, HABIB AMIN: *Selecting the College Student in America*. Teachers College, Bureau of Publications, Columbia University, New York, 1931, x + 124 pp.

LEARNED, W. S.: "Admission to College." *Educational Record*, 14: 23–48, January, 1933.

———: "Study of the Relations of Secondary and Higher Education in Pennsylvania," *Twenty-eighth Annual Report of the Carnegie Foundation for the Advancement of Teaching*, 1933, pp. 39–63.

LEWIS, WILLIAM MATHER: "The Personal Equation," *Bulletin of the Association of American Colleges*, 21: 12–23, March, 1935.

MCCONN, MAX: "A College Dean Looks at the Eight-year Experiment," *Progressive Education*, 12: 454–457, November, 1935.

———: "Freeing the Secondary School for Experimentation," *Progressive Education*, 10: 367–372, November, 1933.

McCullough, Constance M.: "Preparation for College Success in Public vs. Private High Schools," *Education*, 54: 629–631, June, 1934.

Nicolson, Marjorie: "College Statistics May Have Another Interpretation," *Education*, 54: 632–635, June, 1934.

Ogan, R. W.: "Toward Better Recruiting of College Students," *Ohio Schools*, 13: 317 ff., December, 1935.

"Seventh Annual Report of the Committee on Intelligence Tests for Entrance, 1931–1932, *Ohio College Association Bulletin* 82," pp. 1013–1025.

Smith, Eugene R.: "The Work of the Committee on Reports and Records," *Progressive Education*, 12: 441–445, November, 1935.

Stephens, W. B.: "The Conference on College Admissions and Guidance," *Educational Record*, 14: 15–22, January, 1933.

Strang, Ruth: *Personal Development and Guidance in College and Secondary School*, Harper & Brothers, New York, 1934, 341 pp.

Toops, H. A., and H. A. Edgerton: "Opportunities in Ohio Colleges," in *Guidance Manual* 3, Ohio State Department of Education, Columbus, 1931, 203 pp.

Turck, Charles J.: "Report of the Committee on Methods of Student Recruiting," *Association of American Colleges Bulletin* 21: 140–152, March, 1935.

Valentine, Alan: "Problems of an Admissions Office," *Third Educational Conference*, American Council on Education, Washington, D. C., 1934, pp. 38–47.

Walters, Raymond: "Should the Number of Professional Students be Restricted?" *Educational Record*, 16: 412–432, October, 1935.

Wediner, H. S.: "The Universities as Trade Rivals," *Educational Record*, 16: 188–202, April, 1935.

Zook, George D.: "Present Position of Graduate Studies in the United States," *School and Society*, 43: 41–49, January, 1936.

Chapter V

HELPING STUDENTS TO BELONG IN COLLEGE

Orientation

Since the early 1920's there has been a rapid growth of interest in "orienting" students "to college life." This interest was fed by the discovery by a number of institutions that approximately one-third of their entering freshmen were staying 1 year or less, and that only about one-half of those originally enrolled were ultimately graduated. Such losses could not be viewed complacently. It is now generally conceded that the personnel program of an institution should include a program of orientation and freshman adjustment.

An analysis of the problems which the freshman faces when he undertakes his college career reveals some of the reasons why so large a proportion of first-year students are gradually led to give up the struggle.

Consider the complex organization of the new situation into which the student is suddenly plunged. In a given college of a little over a thousand students, an incoming student finds himself on a campus of 200 acres, containing 19 dormitories and cottages and 25 academic or service buildings. There are 15 administrative officers and executive secretaries with whom he probably comes into contact at some early time; 112 members of the faculty and 26 different academic departments. In addition to this, the extracurricular life of the college includes 28 organizations, clubs, and councils. In his own dormitory he lives with from 60 to 100 or more other students. And this is a simple college—comparatively speaking.

Again, from an organizational standpoint, consider how the student has more and more in the last decade been split and split again among the many specialists who have become important members of the college staff. His physical body and his health history may be known to the college physician; some of the same information plus other specialized information about his body is learned by members of the physical education department, who may or may not have full access to the physician's records; the religious counselor may have an understanding of some of his problems; the head of the part-time placement office, the loan-fund committee, or the committee on scholarships may have still further information about him; the admissions committee possesses valuable information about him of which many of the specialists are unaware. The poor student tends to be thoroughly taken to pieces and never reassembled; he is apt to receive excellent counsel from disassociated specialists which he is unable to integrate into a plan that will function for the entire self for which he must act.

From the standpoint of social adjustments, consider what his problems are. If he attends a college away from his home, he finds that all the community affiliations which had helped give him a sense of social support suddenly drop away. Even though he lives at home, the old connections tend to be seriously weakened. He finds his circle of friendships and acquaintanceships practically demolished. He must, as one of a whole group cut adrift from old social moorings, choose himself a new circle of acquaintances and cultivate some of them into friendships. He not only must be a chooser, but he also must act in such a way as to attract the choices of others to himself. He has very few of the means to which he has been accustomed for reestablishing himself socially. He cannot count very much on his family and their status and assets—if they have such things!—to help represent him in this new arena. On the other hand, if his family has been somewhat of a drawback to him socially hitherto, he suddenly may find himself released to represent himself as he wishes. On the whole, the new student is apt to feel rather severely the dislocation that inevitably occurs in all his social adjustments.

His relationship to his family, and all this has meant to him, suddenly must undergo transformation if he is to succeed in his new venture. Until a student leaves home he is apt to have many little things done for him that he has come to take for granted. Some one has probably called him to get up mornings and even taken the responsibility for calling him a second time in order to get him to school on time. Someone has probably still been doing a good deal about dressing him—seeing that he has a whole pair of socks to put on the next morning, that he has a clean shirt, that he changes his underthings regularly, has perhaps even hung up his pajamas after he left in a hurry each morning. Someone has probably taken a very personal interest in what and how much and when he ate, how often he bathed, how much he slept—probably far more than anyone will be able to in college. He may feel relieved to be released from this supervision but may, even so, have a good many adjustments to make because of this release.

He finds that suddenly he has far more freedom than he has ever known before. There are comparatively few time commitments—no regular study times, no definite recommendations as to how to divide his time between the studies he likes best and those he likes least. There is no frequent check by a teacher to see how he is getting along. He has larger sums of money in his possession at any one time than ever before, which sometimes has the effect of making a freshman feel that he has unlimited financial resources, inexperienced as he is in the fact that tuition, board and room expense, books, and other inevitable expenses will fully deplete the amount that at first seems so huge. There is no close supervision of his sleep, of his exercise, of his various activities, and he shakes around in a situation that at first in many ways seems to him free and easy and to offer unlimited possibilities.

He inevitably finds himself in a situation where the competition is much keener than any he has felt thus far. He has competed successfully in his high-school group, but now he has for competition none of the high-school failures with whom he compared so favorably, but rather, only the successes from any number of high schools, all of whom are trying to regain the relatively advantageous positions which they enjoyed in their high schools. A student's best efforts do not seem to take him so far as they used to. This must inevitably lead to frequent periods of discouragement for most of the group. He finds that he does not seem to be able to read so fast, that apparently he had not learned as much in preparatory school as he should have about his subjects, that his fellow students seem extremely competent, and that the professors seem to expect a great deal more than they should.

He finds the curriculum of the college vast and very detailed. He probably does not know it, but he is a victim of a development typified by Harvard where in 1869 there were six courses offered in English; in 1896 there were 40; and in 1924 there were 65 in English alone.

Not only does he find the intellectual standards suddenly advanced far more than he had expected, but he also finds that other standards which prevail on the campus, standards that are fully as important for him to meet, are all at once very different and difficult. In his senior year in high school he was one of those who set the standards for the whole high-school group; they were *his* standards, and he met them easily. Now the standards tend to be those of a group who are three years older chronologically and far beyond him in sophistication, assurance, and maturity of interest. Fashions in clothing are suddenly very different; there are apparently queer but rigidly correct ways of behaving to which he is expected to conform. In the areas of dating, student organizations, athletics, there are a great many mores which he is hectically eager to master so that he may be completely identified with the group of college students of which he is nominally a member. He will rush thoughtlessly into almost any type of behavior in his effort not to be thought by them different and immature.

If he has a roommate, there are further day by day adjustments that must be made. It may be the first time he has ever attempted to get along in the same room for a whole year with anyone so different in his background and general standards and interests as his new roommate. We remember going to see a freshman girl in a college dormitory about ten o'clock one night. We found her at her desk studying, the lamp shade carefully turned to throw most of the room into shadow. In one of the twin beds, tossing and turning in great agitation of spirit, was her roommate *under a big black umbrella,* trying to shut out the light, trying not to interfere with her studious roommate, but firm in her belief that she must be in bed by 9:30 every night in order to get the requisite amount of rest and carry on the habits which had been so well established at home!

The greatest adjustment which any freshman has to make, however, tends to be an emotional one. He has recently been graduated from high school with a fair amount of approval and acclaim, he has been encouraged to feel that he has achieved a sort of climax. When he becomes a freshman in college, however, he suddenly feels demoted, he feels awkward in the midst of apparently serene, self-assured gods and goddesses, he is a bit lonesome, he knows he is unsophisticated, very ignorant, and ill prepared for college life, quite bewildered as to what it is really all about and as to how he should act in this strange and demanding environment.

Colleges have done three things, as they have realized more realistically the situation their new students face and as they have discovered what dire consequences in student mortality this situation was having. They have, (1) organized an intensive preliminary period of freshman orientation, usually designated as "freshman week"; (2) they have reorganized all the provisions for extraclass life of students so as better to provide for their needs; and (3) they have tended to reorganize the curriculum so that students can better find themselves in relation to the organized knowledge which the college presents to them, and so that they can improve their reading, writing, and study skills generally.

What can be accomplished through Freshman Week to help students become oriented to college? There are four main objectives to be accomplished by a freshman week program: (1) The college should take advantage of this period to supplement its information about the incoming student in every way possible; (2) the college should arrange the program for those few days to help the student learn as much as possible about the college; (3) the college should initiate as many processes as possible that will make for the greater emotional security of the student; and (4) the college should take advantage of every opportunity to bring about a heightened college morale through the mobilization of upper-class students and faculty in behalf of the incoming class.

A heavy program of tests during freshman week is probably not the best plan for getting to know the incoming students. It is far better, if possible, to depend upon the results of a series of objective tests, given over a protracted period before the student has actually embarked upon his college career. We would in no way minimize the value of the results of objective tests, but the best results are probably not obtained under the stress of freshman week conditions. It may be necessary to supplement whatever information is available from objective tests previously administered. If so, it is important that the results of the supplementary tests be ready for use by the faculty adviser in helping the student outline his college plans.

It is quite important to have the health staff of the college examine the incoming students as soon during freshman week or immediately thereafter, as can reasonably be done. Family doctors who fill out college health questionnaires occasionally have mistaken notions as to the purposes of these questionnaires, wishing to help the student accomplish his purpose of being accepted by a college, not realizing that too-optimistic evaluations of health may ultimately defeat other important hopes of the student.

If the admissions office has functioned well, there is available when the freshman arrives, a very valuable set of records describing the sort of person he is. On the basis of these records the incoming students should each have been carefully assigned to a member of the personnel staff (who may, of course, also be an academic instructor). These counselors, already fairly well acquainted with the boy or girl through his other records which have been carefully studied, attempt during freshman week to establish a friendly relationship, so that the student may begin to feel at home and to talk about himself, his hopes and fears and plans. It is this counselor who should, during freshman week, help the student make immediate and long-term plans for his college experience.

The faculty counseling plan, however, is not sufficient for accomplishing all the results desired from freshman week. It has been found eminently worth while in a number of institutions to work out in addition a system of upper-class student counselors. Although most institutions still use seniors as counselors, it has been found very advantageous in at least one university to select from the freshman class at the end of the first semester all those freshmen who seem most likely material, to give them a stimulating series of group discussions during the second semester, and to groom them to serve the next year's incoming class. This plan has a number of advantages over that of using seniors; it spares the busy seniors a very arduous duty; it takes advantage of all the emotional identification that those who have just gone through the adjustment process can feel for those who are next to go through with it; it offers the best possible training in leadership to a group who can go on developing within the college for three more years; and it develops within the college three classes that have as their cores leaders who can be counted on.

A good deal has been written about the various programs of lectures, trips, library excursions, etc., that have been developed in various institutions. It does not seem worth while to dwell on these further. We would stress the fact, however, that if freshmen are kept at the end of a one-way telephone wire very much of the time during freshman week, they soon develop the ability to ignore completely what is said at them. It is probably far better to arrange for them to learn about the campus, about its traditions, its geography, its peculiarities, its "who's who," in small, informal groups with student leaders, or in friendly conversation with a faculty counselor, where variation in tempo and the opportunity for response whip up attention and interest.

An outline for discussions which was worked out by a group of prospective sophomore counselors during their freshman training course has proved of very real direct value to the students who worked it out and also of unquestioned value and help to the incoming freshmen, who were, as a result, provided with informed, interesting, and sympathetic sophomore counselors. It is reproduced here for whatever suggestive value it may have.

CURRICULUM FOR SOPHOMORE COUNSELORS AT NORTHWESTERN UNIVERSITY[1]
The College Environment: factors influencing a satisfactory adjustment to it; constructive aids in such adjustment

I. Living conditions
   A. Commuters
      1. Factors affecting their adjustment
         a. Lack of contacts through dormitory and fraternity life
         b. Fatigue
         c. Difficulty because of short periods they spend on campus
         d. Home conditions
             (1) family attitudes toward student and college
             (2) student's attitude toward his family
             (3) amount of work and responsibility at home

[1] This outline was produced at Northwestern University by a group of sophomore counselors-in-training under the direction of Mrs. Alma Stack Persing.

(4) nature and extent of family resources
(5) standing in community
(6) cultural advantages of home
    e. Student's own attitude
        (1) desire to make new contacts and broaden experience
        (2) degree of willingness to make extra effort on campus
        (3) degree of self-reliance and independence
        (4) dependence on family group
        (5) dependence on old social and religious groups
        (6) personality traits (see section II)
2. Constructive helps in adjustment
    a. Suggest places to eat and dress (Union Building)
    b. Suggest places to study (Deering Library should take care of all students)
    c. Organization of time and study
        (1) Organizations and fraternities (see section II)
        (2) Activities (see section II)
        (3) Group leader's help
            (a) personal contacts
            (b) faculty-student meetings that have been partly planned
        (4) Notices of campus life and activities—bulletin boards, newspaper, etc.

B. Dormitories or fraternities
    1. Factors affecting adjustment
        a. Student's own attitudes will to a certain extent be the same as those for the commuter
        b. Attractiveness and convenience of room and house
        c. Ability to adjust and cooperate with the other men in the house
        d. Ability to adjust to roommate
        e. Characteristics of student
            All traits affecting social success (see following sections)
        f. Age, health, and stability of student
        g. Student's background
            (1) Family group
                Only and privileged child
                From large family
                Used to congenial groups
                Used to friction
                Used to assuming responsibility for others
            (2) Living standards
                Neatness, moral values, cultural values, etc.
            (3) Feeling of social security
                If insecure, feels social stigma if not placed in the right fraternity
    2. Constructive helps in adjustment
        a. Change of room or roommates. Before man lives in unapproved house, he should check with dean of men
        b. Cultivation of desirable attitudes

(1) Analysis of reason for misfit. This is often sufficient. Question of breaking of pledge may arise, with attendant question of whether it is better for the man to adjust to the situation or get away from it
(2) Develop sense of responsibility
(3) Relieve possible anxiety concerning social stigma
 c. Necessity of a pledge's observing the fraternity rules
  (1) Explain purpose
  (2) Value of cooperation
 d. Small points in getting along with men in the house and roommates
  (1) Respect others' property
  (2) Respect others' comfort
  (3) Be friendly, tolerant, and tactful
  (4) Be anxious to help, but avoid meddling in others' affairs
  (5) Be willing to take criticism
  (6) Do not be snobbish. (Especially may this be true in case of fraternity man living in an open house)
II. Social adjustment
 A. What is social adjustment?
  1. Liking people, and being liked
  2. Feeling at home with people and adequate to any situation
 B. Factors influencing social adjustment
  1. Social experience
   a. Dress, manners, poise
   b. Background home
    (1) Nationality of family
     Children of foreign-born parents may be at a disadvantage
    (2) Family important in community
     (a) If student depends on this, he may brag, feel homesick, resentful, etc., if he does not do well here
     (b) May be assured and at ease
    (3) Family inferior in community
     May feel inferior and compensate by
     (a) Over aggressiveness
     (b) Withdrawing from contacts
     (c) Choosing undesirable contacts
  2. Town
   a. Locality of
    Difficult for students from other parts of the country to adjust to attitudes, habits, customs, etc.
   b. Small town
    (1) Small-town person used to close personal contacts
    (2) Misinterprets casualness and apparent selfishness of urban life. This is one of the most frequent criticisms of Northwestern University
    (3) Misses seeing familiar faces and places—may become extremely lonely

(4) Unused to distances and excitement—may become tired and distracted
  c. School experience; private, coeducational, military, small state university, etc.
  d. Personal attitudes toward others
   (1) Real interest in others
    (a) Consideration
    (b) Attention to conversation
    (c) Willingness to give and accept favors
    (d) Reasonable conformity to established standards
    (e) Generous, loyal, tolerant
  e. Self-attitudes
   (1) Self-confidence and self-respect obviate bragging, aggressiveness, oversensitiveness, jealousy, extreme shyness
   (2) Self-control—the spoiled-child attitude
   (3) Lack of undue self-interest
   Has the maturing personality been blocked at the adolescent stage?
  f. Other personality traits and habits as factors
   (1) Adaptability; ease with which individual adjusts to new personalities and environment
   (2) Method of meeting problems
    (a) Does he face problems (social or otherwise) and meet them or
    (b) Does he evade all issues and withdraw?
C. Constructive help in making social adjustment
 1. New Student Week. Group leaders' part
  a. Personal friendly welcome
  b. Introduction to others
  c. Develop group possibilities as far as possible—eat together, go places together, get men acquainted
  d. Help to develop other contacts
  e. Emphasize own well-established position
  f. Overcome unfamiliarity with campus
  g. Take plenty of time for individual conferences
 2. New Student Week. New student's part
  a. Get to meetings and appointments on time
  b. Do not be upset by tests, etc.
  c. Make the most of opportunity to make friends—concentrated attention of campus does not last
  d. Take responsibility about attending activities—they are planned for new students. Do not be afraid to mix
 3. Fraternities as a constructive help in social adjustment
  a. Choose group for personal development and friends, not national standing only
  b. Do not limit friends to one group
  c. Do not limit ideas to one group
  d. Do not think that the fraternity has "made you"

Justify your choice and existence by amounting to something yourself
- e. Attitude of the pledge
  - (1) Do not complain of the chapter
  - (2) Stand on your own feet. Rushing does not last
  - (3) Transfers must expect same treatment as frosh
  - (4) Be a good sport about pledge duties
- f. Man who gets into wrong fraternity
  - (1) Admit mistake frankly, without ill feeling, if adjustment is really impossible
  - (2) Recognize the fact that plenty of desirable people are not congenial with everyone. Do not criticize group or self
  - (3) Serious for transfer to break pledge as the chances of repledging are small
4. Activities as a help in social adjustment
   - a. Purpose of activities
     - (1) Develop the individual
     - (2) To help make a campus situation which will offer opportunities for physical, intellectual, and social recreation and development of all students
   - b. Advantages from participation in activities
     - (1) Friends
     - (2) Training
     - (3) Experience
     - (4) Recreation
     - (5) Service
   - c. Best way to choose activities
     - (1) Choose with purpose, then concentrate efforts
     - (2) Do not necessarily choose to do familiar things Broaden experience, develop new powers
   - d. Things to do to get into activity
     - (1) Get definite information about when and how to join. Ask assistance from group leaders, activity heads, personnel office, etc.
     - (2) Be dependable, resourceful, and interested
   - e. List of activities with officers will be presented to group leaders at the meeting before New Student Week.
   - f. In advising activity for a man, consider his needs and ability

III. Financial adjustment
  A. Working outside for room and board
  1. Advantages
     - a. Saves living expenses
     - b. Sometimes more pleasant than in an undesirable campus house
  2. Disadvantages
     - a. Four hours time required per day for room and board; and lesser amounts for room or board
       - (1) Necessitates easy program
       - (2) Taxes strength

(3) Consumes time that might go to extracurricular activities
    b. The student may become a commuter without the advantages of home
3. Constructive help
    a. Be sure relation with employer is satisfactory
    b. Should carry light program
    c. Discourage too much participation in activities, but urge at least one contact
    d. Help to make friends, and if attitude is defensive be sure to go more than halfway

B. Other employment
1. Means of securing
Personal effort or through employment bureau in personnel department
2. Types of work
Odd jobs, clerking, typing, sign painting, switchboard, etc.
3. Advantages
    a. May permit more desirable living conditions than a job for room and for meals
    b. May be more educational and desirable
    c. Less apt to result in an undesirable attitude on part of the student than working for one's room
4. Disadvantages
    a. Usually less remunerative than above
    b. Less regular employment
    c. More difficult to secure

C. Scholarships and loans
1. How secured
    a. All information can be secured from Mr. Nims in personnel office
    b. Desirable first to consult personnel counselor or some faculty member who will make personal investigation
2. Advantages
    a. Allows full time for study and normal student life
    b. Stress necessity for good grades. Demand so great that selection is now very high
3. Disadvantages
    a. Not advisable to assume too large a debt. May be better to stay out of school a year, or transfer to cheaper school

D. Management of allowance
1. Spending too much owing to
    a. Inexperience in handling money
    b. False standard of value
    c. Feeling of social insecurity
    d. Desire to "keep up" with some individual or group
2. Constructive aids
    a. Budget may be planned
    b. Desirable friends are not "bought"

  c. Emphasize desirable campus opinion—campus leaders have arrived because of intelligent effort not because of foolish spending—or have they?
  d. Stress own economies
  e. Give practical information about
   (1) Good places to shop
   (2) Unnecessary campus expenditures
IV. Health
 A. Major illnesses
  1. Infirmary and health service
  2. Explain regulations about infirmary and doctor's excuses to be presented to instructors for absences
 B. Physical defects (speech, blemishes, crippled, etc.)
  1. As factor in adjustment
   a. Makes a man different
   b. May make participation in studies or activities difficult
   c. Limits opportunities for social contact—through the nature of the defect as well as the man's attitude
  2. Constructive help
   a. Discuss with personnel counselor
   b. Use of agencies on campus to correct such defects—corrective gym, speech clinic, clinics at medical school, etc.
   c. Group leader's cooperation in helping to make possible social contacts
 C. General lack of vitality
  1. Causes
   a. Poor arrangement of time, loss of sleep, late hours, etc.
   b. Worry, emotional strain, etc.
   c. Fatigue due to too heavy schedule
   d. Poor vitality due to some physical trouble
  2. Results
  Poor achievement and adjustment in any college situation
  3. Constructive help
  Report cases as it is necessary to analyze cause for condition. A man may "drag along" for entire year without anyone's knowledge
V. Scholastic adjustment
 A. Factors influencing
  1. Objectives of students in the university
   a. Cultural, social—the gentleman's college
   b. Pure knowledge—education for its own sake
   c. Constructive thinking—knowledge as a means of evolving a better social order
   d. Vocational or professional training for purposes of earning a living
  2. Previous school training
   a. Scholastic standards of the school
   b. Closeness of supervision and faculty contacts

c. Student on probation because of grades, or of unaccredited college or preparatory school
d. Type of school: finishing, night, denominational, state university, etc.
3. Power to accomplish scholastic adjustment depends on
   a. Study habits—regularity, keeping up to date, reviewing, organizing, place of study, etc.
   b. Mental discipline—ability to concentrate: influenced by relaxation, physical condition, emotional state, mental content, etc.
   c. Ability to grasp printed material
      (1) Reads without grasping
      (2) Reads too slowly
      (3) Reads words
      (4) Reads ideas but does not see relation
   d. Interest in subject matter and in learning
   e. Motivation
   f. Thoroughness of preparation
   g. Degree of mental ability
4. Campus attitude
   Is it hostile to intellectual success?
5. Personality factors and attitudes in scholastic success
   a. Independence, dependability, working honestly, getting things in on time
   b. Enthusiasm
      Interest is not inherent in any course
   c. Taking responsibility for success
      (1) Do not blame situation
      (2) Teachers-pick-on-me attitude
      (3) The student who seeks favors
   d. Open-mindedness
      (1) Intellectual curiosity about new ideas
      (2) Desire to examine ideas and modify points of view if convinced

B. Constructive help
1. New student must learn at once to
   a. Depend on self without supervision
      (1) Plan time and study program
      (2) Choose between the many things offered
   b. Recognize the standard of work required
      (1) Check on progress with professor if uncertain
      (2) Realize importance of mid-semester grades
      (3) Understand nature of grading system, curve of distribution, what "A" means, etc.
2. Know faculty
   a. Make definite appointments for help. Do not expect the instructor to stop after class
   b. Do not be afraid to consult faculty members

ORIENTATION

        c. Recognize value of knowing faculty. They are willing and glad to see students but cannot seek them out
     3. If poorly prepared or failing without knowing why
        a. Do not wait before doing something
        b. Consult personnel counselor if you do not make a successful faculty contact
     4. If on probation or failing at mid-semester (same as above)
VI. Technical adjustments
   A. Program planning
     1. Transfers' difficulties
        a. Getting credit from former school. Adjusted through registrar of particular school. Consult with personnel counselor if desired
        b. Arranging courses in field of concentration and required subjects
           (1) Results in discouragement and uninteresting courses for some transfers
           (2) May make too heavy program for new student, especially for one entering on probation or working outside
     2. Constructive help
        a. Group leaders can best help by being on the lookout for badly planned programs, supposed errors in credit, etc. Consult with counselor
        b. Stress fact that all adjustments of program must be made early and that a bad program does not necessarily have to be carried
        c. Suggest good professors
        d. Tell student not to wait for help; go for help
   B. Registration
     1. Difficulties obvious
     2. Constructive help
        a. Advise student to have clear idea of what he wants to take, what the requirements are, etc. before going and to be familiar with bulletin
        b. To expect some confusion, take time, do not worry, be pleasant
        c. Not to be alarmed if mistake is made. It can be corrected
VII. Adapting of new ideas
   A. Aspects of new environment which may modify students' standards and value concepts
     1. Urban community
     2. Highly gregarious coeducational school
     3. Freedom from restriction and supervision
     4. Set of campus traditions and nature of campus opinion
     5. Few ideas and information secured in classroom through student contacts
   B. Possible results of above
     1. Modifies ideas of own importance. May feel inadequate, insecure, inferior for first time. Sympathy

2. May be unable to fit self to new standards
    a. Entirely discards old, without real grasp of new
    b. Fails to adjust old to new—clings entirely to old
    c. Questions both old and new value concepts. Period of uncertainty and depression
C. Standards and ideas commonly in conflict
  1. Attitudes to opposite sex
    a. Campus attitude toward necking as means to popularity
    b. How much companionship is usual
       Many men develop inferiority because no "dates"
    c. Place of emotional experience in well-balanced life
  2. Attitude toward religion
    a. Conflict often results when student has come from conventional religious home
    b. May result in feeling guilt, indecision, or bitterness and loss of idealism
  3. Conventions of dress, manners, smoking, etc.
  4. Attitude toward material things
    a. Idea that everyone on campus is rich
      (1) Must pretend to be well off
      (2) Discouraged because feels unable to compete
    b. Comes to school with false standards and objectives
       Explains much undesirable social behavior
  5. Attitudes toward educational objectives
    a. May meet with campus opinion that it is silly to study, all right to cheat, socially unacceptable to get grades
    b. Results in feeling of not belonging, of being queer, or in destroying scholastic interests and ambitions
D. Helps in these readjustments
  1. Foster wholesome campus opinion
  2. Student must recognize that
    a. All worth-while people continually modify their ideas
       To be static is to be dead
    b. Harm is done if student feels shame or guilt because ideas are changing
    c. Encourage free discussion of questions with other students, interested faculty, and others

During the summer, as applicants for admission are accepted, they are assigned not only to adult personnel advisers, but also to the sophomore counselors who have been groomed to serve them. It is well not to assign more than 10 advisees to any one sophomore counselor. The sophomore counselor, as well as the faculty-personnel counselor, should, in advance of meeting him, be given pertinent information about his advisee from the admissions data.

The freshman-week program may well use these groupings of from 6 to 10 freshmen as its units of structure. There should not only be discussions, during which most of the information now offered in lectures is touched upon, but there should also be a variety of social activities and good times planned for these groups as units. In one institution the director of such a program said that, when a group of six freshman boys and their sophomore counselor and a group of six freshman girls and their counselor got together for lunches, movies, games, library trips, etc., the boys always wisecracked and the girls giggled, everyone had a good time, and all began to feel very much at home.

A plan for social activities in small groups, with plenty of variety of activity so that everyone has opportunities to participate and everyone has opportunities to focus his attention on a few instead of a mass of individuals, can do a great deal for the feelings of belonging and security of the incoming student.

In this sort of organization, it is easy for each sophomore counselor to learn his freshmen immediately in a way that often is not accomplished by anyone in the college until much later in the year—until perhaps too late. The personnel officer in charge of freshman week should keep in close touch with all sophomore counselors throughout freshman week to avail himself quickly of information which he may be able to use helpfully in behalf of freshmen.

A calendar of preparations for freshman week may, perhaps, suggest further detail:

September	Get acquainted with incoming freshmen
September–February	Continue study of freshmen for leadership possibilities
February	Invite outstanding freshmen to prepare to become sophomore counselors for next year's freshmen
February–June	Hold regular, informal discussion groups of prospective sophomore counselors. Have groups no larger than 15 or 20 and encourage them to work out their own discussion outline

February–June	Review the college handbook critically and revise with suggestions from the staff counselors and student counselors
February–June	Review catalogue or college bulletin of information and revise in the light of suggestions from staff counselors and student counselors
February–June	Review personnel records and revise, if necessary, in the light of the experience to date
February–June	Review system of faculty counselors and revise, if desirable
April or May	Plan program for fall with student government officers, heads of religious organizations, athletic association officers, Panhellenic, interfraternity council, heads of dormitories, other personnel officers, etc.
July–September	Work on admission of new students; send new students carefully worked-out information; assign new students to faculty and student counselors; write sophomore counselors about fall program and any further instructions; work out further details of fall program
September	Reception of incoming freshman. Freshman week program. Keep in close touch with both faculty counselors and sophomore counselors in order to learn immediately of any incipient problems for which the resources of the institution might be of help.

Other means which the college may use in its attempt to start the student off to a less hazardous future follow:

1. A closer relationship with "feeding" high schools. Better descriptive material sent the high schools; more visits back and forth of both students and staff (see also discussion in Chapter IV on Selection and Admissions, pages 54–67).

2. A closer relationship with parents of students.

3. The organization of a more effective faculty advisorial system than the usual one which utilizes academic officers who have no talent or training in personnel work.

4. The organization of the student living units for better orientation and better living (see discussion in Chapter XII on Housing).

5. The better coordination of all the efforts of the personnel specialists, the admissions officer, the physicians, the

financial-aid office, the director of extracurricular activities, the director of religious activities, the faculty counselors, the heads of dormitories, etc.

6. More effort to learn the student in order that the institution may aid his development more wisely; cumulative records recognized as indispensable; objective tests more widely used.

Undoubtedly, one of the most significant efforts that the colleges are making to enable the student to adjust more satisfactorily to college opportunities is, instead of merely adjusting the student to the college, to reorganize the opportunities the college offers him also. We find junior colleges springing up all over the country, differentiation of objectives getting under way, general colleges, horizontal and vertical divisions of the curriculum, cooperation with the Aiken commission of the Progressive Education Association, the organization of new and different curricula, cooperative state and national testing programs, revision of teaching methods, the introduction of "house plans," as well as the organization of "orientation courses" designed to help students see the woods in spite of the trees. Discussion of all of these innovations is to be found in books and periodicals. Another tendency which seems to be developing is the offering of individual diagnosis and both individual and group instruction in such "enabling" courses as corrective speech, how to study, how to increase reading speed and comprehension, corrective exercise, and appearance and manners.

It must not be thought that "orientation" is something that is done to freshmen at the beginning of their college course and then to be considered finished and over with. The sort of efforts outlined in this chapter, well organized and conscientiously carried out, will do a great deal to insure that the new student start out under the most favorable conditions possible. He will more surely possess information pertinent to his successful adjustment, he will be emotionally fortified, he will be well launched toward satisfying social adjustments, and the college will know far more about him than it used to learn about its students for several months. A really effective program of orientation, however, will continue, not only throughout the first year of a student's college career, but also through the subsequent years, its efforts to help students avoid difficulties, scholastic, health, social, economic, vocational, and emotional. Suggestions for what might legitimately be termed the continuation of the orientation program are to be found in other chapters of Part II of this book.

BIBLIOGRAPHY

ANGELL, ROBERT C.: *A Study in Undergraduate Adjustment*, University of Chicago Press, Chicago, 1930, ix + 164 pp.

BENNETT, M. E.: *College and Life*, McGraw-Hill Book Company, Inc., New York, 1933, xiv + 456 pp.

———, and H. C. HAND: *Problems of Self-discovery and Self-direction.* McGraw-Hill Book Company, Inc., New York, 1935, xi + 171 pp.

BLAKE, MABELLE BABCOCK: *Guidance for College Women*, D. Appleton-Century Company, Inc., New York, 1926, xviii + 285 pp.

BOOK, W. F.: *Learning How to Study and Work Effectively*, 18–475 pp., Ginn and Company, Boston, 1926.

———: *How to Succeed in College*, Warwick & York, Inc., Baltimore, 1927, 192 pp.

———: "Newer Personnel Practices in College," *Personnel Journal*, 7: 38–53, June, 1928.

BOUCHER, C. S.: "Orientation and Survey Courses at the University of Chicago," *School and Society*, 27: 760–761, June, 1928.

BRAGDON, H. C.: *Counseling the College Student*, Harvard University Press, Cambridge, Mass., 1929, 11 + 162 pp.

CHARTERS, W. W.: "The Troubles of the Freshman," *Journal of Higher Education*, 4: 331–332, June, 1933.

DOERMANN, HENRY J.: *The Orientation of College Freshmen*, Williams & Wilkins Company, Baltimore, 1926, 162 pp.

EMME, E. E.: *Adjustment Problems of College Freshmen*, Cokesbury Press, Nashville, Tenn., 1933, 152 pp.

FITTS, CHARLES F., and F. SWIFT: "Construction of Orientation Courses for College Freshmen," *California University Publications in Education*, 2: 145–250. 1928.

HIBBEN, JOHN G.: "Report of the President for Year Ending July 31, 1925," *The Official Register*, Princeton University, 1925, 88 + pp.

KNODE, J. C.: *Orienting the Student in College*, Teachers College, Bureau of Publications, Columbia University, New York, vi + 140 pp., 1930.

LEONARD, EUGENIA A.: *Problems of Freshman College Girls*, Teachers College, Bureau of Publications, Columbia University, New York, 1932, 139 pp.

NEWMAN, H. H.: "An Orientation Course," *Journal of Higher Education*, 2: 121–126, March, 1931.
ODELL, CHARLES W.: "Predicting the Scholastic Success of College Students," *University of Illinois Bulletin* 52, 1930, 44 pp.
PFENNIG, HAZEL T., and JOY M. LACEY: "Orientation Course in College Curriculum," *Teachers College Journal*, 2: 47–55, November, 1930.
"Report of Committee G," in *American Association of University Professors Bulletin* 8: 350–380, October, 1922.
RIGHTMIRE, GEORGE W.: "The Floundering Freshman," *Journal of Higher Education*, 1: 185–192, April, 1930.
STEPHENS, WINSTON: "The Conference on College Admissions and Guidance," *Educational Record*, 14: 15–22, January, 1933.
STODDARD, GEORGE D., and GUSTAF FREDEN: "The Status of Freshman Week in Large Universities," *School and Society*, 24: 586–589, Nov. 6, 1926.
STRANG, RUTH: *Personal Development and Guidance in College and Secondary School*, Harper & Brothers, New York, 1934, vii + 341 pp.
WERNER, OSCAR H.: *Every College Student's Problems*, Silver, Burdett & Company, New York, 1929, xi + 370 pp.
WILKINS, ERNEST H.: "The Orientation of the College Student," in *Problems of College Education*, pp. 247–260, University of Minnesota Press, Minneapolis, 1928.
WILLIAMSON, E. G., and J. B. DARLEY: *Student Personnel Work*, McGraw-Hill Book Company, Inc., New York, 1936, 313 pp.

Chapter VI

HELPING STUDENTS TO LEARN SOCIAL WISDOM AND SKILL

The Social Program

Among the persistent needs of all normal individuals at all ages and stages of development are the securing and giving of affection, the accomplishment of a series of social belongings, the achievement of a certain amount of likeness to other people, the progressive assumption of responsibility for the welfare and happiness of others, and the progressive development of a sense of selfhood based on the maturing of value concepts. Although many prophets in higher education have seemed to believe either that these needs are relatively unimportant or else that college students are peculiarly exempt from them, the contention of many thoughtful people is that this is by no means the case. The need of college students for social education, even though it be at a higher level, is as real as that of nursery-school youngsters.

One of the reasons why the importance of social education has been so neglected in higher education undoubtedly is the fact that scholars traditionally are supposed to be entirely above and beyond recognizing such a thing as social and affectional relationships. This is a grotesque role wished on scholars during the Middle Ages, which they have never had the good sense to disown completely. Contemporary affectional relationships are, with few exceptions, more real and more important to any normal person than the study of any sort of subject matter, no matter how fascinating in itself and how interestingly presented. It is difficult to understand how higher education could have failed so completely to take these relationships into consideration in its educational plan. It is our contention that the college which includes prominent consideration of social education in its total program of education is contributing to civilization values as important as any that come out of scientific discovery or artistic creation.

Consider the human material that enters a college. Each student, to a fairly large degree, finds himself totally disrupted socially from those ties and relationships in which he has found opportunity to give and receive affection. He usually finds that he is in a much more heterogeneous group than he has hitherto known; he usually finds that it is a group with which at first he feels alien. Each, inevitably and immediately, begins to put out social feelers toward others in his group, hoping to meet with a response to some of his projections so that he can begin to reestablish himself in the social fabric. He wants to end his social isolation as soon as possible. Just as nature abhors a vacuum, so all normal individuals abhor social disconnection.

Someone should undertake a study of the factors which determine the social connections that college students make with each other. Is the matter of projecting social impulse entirely haphazard or are there certain discoverable factors that guide projection and reception in the first days of each student's college life? How, and on what bases do college students attempt to perfect (from their standpoint) their social relations? Although the whole field of social dynamics is one of the most important areas within the personnel field, there is still woeful ignorance concerning its simplest aspects and an amazing lack of interest in its possibilities.

It is apparent to the discerning eye that one of the projects prosecuted by every student with the most energy and the most persistence is work on his "social belongingness." For the most part without thoughtful, conscious plan, but none the less purposively, each student tries to attract the favorable regard of this or that person, receives encouragingly the social advances of certain ones and ignores discouragingly or repels the advances of others. Each tries to relate himself to one or another nebulous or well-formed social group. Each tries to root himself socially; each wants to feel comfortable and secure, attached socially to others, with others dependent socially on him.

The lines of stratification along which social divisions occur in the college group are not sufficiently understood. The Lynds in *Middletown* and Sorokin in some of his studies have demonstrated how divisions in communities outside the college occur along occupational lines. For very young girls, age seems to be one important stratification force; for newly arrived immigrants and for many second generations, nationality is the outstanding determinant—much more effective than occupation or age or neighborhood. We have not yet sufficiently distinguished the major bases for social grouping in college communities, or the bases for the minor groupings that appear within the major groups. What are the principles of major and minor cohesion in the already sifted group of those attending college?

Each new student, as he becomes one of the inchoate mass of new students, finds discomfort in not feeling sufficiently like others he sees around him. One of the early discernible efforts which each new student makes is to achieve a certain amount of identification with others by attempting to be like them. At the college level, this phenomenon, too, has received little attention. Certainly, few college administrators have consciously attempted to engineer and utilize the social force that exists in this situation for the production of greater social power and individual development.

How many college presidents in their welcoming addresses at the beginning of the academic year have pointed out the dangers of a lack of social responsibility on the part of those generously endowed by nature, and privileged beyond their noncollege contemporaries! And how frequently are students exhorted to feel a sense of responsibility for the welfare and happiness of others! And yet too few college programs are set up to provide practice and growth in this respect. A few really effective programs of student-faculty cooperative government, a few programs of student participation in industry and in community projects, provide praiseworthy exceptions. It should be possible, however, to redesign the total college experience with due regard to the opportunity it affords each student to accept and discharge satisfactorily his social responsibilities. College students frequently find no obstacle and even find encouragement to living in a completely egocentric way that seriously retards their normal emotional and social development. Certainly one of the norms of adulthood is the ability to think and behave in the broader interests of others. Colleges should reconsider seriously their programs for advancing along this line the picked group of youth entrusted to them. Exhortation alone will not prove effective. Living conditions, social groupings, college traditions, extracurricular activities, the curriculum per se should all reinforce each other in the interests of this objective.

According to a preliminary study made by one of the authors for the American Council on Education,[1] the college years constitute a period during which young people advance their value concepts in three important respects: (1) they learn to distinguish values in terms of better and worse, instead of categorically in terms of right and wrong; in other words, they become sensitized to values; (2) they come to recognize their own inescapable responsibility for making choices—they recognize that they can no longer evade responsibility for honest value choices by delegating this authority to some convenient value authority; and (3) most college students during the four years of college are powerfully influenced to want to choose the better

[1] LLOYD-JONES, ESTHER, "College and Character," unpublished manuscript.

values (as they see them) in preference to the poorer ones. This same study also revealed how little colleges understand of the forces on their campuses that aid and hinder in this process. The study demonstrated that most colleges do not have any accurate notion of which faculty members, which student groups, which traditions, which extracurricular activities, which courses of study, etc., are the most potent forces for this sort of growth in individual students. Instead of placing the emphasis on this sort of educational influence, college executives still show most appreciation of those faculty members who produce the most books, still disregard in this respect the living conditions they provide for students, still appoint to their teaching faculties many men and women who have Ph.D.'s but who possess inferior personalities, still ignore the power that exists in student mores, in extracurricular activities, and in social life for the student's growth in value concepts.

The student personnel program should include within its scope consideration for the social education of students in the ways outlined above. One of the main concerns of the director of student personnel work should be the direction of a total program that will adequately advance the development of college students in these respects. The selection of new members of the college staff should prominently involve consideration of their usefulness in the social education of students. As already discussed in the chapter on housing of students, it is not sufficient for our highest educational institutions to be satisfied when they have warmly sheltered and adequately fed their student population; living arrangements should be planned in the important interest of social education (in the broad sense in which we are using the term). Directors of residence should not be thought of as guardians of student morals or as policemen but rather as tutors in an important phase of student education, as social engineers in behalf of social values. Physicians should not be appointed merely because they have M.D. degrees and are willing to work for the salary the college can designate, or merely because they are interested in public health; colleges should recognize the unusual opportunities open to the right sort of physician to do health counseling, to make valuable contributions to the value concepts of students. Colleges should not look with either idle toleration or active hostility on student traditions and mores; these should be carefully evaluated and utilized as powerful instruments for the social education of students. Extracurricular activities are far more than safety valves for young energy; properly viewed, they are as valuable as laboratories for social living as are science laboratories for scientific discovery.

Many writers, possessed of sensitive social conscience, are indicting colleges and universities because they are aloof from the real world; they accuse them of being ivory towers, of making possible a kind of living among an important youth group that is not only unrealistic but is also productive of social irresponsibility and emotional regression. There is no doubt but that much of this criticism is deserved. The college does need to relate itself—not only its faculty but, even more, its student body—to real life outside the cloistered walls that enclose many colleges. A thorough reexamination which takes this criticism into account is past due.

It must not be forgotten, however, that the very isolation of the college, the fact that it is quite self-contained, makes it an extraordinarily good laboratory in which the personnel and instructional staff can experimentally work out a program of social education. How can lines of social cleavage, which seem inexorably to form, but which are not yet fully understood, be conserved and strengthened? How can these same principles of major and minor cleavage be so influenced within the four-year span as to bring about social diversity—a result that is seemingly antithetical to the purpose of cleavage lines? How can every student be provided with the kind of group esteem that inevitably tends to raise him to a higher level of self-esteem and self-confidence and which at the same time releases him from egocentricity as can no other experience? What methods and techniques do we have to enable each group, whether separated by minor or major cleavage lines, to contribute to the social whole? Does the program, as a whole, provide example and practice in those principles of social relationship—sincerity, consideration of others, friendliness, reserve —which must be deeply ingrained in the attitudes and habits of an individual if he is to live harmoniously with himself and others? Does the social program provide example and practice in those amenities of social living, which, when based upon fundamental principles of social relationships, give to life an added grace?[1] Is the total campus situation rich with opportunities for students to exert leadership efforts? Is there ample opportunity for each to initiate and to lend support to worth-while, socially-beneficial undertakings? Do students receive unspoken encouragement (which is even more effective than oral suggestion) to mature emotionally in keeping with their superior intellectual maturity? Do students find during their college years a mature interpretation of selfhood in terms of social obligation and superior value concepts?

We have tended to neglect social education in higher education. To some degree our neglect is understandable. In very much the same way that the atom, which is invisible, was ignored by physicists until science discovered enough about it to give them some knowledge of its behavior and of how it could be controlled, so social relationship has been ignored by educators. Increasingly we will come to understand the patterns of social behavior appropriate for individuals of college level, and increasingly we will experiment with methods which induce desired social behavior. We will learn in what ways and by what methods to influence social environment within the laboratory that is the college.

[1] On the other hand, the social program is too often conceived narrowly as merely drill in how to hold a teacup, how to dance correctly; it is thought of as synonymous with the program of parties that are held each year.

We will learn how to apply constructively the truth that Alexis Carrel expresses in his *Man, the Unknown*:[1]

The psychological state of the social group determines, in a large measure, the number, the quality, and the intensity of the manifestations of individual consciousness. If the social environment is mediocre, intelligence and moral sense fail to develop. These activities may become thoroughly vitiated by bad surroundings. We are immersed in the habits of our epoch, like tissue cells in the organic fluids. Like these cells, we are incapable of defending ourselves against the influence of the community. The body more effectively resists the cosmic than the psychological world. It is guarded against the incursions of its physical and chemical enemies by the skin, and the digestive and respiratory mucosas. On the contrary, the frontiers of the mind are entirely open. Consciousness is thus exposed to the attacks of its intellectual and spiritual surroundings. According to the nature of these attacks, it develops in a normal or defective manner. . . . The education of the intelligence is relatively easy. But the formation of the moral, esthetic, and religious activities is very difficult. The influence of environment in these aspects of consciousness is much more subtle. No one can learn to distinguish right from wrong and beauty from vulgarity, by taking a course of lectures. Morality, art, and religion are not taught like grammar, mathematics, and history. To feel and to know are two profoundly different mental states. Formal teaching reaches intelligence alone. Moral sense, beauty, and mysticity are learned only when present in our surroundings and part of our daily life. . . . The growth of intelligence is obtained by training and exercise, whereas the other activities of consciousness demand a group with whose existence they are identified.

We would add to Carrel's statement the fact that "the social group"—"the social environment"—"the habits of our epoch" are, to a large degree, actually amenable to control. Especially are they amenable to control within the college community because, to an interesting extent, the college constitutes a small world of its own, partially isolated from the larger community.

[1] CARREL, ALEXIS, *Man, the Unknown*, pp. 150–152, Harper & Brothers, New York, 1935.

We would add also, that in the final analysis, "the social group" and "the social environment" are made of no other stuff than human relationships, and whatever quality the social environment possesses can be reduced in the final analysis to a matter of the patterns, number, direction, and strength of these relationships.

The social education of students should be an objective upon which higher education concentrates a good deal of attention during the next decade. A program of social education will not, however, survive regimentation. It will not be mastered by "trick" methods. A good program developed in one situation cannot be taken over bodily by another with any hope of success. The field should be carefully protected from many who will, with the utmost willingness, dub themselves "social engineers," and undertake to solve all problems in this field. The program of social education should be recognized as lying within the area of responsibility of the vice-president of the institution or the director of student personnel, but results can be accomplished only as it receives thoughtful, persistent, cooperative attention and effort from instructional as well as personnel staff members.

BIBLIOGRAPHY

ANGELL, ROBERT COOLEY: *The Campus*, D. Appleton-Century Company, Inc., New York, 1928, xii + 239 pp.

BLITZ, ANNE D.: "Social Conditions Arising from Inter-racial Contacts on the Campus," *Report of Tenth Annual Meeting of the National Association of Deans of Women*, Cleveland, 1923, pp. 73–79.

MOFFETT, M. L.: *Social Background and Activities of Teachers College Students*, Teachers College, Bureau of Publications, Columbia College, New York, 1929, 133 pp.

MORENO, J. L.: *Who Shall Survive?* Nervous and Mental Disease Publishing Company, Washington, D. C., 1934, xvi + 437 pp.

PRESCOTT, DANIEL: "Affective Factors in Education," *Official Report of the American Educational Research Association*, 1936, pp. 176–180.

———: "Non-intellectual Education," *Educational Record*, 17: pp. 248–258, April, 1936.

Sociometric Review, New York State Training School for Girls, Hudson, N. Y., 1936, 62 pp.

Sociometry, a Journal of Inter-personal Relations (Beacon, N. Y.: Sociometry), 1: pp. 1–267, July–October, 1937.

TUTTLE, H. S.: "The Campus and Social Ideals," *Journal of Educational Research*, 30: pp. 177–182, November, 1936.

VAN CLEVE, C. F.: "Thrill of College Life," *Junior College Journal* 5: pp. 151–152, December, 1934.

Chapter VII
GIVING STUDENTS INDIVIDUALIZED HELP

Counseling

Cowley sees three reasons why programs of counseling are being adopted by colleges and universities with increasing frequency: (1) counseling personalizes education; (2) counseling integrates education; and (3) counseling coordinates the various student personnel services.[1] He points out that about 1850 higher education in this country tended to become more and more impersonal as professors spent more time in their studies in imitation of European scholars. The curriculum has now become "literally thousands of times more extensive than that in vogue in the pre-Civil War College" and urgently needs integration if it is to serve as an effective educational instrument for the student instead of primarily a platform for professorial exhibitionism. The many personnel services that have grown up, on the one hand, give the student expert assistance for his various separate problems, but, without counseling, they also threaten to split him up into many parts which he finds difficult to reassemble. There seems little doubt that counseling has an important and increasingly recognized role to play as a function of higher education.

Various organizational plans for counseling have been presented elsewhere in this book (see Chap. III). It is purposed here to discuss the functions, principles, and problems concerned with counseling.

[1] Cowley, W. H., "Preface to Principles of Student Counseling," *Educational Record*, 18: 217, April, 1937.

Because of the very practical importance of vocational considerations and because education, in the good old classical tradition, tended to ignore them, we have in the last 20 years, intensified our interest in vocational counseling. Counseling with respect to vocational interests and plans is important (see Chap. IX); it provides for the personal consideration of each student's vocational problems; it serves to integrate the resources of the curriculum for the solution of those problems; and it coordinates the various personnel services in their behalf. A few educators have been so impressed with the value of vocational counseling that, for them, "counseling" has become synonymous with vocational counseling. Counseling, however, is just as truly and directly concerned with the curricular, social, religious, financial, physical, and emotional problems that students face as it is with the vocational. The province of counseling extends over every problem which the college students may have and is not limited even primarily to any one sort of problem.

Every problem, no matter what its superficial aspect may seem to be, must involve consideration of other aspects. Every counselor is under constant temptation to diagnose student problems as lying most importantly within the areas in which he feels (paradoxical as it may seem) either best informed, or personally most insecure. If a counselor, for example, has had training in health he is apt to see every problem first, and possibly too exclusively, from the standpoint of physical health. There is certainly psychological truth if not stark realism in the story of the country physician who confessed that he diagnosed every case that he possibly could as grippe because he was "a wow" on grippe. On the other hand a counselor is also apt to diagnose students' problems in terms of his own personal insecurities. If a counselor has personally experienced the panic that may come with not having a job, he may tend subsequently to focus every student problem in terms of vocational prospects. It is certainly important in counseling not to take the problem of students too innocently at their face value, but it is equally important that the counselor should not twist interpretations in terms of his own inexperience or his own insecurity.

It is essential, if counseling is to serve the purposes of higher education as it should, that it should not be forcibly fed. Nor should counseling be organized and administered in such a way that it may seem to the student body like medicine, no matter how sugar-coated. Counseling should be a casual, although by no means neglected or naïve, part of the whole educational plan.

Several examples may serve to make these points clearer: In institution A the personnel director is charged with responsibility for the counseling program. He has found it so difficult to interest a faculty, obsessed with its own scholarship, in counseling students that he has attempted to do most of it himself. Records of his interviews, electrically recorded on aluminum phonograph records, have convinced a number of impartial judges as well as himself that his interviews cannot possibly occasion any significant results. His interviews with students average about 10 or 15 minutes in length. In this short time he feels he cannot attempt to learn any additional facts about the student's problems; all he can do is to recite a number of obvious truths, most of which the student already knows in the same general way in which the counselor recounts them, and to exhort the student generally to renewed effort or to a better way of life, occasionally varying his technique with more or less veiled threats of possible dire consequences. The main result of this counselor's efforts is his own righteous feeling of having worked hard in the performance of duty, which he has mistaken for an indication that he is accomplishing his purposes.

In another institution, B University, much is made of the counseling program; students are summoned for elaborate conferences in which they are scientifically taken apart and put back together again. The counselors are all highly trained, and they take their work seriously. A student, summoned for one of these conferences, knows that a crucial moment in his life has come. Some students are tense and scared; others are defensive; still others endow the counselors with an unjustified omniscience, abandoning their own self-direction, initiative, and critical faculties to a group of counselors who are fitted out with every show of scientific authority.

In C College, the administration felt that it had provided satisfactorily for the counseling of students when it delegated members of the faculty as special counselors. Having named these counselors, it supposed that counseling was adequately provided for. There was no special head of the counselors; there was no compensation in increased salary or decreased teaching load which acknowledged counseling as an important professional activity. These "teacher counselors" continue to feel keenly the competition of the "teacher scholars" of the faculty and continue to devote their major effort to research, lecturing, and writing, with less and less time and interest given to counseling.

In still another institution a number of the most interested and talented members of the faculty have been designated as counselors. They are relieved of a fair share of their teaching load and understand that promotion is dependent on their contribution as counselors as much as it is upon their scholarly publications. In their capacity as instructors they are responsible to the dean of their division; in their capacity as counselors, they are responsible to the head of the student personnel program of the institution who holds regular meetings with them, discussing principles of counseling, steadily increasing their interest in counseling and their ability to contribute to the sound growth of students through counseling. Through the personnel director they are effectively articulated with the social program of the institution, the testing program, the various student organizations, the housing program, the health program, religious program, the records system, etc. The possibilities for the effective adjustment of students, for their stimulation and all-round development, are greatly increased.

Students in this last institution have frequent, natural contacts with the counselors. There is no tenseness about going to talk to a counselor; he is merely a personalized teacher. But he is at the same time a naturally gifted counselor who is receiving official encouragement and help in developing his counseling skill. This counselor who works as part of an organization has at his command all the help that science can give him, but the student is never made to feel as though he were being put into a test tube. This counselor is not working as a lone hand; he can quickly and easily bring into play the facilities of the social program; he can readily bring to bear the facilities of the health office; his efforts are augmented because many clerical details are taken care of for him. In addition, he is a member of a council which also includes interested, expert, trustworthy co-counselors. In this council each member discusses any especially interesting or difficult problems that emerge in the course of his work with students.

There are, of course, two general approaches for the counselor working with individuals; he may rearrange or change the individual's environment, or he may change the individual directly. In the case of the college student, rearranging the environment may mean a change of curriculum, change from one professor to another, a change of roommates, a change of place to study, a change of student organizations, a short vacation, a change of institution. The counselor may attempt to change the individual directly by having his diet modified, by obtaining medical treatment for him, by giving him individual instruction in speech, study methods, human nature, social technique, special tutoring in subjects in which he is deficient. Or he may attempt to help him by less overt methods that depend for their efficiency primarily on the way in which the counselor is able to relate himself to the student.

The skilled counselor soon comes to recognize that there are various levels on which counseling may take place: there are those casual contacts, for instance, between counselor and student when one brief bit of information is wanted by the student—there are no other needs. There may be a somewhat more prolonged contact, one that involves a greater degree of dependency, when for instance, it is a question of change in curriculum, change in vocational plans, but this sort of contact frequently need not run very long or very deep. The discovery of the need for a course of remedial instruction and the subsequent program may result in a counseling contact that is somewhat protracted. In such a case there is every justification for the counselor to assume a larger degree of responsibility for investigating the assets and liabilities which the student possesses (although this investigation may still be more specific than general) and to assume a large degree of responsibility for the leadership of whatever project the counselor and student agree to embark upon as a result. The skilled counselor will find a considerably deeper level of counseling indicated in a few cases where students, usually because of some emotional deprivation, are unwilling or unable to meet conditions which their abilities and the expected degree of maturity would demand of them. Such cases do not develop in any great number in those environments where a calm assurance prevails that each person can and will measure up to the responsibilities that seem appropriate for him *and* where "appropriateness" is a matter of individualized concern. These cases, as a matter of fact, are especially sensitive to suggestion and tend to become worse under the influence of an overanxious counselor. It is unquestionably the safe practice for most counselors to adopt a generally benevolent, optimistic, even somewhat naïve attitude, if necessary, in their counseling, rather than to run the risk of being apprehensive and oversympathetic. The latter attitude actually encourages the development of supersensitivities and inadequacies in students, while the former attitude is, in almost all of the cases represented by college-selected material, entirely harmless and, in most instances of college students, even beneficial.

The college population on the whole represents superior stock. The best psychological environment that the college can set up is to expect confidently that each of its members will shoulder responsibility, give himself gladly to the discharge of the responsibility, and develop in so doing. Counseling should be consistent with this general attitude.

There will always be an occasional college student who, because of neurological or other physical weakness, or because of some other serious inadequacies, is not able to meet the demands that his life makes. A counselor, after some experience, especially if he professionalizes his counseling by study and conference with his co-counselors under the leadership of a trained director of personnel, will soon come to recognize those cases which must have deeper therapy and also will recognize the cases which he is not qualified to handle. It is idle to assume at the present time, however, that there is any school or group of therapists, to whom all such cases should be referred, who are able to work miracles with all those mentally harassed.

There are available a very few specialists who have both medical and thorough psychological training. Those few so trained can be of invaluable assistance.

There are available a larger number of medically trained individuals, who properly call themselves psychiatrists, who have had experience in institutions for the insane but who may not be thoroughly trained in psychological and educational methods. Such men may prove useful insofar as their medical training and general experience afford them authority for procedure; they are qualified to deal with pre-psychotic and psychotic students; they may also be useful, because they are physicians, in diverting the unfavorable criticism of those who are rightfully concerned that health considerations should be faithfully guarded at every turn.

There are available a few psychologists who have had thorough clinical experience not merely in mental testing, but in all aspects of psychology, as well as sound training in educational method. Psychologists so trained are usually particularly cautious to obtain medical assistance in their work with individuals and are sometimes very useful as consultants to the college counselor.

The counselor of college students should investigate carefully to discover the best resources available to him for those cases for which the ordinary resources of the college —the medical experts, the religious counselor, the teacher of remedial speech, etc., do not seem adequate.

Some college officials seem to feel that if they can delegate a large proportion of their counseling program to a medical officer who calls himself a psychiatrist, their responsibility for counseling is adequately discharged. It is our belief that this is an inferior plan. Students do not go as readily and casually to a psychiatrist as they do to a teacher counselor. There is always in the mind of the student the idea that a psychiatrist deals with the abnormal; this has unfortunate suggestive value for the student who might with more positive suggestion be able to deal successfully with his own problems and might, furthermore, be able to do it on a less radical basis than that on which any other person can work with him. Another reason why this seems to us a doubtful plan is that there are not a sufficiently large number of medically and psychologically trained experts available to staff college counseling programs as they should be staffed. One person, no matter how expert, can not possibly meet the counseling needs of the college of ordinary size. Not many of those who have spent four years in medical school plus another two or three in the study of psychology and educational method can afford to accept a full-time position on the staff of a college. To have a physician who is also trained in clinical psychology and educational method; to have him as a member of the counseling council; or (if he has administrative ability and can give enough time to identify himself thoroughly as a member of the college staff) to have him as chairman of the counseling program is far preferable to merely appointing a psychiatrist to the college staff as counselor-at-large, expecting that, alone, he can effectively carry the counseling program of the college.

There are a number of excellent books emerging in the field of counseling. Some of those which should prove most helpful to the college counselor are listed in the bibliography at the end of this chapter. Others are listed in the bibliography of Chap. IX on Vocational and Educational Counseling. It may be worth while, however, to stress here briefly some of the points that are especially pertinent to counselors of college students.

1. Education, even on the college and university level, is fully as much a matter of the student's emotions, social habits, attitudes and skills, and physical equipment and appearance as it is of his mind and his store of information. The kind of counselors to be discovered within college faculties will usually find it necessary to guard consciously against the overintellectualization of the counseling process. Along with the desire to overintellectualize the counseling process, one usually finds a tendency to oversimplify the emotional pattern. The best safeguard against this is the practice of holding regular discussion meetings with a council of counselors who, out of their study and experience, will be able to raise questions, offer suggestions and increase each other's insight.

In this connection it seems to the authors that the kind of counselor who comes to college counseling via the academic route will do well to revise completely many of his ideas of what an interview should be. Frequently an interview has only the following effects: it may merely discharge a feeling the interviewer has that he ought to do something about a certain situation; it may satisfy some sadistic tendency that the interviewer has; it may give him an opportunity to verbalize himself into a rosy glow; it may offer the best outlet his life affords for his managerial drives, his will to power, his urge toward tidiness, his evangelistic drives. It may, for the student, be merely an experience of acute humiliation; or it may give him an opportunity to rationalize or strengthen a role he is attempting to play; or it may serve as an opportunity to increase his resistance level or afford him an opportunity to feel martyred, pursued, and harassed—in other words, it may actually satisfy some masochistic tendency on his part, or it may give him, also, an opportunity to verbalize himself into a rosy glow.

On the whole, the interview has recently been assigned too much importance in college counseling. It has been too exclusively the source of information, for instance. And yet experiment after experiment shows that it is not a completely reliable method for securing information. Observation, carefully directed, and records, carefully kept, are invaluable supplements for securing information. The interview is as inadequate an instrument for therapy, if relied on alone, as it is for fact finding.

The reason why the interview has been glorified in college counseling is because it is essentially a structure of words and words are the chief implements of intellectualization. Counseling, even in colleges and universities, should concern itself as well with that great part of living that does not take place on an intellectual, verbal level. The interview should be used for its positive values,[1] but counseling should not be thought of as consisting primarily of words.

2. Anyone, even a college student, has the right to reject the help of a would-be counselor. It is far more important that the counselee should evolve his own plan of action than it is that he adopt any plan, no matter how perfect, that someone else attempts to impose on him. A few counselors are very successful in persuading the recalcitrant, shortsighted student to modify his plans in favor of plans that are socially more acceptable, plans that offer more chance

[1] See books on the interview included in the bibliography at the end of this chapter.

of genuine development for the student himself; but most counselors are successful only in imposing their own standard of conduct on the student, against his will and his actual acceptance of it. Counselors, in their eagerness to teach social wisdom and to insure the immediate well-being of the student, should guard carefully to be sure that the exclusive result of their efforts is not the increased resistance of the student to the sort of suggestions which the counselor initiates. Personnel officers, especially those who hold the title dean, may find it difficult, for a number of reasons, to be good counselors: because of the authority and disciplinary function which adheres traditionally to their office; because they will be tempted constantly to want to take short cuts to progress; and because they will feel an obligation to keep the social situation as neat and tidy as possible, even though this may actually be at the expense of genuine understanding and development on the part of the students.

Concede always the right of the student to refuse help. Independence is one of the qualities which a college student should possess. Reticence, also, plays an important role in the normal personality. It is a serious matter for any counselor to attempt to break it down. The counselor who engages in gratuitous probing is usually either very inexperienced or he is animated by an unwholesome curiosity.

3. Try to retain a sympathetic point of view with students. Some successful counselors find that working actively with groups of students in extracurricular activities where student thinking and action are spontaneous and vigorous is excellent training for counseling. Student generations roll round and round, but, like the waves in the ocean, they do not actually go any place. There comes to be a perfectly wholesome desire on the part of many who work with college students to want to see progress beyond the college-senior level of development. Many counselors who mature wholesomely into middle age find themselves becoming bored by continual preoccupation with a group

which seems to remain forever adolescent. The best insurance against the danger that the counselor may become retarded in his own personal development, and against the danger that he may become impatient of the group with which he works, is for him to incorporate richly in his own personal life those experiences with people, with ideas, with activities which rightfully belong to the well-endowed, mature person. Thus he will be able to live a life that is personally satisfying and that keeps him from being stunted as a person and will also be able to return constantly with patience and real interest to the needs and problems of the students.

4. Try not to fall into set routines in counseling. Be familiar with a wide range of clinical techniques but always adapt clinical instruments to the needs of the individual and his particular situation rather than enforce any one or a few patterns routinely upon all students. The use of carefully thought-out sequences of questions to be asked students who seem to present certain sorts of problems, the use of blanks and forms, is worth while, but these should be instruments in the counselor's plan rather than determinants of the counselor's plan. The counselor should have philosophy of method rather than polished routines.

5. College counselors are fortunate in that they have a reasonable expectation of a four-year contact with their counselees. In clinics and in the private practice of professional counselors there is rarely this long a contact between patient and counselor. It is frequently important, from a standpoint of expediency, especially in clinics, to try to secure an adjustment to immediate situations and problems. The college counselor has a very real advantage in that he can view adjustment to contemporary situations as symptomatic and can key his counseling efforts to the ultimate goal of "adjustability" rather than merely to immediate adjustment.

6. Be willing readily to recognize the fact that no one can be all things to all college students. Many successful

professional counselors make it a practice not to accept any case for therapy until after a two-week trial period during which the counselor attempts to discover more fully the true nature of the problem and the effect his personality has upon the counselee and the problem itself. Be grateful if, as a counselor, you can connect the student with some other source of help, instead of feeling challenged always to undertake the counseling process yourself.

7. Discourage the students whom you counsel from psychologizing about themselves; this type of activity is usually interesting and diverts the counselee quite effectively from facing his problems honestly: this is, of course, his unconscious reason for being willing to put so much intellectual energy into psychologizing about himself.

8. Stay strictly away in your counseling from the use of psychological terminology. Labeling patterns for a student is not useful to him and sometimes has undesirable suggestive value—especially for those students who have studied one or more courses in psychology. Avoid making diagnoses for the student insofar as possible. Always attempt to secure the student's cooperation in determining upon and describing experiences, behavior, and other factors that combine to block development. As a matter of fact, clinics are recognizing that it is impossible to make any final classification of human problems; every person represents a unique combination of potentialities and tensions which it is more helpful to describe than to label.

9. Avoid emotional entanglements in counseling. The experienced counselor comes to recognize the nature of the counselee's emotional need in the counseling relationship. He also knows his own; and he is able to resist playing a Jehovah role, for instance, even though he is invited to do so and even though it is a pleasurable role, because he knows it will not actually contribute anything to the student's growth. It is desirable that a thoroughly cordial relationship exist between counselor and counselee, but this should be carefully controlled by the counselor so that it

remain within the feeling range that is most favorable to counseling results.

10. There is no excuse for a counselor's ever having an appointment with a student under conditions that do not insure that he have additional assistance with the occasional student who becomes hysterical or who has a seizure of some sort, or who is lacking in self-control to an unusual extent. We know of one outstanding college counselor who was a victim of his own carelessness in this respect. One day he scheduled an appointment with a student at a time when his secretary was not in the office. He thus had no witness to deny the highly imaginative story told subsequently by the student. The student was of the type who so enjoyed attracting attention that the counselor's reputation was seriously hurt and it seemed best to the administration for him to move to another university.

11. Many successful counselors are finding it wise to be eclectic in their use of various systems of psychology; they do not commit themselves to any one "school" of mental therapy but find useful principles in all of them. The most stimulating council of counselors will be that one whose members are not overwhelmed by any one point of view but, conversant with various schools of psychology, turn their minds freshly upon each new problem which they discuss together.

12. The value of the synergistic principle has not been recognized in counseling as it has been in medicine. It is probable that it is as operative psychologically as it is physically. It is probable, for instance, that direct, forceful suggestion is not often necessary or desirable. It is probable that the administering of one slight suggestion plus a concomitant slight alteration in environment, plus, perhaps, some other seemingly unimportant therapeutic measure, can, with the resultant reactions of the student, bring about the desired results in the total situation without recourse to more radical technique. It is our opinion as a result of the clinical practice of counseling that the

synergistic principle is a valuable one and should be consciously used in counseling.

13. Questions with regard to the counseling process—whether to write or not during an interview, whether one or the other should face the light, how long a period should be spent in each interview—all are superficial. We have tended to become too bundled up in technique. As Levine[1] has recently said: "The personality of the counselor is infinitely more potent . . . than the mastery of therapeutic technique." College counselors should make themselves masters of counseling technique, but, much more importantly, they should live so that their own continued maturing is not hindered; they should live and think and act in such a way as continuously to be testing out for themselves the best values of life. Only thus can they remain fit counselors to youth.

14. Problems of development and adjustment are more and more being recognized as inhering primarily neither in the person himself nor in environment, but rather as existing in the ratio of the person to his environment. College counselors, far more than any other group of counselors, possess an unusual advantage in that, not only can they ordinarily have contact with students for four years, but also they have that protracted contact in an environment that is, in the first place, an unusually controlled one and which, furthermore, is amenable to a great deal of manipulation in the interest of individuals. It is not unreasonable to expect that out of thoughtfully directed programs of counseling in colleges may come increased understanding of individual and social dynamics.

BIBLIOGRAPHY[2]

American College Personnel Association, "College Personnel, Principles, Functions and Standards," *Tenth Annual Report*, 1933, 81 pp.

[1] LEVINE, ALBERT J., *Fundamentals of Psychologic Guidance*, p. 18, Educational Monograph Press, Brooklyn, 1936.

[2] See also bibliography for Vocational and Educational Guidance, Chap. IX.

ARLITT, ADA HART: *Adolescent Psychology*, American Book Company, New York, 1933, 246 pp.

BELL, HUGH M.: *The Theory and Practice of Student Counseling*, Stanford University Press, Stanford University, 1935, 138 pp.

BINGHAM, WALTER VAN DYKE, and BRUCE VICTOR MOORE: *How to Interview*, Harper & Brothers, New York, 1934, 308 pp.

BLUEMEL, CHARLES SIDNEY, *Mental Aspects of Stammering*, Williams & Wilkins Company, Baltimore, 1930, 152 pp.

BOUCHER, CHAUNCEY S.: *The Chicago College Plan*, University of Chicago Press, Chicago, 1935, xi + 344 pp.

BRAGDON, HELEN D.: *Counseling the College Student*, Harvard University Press, Cambridge, Mass., 1929, 147 pp.

BRUMBAUGH, AARON J.: "Selection and Counseling of Students at University of Chicago," in W. S. Gray, *Provision for the Individual*, pp. 55–67, University of Chicago Press, Chicago, 1932.

BURNHAM, WILLIAM H.: *The Wholesome Personality*, D. Appleton-Century Company, Inc., New York, 1932, xxvi + 713 pp.

COWLEY, W. H.: "A Preface to the Principles of Student Counseling," *Educational Record*, 18: 217–234, April, 1937.

DAVIS, JOHN E.: *Principles and Practice of Recreational Therapy for the Mentally Ill*, A. S. Barnes & Company, New York, 1936, 206 pp.

DOLLARD, JOHN: *Criteria for the Life History*, Yale University Press, New Haven, 1935, iv + 288 pp.

ELLIOTT, HARRISON SACKET, and GRACE LOUCKS ELLIOTT: *Solving Personal Problems*, Henry Holt & Company, New York, 1936, vii + 321 pp.

FLANAGAN, JOHN CLEMANS: *Factor Analysis in the Study of Personality*, Stanford University Press, Stanford University, 1935, x + 103 pp.

HARRIMAN, PHILIP: "The Dean of Women in the New Social Order," *Journal of Higher Education*, 4: 367–369, October, 1933.

HORNEY, DR. KAREN: *The Neurotic Personality of Our Time*, W. W. Norton & Co., New York, 1937, v + 299 pp.

LEVINE, ALBERT J.: *Fundamentals of Psychological Guidance*, Educational Monograph Press, Brooklyn, 1936, 96 pp.

LOUTTIT, C. M.: *Clinical Psychology*, Harper & Brothers, New York, 1936, xx + 695 pp.

MARCUS, GRACE: "The Individual and His Family Relationships; Some Newer Concepts in Social Case Work," *Mental Hygiene*, 17: 353–368, July, 1933.

MOFFETT, MARY LEDGER: *The Social Background and Activities of Teachers College Students*, Teachers College, Bureau of Publications, Columbia University, New York, 1929, vi + 133 pp.

MORGAN, JOHN J. B.: *Keeping a Sound Mind*, The Macmillan Company, New York, 1934, ix + 440 pp.

PATERSON, DONALD G.: "Analysis of the Individual," *Occupations*, 12: 5–7, April, 1934.

PLANT, JAMES S.: *Personality and the Cultural Pattern*, The Commonwealth Fund, New York, 1937, 432 pp.

PRESCOTT, DANIEL A.: "Affective Factors in Education," *Occupations*, 14: 723–732, May, 1936.

———: "Non-intellectual Education," *Educational Record*, 18: 248–258, April, 1936.

———: *Emotion and the Educative Process*, American Council on Education, Washington, D. C., 1938, 323 pp.

PRESSEY, L. C.: *Some College Students and Their Problems*, Ohio State University Press, Columbus, 1929, 97 pp.

REYNOLDS, O. EDGAR: *The Social and Economic Status of College Students*, Teachers College, Bureau of Publications, Columbia University, New York, 1927, v + 57 pp.

RIVLIN, HARRY N.: *Educating for Adjustment*, D. Appleton-Century Company, Inc., New York, 1936, 419 pp.

ROBINSON, VIRGINIA P.: "Treatment Possibilities in Short Interview Contacts," *Visiting Teaching Bulletin* 7: 1–4, October, 1932.

SHAFER, LAWRENCE F.: *Psychology of Adjustment*, Houghton Mifflin Company, Boston, 1936, 599 pp.

STRANG, RUTH: "Investigations Relating to Work of Dean of Women in Normal Schools and Teachers Colleges," *National Association of Deans of Women, Seventeenth Yearbook*, 1930, pp. 113–114.

———: *The Role of the Teacher in Personnel Work*, Teachers College, Bureau of Publications, Columbia University, New York, 1935, 417 pp.

———: *Counseling Technics in College and Secondary School*, Harper & Brothers, New York, 1937, x + 159 pp.

SYMONDS, PERCIVAL M.: *Diagnosing Personality and Conduct*, D. Appleton-Century Company, Inc., New York, 1931, 602 pp.

TAFT, JESSIE: *The Dynamics of Therapy in a Controlled Relationship*, The Macmillan Company, New York, 1933, ix + 296 pp.

TOWNSEND, MARION E.: *Administration of Student Personnel Services in Teacher Training Institutions of the United States*, Teachers College, Bureau of Publications, Columbia University, New York, 1932, no. 536, 115 pp.

WALLIN, J. E. WALLACE: *Personality Maladjustments and Mental Hygiene*, The Macmillan Company, New York, 1935, xii + 511 pp.

WALTERS, JACK E.: *Individualizing Education*, John Wiley & Sons, Inc., New York, 1935, 278 pp.

WILLIAMSON, E. G., and J. G. DARLEY: *Student Personnel Work*, McGraw-Hill Book Company, Inc., New York, 1937, xvi + 313 pp.

YOUNG, PAULINE V.: *Interviewing in Social Work*, McGraw-Hill Book Company, Inc., New York, 1935, xvi + 416 pp.

ZACHRY, CAROLINE: *Personality Adjustment of School Children*, Charles Scribner's Sons, New York, 1929, 306 pp.

Chapter VIII
MORE ABOUT GIVING STUDENTS INDIVIDUALIZED HELP

Discipline

There is a wide range in the point of view and practice concerning discipline in the colleges and universities of the country. There are a few institutions which, in terms of their philosophy of higher education, consider the behavior and conduct of students entirely outside their province. All that these institutions purport to be interested in is scholarship, transmitting culture via the intellect (narrowly conceived), and maintaining academic standards through the rigorous use of written and oral examinations. How students behave in their personal and social life is, they believe, in no way their concern.

Another extreme type of institution conceives of discipline in terms of a system involving precise and complete laws or rules, each of which has attached to it an automatic penalty for infraction. In between these two extremes there are other philosophies and plans for the discipline of students that, in our opinion, are consistent with a more adequate philosophy of higher education and which are more consistent with what psychology has shown to be the nature of the individual and his methods of living and learning.

The kind of person which the disciplinary program of the institution should aim to produce is one whose actions are controlled and integrated; who is able to exert his efforts purposefully, with foresight, and with self-directed orderliness; who is truly sophisticated with regard to relative social values; and who is benevolently disposed to assume his share of responsibility for creating socially satisfactory situations (see also the chapter on Social Education, pages 95 and 96). Certainly, the development of a truly disciplined individual should be an important purpose of education. Such an individual is produced neither by a rigid set of precise rules nor by a program of education which is exclusively intellectualistic.

Any program must rest back upon basic assumptions. What assumptions might well underlie the disciplinary program of an institution of higher education? The following are offered as suggestive. They are necessarily presented briefly and, as a result, somewhat too dogmatically. Their proper treatment would alone merit a whole book.

1. No individual can function as abstract intelligence. All that one thinks or believes in any effective sense is related to how he behaves, how he has behaved, and how he will behave. Behavior and thought are inseparably related.

2. All behavior of an individual has social implications.

3. College students differ in their willingness to cooperate in common enterprises and their willingness to live conformably with the social standards which are obviously essential to the welfare and survival of the group. They also differ in their knowledge of what the social standards are and in their knowledge of how to meet them.

4. Certain social standards are so nearly universal—at least in our culture—and so clearly essential to social life that they may be regarded as having enduring value.

5. Education with respect to the rights which society grants the individual and his duty to respect these rights in others is by no means satisfactorily concluded in the elementary school or in the high school. Nor can the college expect to have concluded a student's education along these lines satisfactorily by the time he is graduated.

6. This area is a legitimate educational concern—even an educational obligation—of higher education.

7. Knowledge and skill in the area of social standards are amenable to educational method.

8. Influence as to what to believe are the acceptable social standards and how to act with respect to them is ineffectually

derived from written rules but is strongly derived from collective opinion.

9. Collective opinion is amenable to leadership and direction.

10. It is socially desirable that the collective opinion which is inevitably and constantly generated should have the direction of benevolently disposed, experienced, wise leadership.

11. The college or university constitutes, sociologically, a situation which has great possibility as a laboratory for education in social standards, foresight, attitudes, skills, followship, and leaderships.

12. It is the wholesome need and desire of every normal person to assume increasing responsibility for the welfare and happiness of others.

13. Any student may fail to make satisfactory social adjustments occasionally or repeatedly for any one or all of a number of reasons: (a) collective opinion may not be sufficiently strong to help him to know what is expected of him; (b) he may be retarded in his sensitivity to social standards, and, though collective opinion be strong, he may still fail to understand what the acceptable standards are; (c) he may be inept and inexperienced in knowing how to meet the social standards even though he recognizes what they are; (d) he may have an impulsive or a somewhat deliberate drive to deviate experimentally in the area of social standards and method.

14. Failure in this area should be handled on an educational basis just as should failure in other areas.

A program based on the foregoing assumptions would have very different aspects than have the disciplinary programs (if they can be called that) that are now generally prevalent. It is worth while to inquire in what respect it would be different.

The futility of depending upon a large body of detailed written rules would need to be recognized. The system of rules and penalties which now exists in most of our institutions probably constitutes a kind of hand-washing gesture on the part of the administration which either does not desire or does not know how to handle discipline by methods more truly educational. One readily concedes that it is relatively simple to write down detailed directions, which, if meticulously obeyed, would result in a minimum of social friction. Any office clerk can also make up a list of penalties for the infraction of each of these rules. It then becomes a relatively simple matter for any dean or faculty committee, no matter how lacking in imagination and teaching skill, to assign punishment to individuals in terms of rules and punishments, without much jeopardy to the punisher's feeling that his duty to society is being righteously fulfilled. This is apparently pretty much the theory upon which some of our modern political states are basing their government, but we would dispute any contention that it is the most educational basis on which the whole matter of building disciplined individuals might be handled.

An increasing number of institutions are veering around to quite a different program from the foregoing in an attempt to help their students become truly self-directing, disciplined individuals. A different type of program would be based on such assumptions as the fourteen offered earlier in this chapter. The only rule in these institutions is the announced or tacit expectation that students will behave like ladies and gentlemen. This, admittedly, allows each student a good deal of leeway when behavior comes down—as it always does—to a matter of alternative choices. It is believed to be a desirable thing, however, educationally speaking, for students to be free to make choices. Only when a student is free to make choices is it possible to enlist his whole intelligence and his initiative in the situation.[1] It is important for a college individual to learn to weigh values wisely; it is important for him to realize that he is responsible for making choices—that no one else can continue to take that responsibility for him; it is important for him to learn to want to incorporate the better values into his plan of living.

Experience demonstrates that it is not very effective merely to tell young people, even of college caliber, about

[1] DEWEY, JOHN, *How We Think*, D. C. Heath & Company, New York, 1933, x + 301 pp.

the desirability of weighing values, of recognizing their responsibility for making choices; nor does it profit much to exhort them to be well motivated. But experience does show that there are many influences that can be brought to bear in the college environment that unquestionably are effective in these respects.

One of the most important influences in this regard is the college faculty as individuals. No thoughtful person denies that students learn a great deal more from their teachers than is contained in their lecture notes. Incidental precept, example, "subtle indoctrination," the communication of attitudes of appreciation or deprecation, response to personality based on sympathetic identification, admiration, scorn and rejection, understanding—all these factors are powerfully at work constantly, acting as determinants of students' attitudes and action choices. One can make a very powerful case for the importance of taking the personality of faculty as well as their scholarship into account in assessing an educational situation.

There is a tendency which the authors think they discern in certain colleges and universities that should cause concern in this respect: this consists in the functionalization of the personnel program itself to such a point that technical skill is assigned importance at the expense of interest in what sort of person the man or woman is who is responsible for the discharge of that function. To lose sight of either proficiency in technical skill or quality of character and personality in a personnel officer is to defeat either of the equally important considerations of the personnel program, *i.e.*, the development of students and service to students.

The character and personality quality of the teaching and personnel staff can be influenced in two ways: careful consideration can be given to these qualities when new appointments to the staff are being considered; and the president and his chief assistants can maintain a steady insistence that education is something more than book learning and that the faculty are important in the educational plan of the institution in more respects than the purely academic one.

Another powerful influence (as we have already stated under assumption 8), in developing disciplined individuals in our colleges, is the pressure of collective opinion. As we have also stated, collective opinion is amenable to leadership and direction, and it is socially desirable that it should have this direction at the hands of a benevolently disposed, experienced, wise leader, who is himself very well balanced.

There are those who would think it better to let collective opinion form without deliberately attempting its direction —who believe that there is a preordination and a rationale in it that cannot and should not be interfered with. Many others, however, believe that there are, in the formation of collective opinion, so many random and capricious elements, that it is highly desirable from a social and educational point of view, to attempt to improve its quality, its consistency, and its influence in behalf of bewildered individuals.

Perhaps the most important difference between a successful director of personnel and one who merely does a little rearranging occasionally lies in his or her ability to influence collective opinion. Collective opinion is not usually developed most effectively by direct exhortation and admonition—although on rare occasions it may be necessary to adopt this method with respect to some one important issue. The wise leader of collective opinion, on the other hand, usually has no detailed, specific list of opinions to which he is determined the group must subscribe. He is rather concerned that the campus be so knit together in major and minor social groups, and that the lines of communication between these groups be such, that the generation of some collective opinion is possible. He is also concerned that the situation be so arranged as to provide continual tests for potential student leaders. He uses his influence to ensure that those students who have earned it should receive recognition by their fellows for effort and success in leadership as they progress through college. This by no means implies that the director of personnel should suggest names to nomination committees or attempt to "write tickets." No efforts along this line should be made or will be necessary if the whole system of extracurricular activities is set up in such a way that leadership ability is given a chance to function and if, from the freshman year on, students learn to respect and give recognition to those who successfully attempt tasks in behalf of the general campus welfare.

Those students who, after 2 or 3 years of such valuable laboratory experience in group leadership, come to positions of importance among their fellows are, of course, individuals whom the personnel director will want to know well and to whom he will want to give a good deal of attention. These students are usually among the most gifted individuals the country will produce. They are worthy of the personal attention of those members of the college staff who are themselves most gifted in leadership, for the same reasons that the student gifted in writing deserves the especial attention of the faculty who are gifted and interested in literary effort.

Collective opinion, generated out of a democratically arranged situation in which the best individuals of the group are able to come to positions of leadership, sets a tone and provides a morale which are the most powerful disciplinary forces that can be brought to bear. It enables the floundering freshman and other needy students to lay hold on the best social experience of his peers without wasting too much time and energy in trial and error. If the student decides he wishes to make some trials, he at least knows what the route of social wisdom is from which he departs. Collective student opinion, in fact, represents a broad, well-charted route which all students, on the whole, may profitably follow. The student who wishes to experiment with some of the interesting bypaths is able to know how his direction lies with reference to the big highway and is, therefore, better able to return to it in case he does not find his excursion worth while.

There are bound always to be those individuals who make a poor showing occasionally or chronically in getting along congenially and productively in their social groups. These cases call for individualized treatment just as truly as would failure to progress satisfactorily in their academic program. Failure may be due to sheer ignorance, lack of background, ineptness, lack of skill; or it may be due to a sort of perversity that unquestionably goes back to emotional inadequacies—either immaturity, or the desire to "show someone," or the desire to attract attention at any cost, or a natural or compulsive desire for excitement and adventure.

No matter what the cause of social failure, the majority of colleges and universities now tend to "handle" such cases by having the culprit appear before a group of students, or students and faculty, or before a faculty committee to explain himself. The penalty for the misbehavior is usually imposed much after the manner of our better courts, after the defendant has had an opportunity to appear and after all evidence has been carefully gathered and presented.

It seems to the authors that there is an educational way of dealing with failure in this realm that does not involve the student's appearing before a group. A few institutions have been so fortunate as to discover a person on their staffs endowed with a fine sense of morality but also so gifted in getting along with college boys or college girls that the college has been able to see the wisdom of leaving problems of failure in this realm to him or her for appropriate educational treatment. Anyone with experience in any of the better behavior clinics would understand that it may be possible to secure specific outward conformity by exerting external authority but that, if the behavior failure is due either to ignorance or lack of skill or to some underlying emotional cause, it is futile to expect results of a lasting character through the imposition of a group's authority. The chances are, in fact, that real harm is done to the individual by this course insofar as any genuine possibilities of reeducation and rehabilitation are concerned.

While we believe that students in need of disciplinary help can always secure that help much more effectively from an individual rather than from a number of individuals sitting in solemn conclave (just as, if the student needed remedial help in reading, he could get it much more effectively from an individual than he could from a group of "experts" all working on him concomitantly), we also recognize the fact that there is a dearth of individuals mature enough and wise enough and sufficiently trusted by faculty and students to carry this responsibility. We also recognize the fact that any disciplinary officer, no matter how wise (perhaps the wisest ones will seek help all the faster), will need and want a group of advisers with whom he can regularly discuss many of the cases of behavior failures with whom he is required to work. This advisory council might well be made up of a small group from the larger council of student counselors (see Chapter VII, on Counseling). Such a group should be willing and able to give time to considering with the dean or head of counselors just how to help individuals who are having difficulties in getting along comfortably and constructively in the social group. The dean or head counselor would, under this plan, be responsible for seeing every student who gets into any serious difficulty, would be responsible for trying to understand the whole situation fully, and would then discuss the case, either by name or anonymously, with his advisory council. This advisory council would help him see what sort of educative plan he might attempt to work out with the student to help him remedy his weaknesses. This council should not obtrude itself in any way on the student's consciousness; all the student's dealings would be with the one counselor to whom in the first place he had reported—whether voluntarily or by compulsion. This dean or head counselor should have the power, usually after discussion with his council, to expel a student from college, if it seemed that the student probably could not be helped by an amount of time and energy that the college could afford to spend on him.

In one college where some such plan for handling individual cases of behavior failure is a success of years' standing, the chief counselor who handles these cases does not consider that his work is complete until the student himself understands wherein the failure lies and begins to feel genuinely appreciative of the help that has been given him to overcome his weaknesses. At this point, of course, the student's genuine cooperation usually begins to be felt and progress proceeds more rapidly. Rarely, in many years in this institution (although there have had to be some expulsions) has any student failed to understand and genuinely cooperate in whatever plan was finally agreed upon.

Certainly any teacher or counselor who can secure this sort of insight and cooperation on the part of an erstwhile social moron or social rebel is an educationist of the first order and a heavy producer of social values—a disciplinarian worthy of the title in its finest sense.

BIBLIOGRAPHY

DEWEY, JOHN: *How We Think*, D. C. Heath & Company, New York, 1933, x + 301 pp.

GAUSS, CHRISTIAN: *Life in College*, Charles Scribner's Sons, New York, 1930, xv + 271 pp.

HAWKES, HERBERT E.: "Constructive Discipline," *Association of American College Bulletin* 14: 180–186, April, 1928.

———: "College Administration,'" *Journal of Higher Education*, 1: 245–253, May, 1930.

HEALY, WILLIAM, and AUGUSTA F. BRONNER: *New Light on Delinquency and Its Treatment*, Yale University Press, New Haven, 1936, vii + 224 pp.

Oberlin College, *Report of the Joint Committee on the Honor System*, Oberlin College, Oberlin, 1930.

SEARS, LAURENCE: *Responsibility: Its Development through Punishment and Reward*, Columbia University Press, New York, 1932, 198 pp.

TUTTLE, HAROLD S.: *A Social Basis of Education*, The Thomas Y. Crowell Company, New York, 1934, 600 pp.

Chapter IX

HELPING STUDENTS TO MAKE AND TO REALIZE EDUCATIONAL AND VOCATIONAL PLANS

Educational and Vocational Guidance

In higher education, our attention is focused upon a selected group of persons whose range of possibilities, vocationally and educationally speaking, tends, in contrast to that of the total population, to be limited. As the demands of education beyond the secondary level tend progressively to sift out the more gifted group, so, at the same time, the occupational probabilities for this group tend to be restricted more and more to the upper range. While students in higher education are potentially more capable of self-direction, of discovering their own goals and occupations, experience with them usually brings the conclusion that many are in need of stimulation and information which will aid them to make satisfactory adjustments both in college and after graduation. These students are socially and economically of great potential value and should be utilized in the most productive directions possible by education and society.

Vocational guidance has been defined as "the assistance given to an individual in connection with choosing, preparing for, entering upon and progressing in an occupation."[1] Success in an occupation is important, but, as Williamson points out, the average adult spends considerably less than one-third of his hours at work.[2] He goes on to say: "Viewed clearly, general education is the

[1] Definition given by the National Vocational Guidance Association.
[2] Williamson, E. G., *Students and Occupations*, p. 1, Henry Holt & Company, New York, 1937.

basis, not only of all specialized work, but is itself the training for the most important of all professions, the one profession none can escape. This profession is the living of a life satisfying to us and to those around us."[1] Education should offer a broad training for living. Some of the important problems of living, however, may be alleviated if the student is given some assistance in connection with choosing, preparing for, entering upon, and progressing in an occupation.

The purpose of the educational and vocational guidance program is to organize and make available educational and occupational information in order that students may profit by their collegiate experiences to their fullest capacities. Educational and vocational guidance cannot be imposed upon individuals; each student, after all, is at the helm of his own ship and may sail to a flying finish or sink in the attempt. It is utterly futile to attempt to coerce any student into setting his course, no matter how gently the persuasion may operate. True education demands that decisions be of the student's making. Still, educational and vocational guidance can assist him in making intelligent decisions by supplying essential and valuable information. Such guidance should supply the student with "a guided and professional inventory of personal assets and liabilities and a frank appraisal of job requirements and opportunities"[2] and thus increase the probability of success in all-round development for satisfactory living.

The selective principle of education has long been recognized; there are constant selective factors at work that inevitably tend to grade the human material of the schools and colleges more and more finely. This principle has already operated fairly drastically on the group that finally gets to college. Even so, there is plenty of evidence that many students get in to college who are not qualified to compete under college conditions with the

[1] *Ibid.*, p. 9.
[2] *Ibid.*, p. xiii.

kinds of groups that have been sifted to the top by the high schools. Toward these students the college may adopt an attitude of ruthlessness or one of helpfulness. The personnel point of view would encourage the most realistic and constructive educational guidance of each individual throughout his elementary and secondary periods; it would desire for each individual that, at the conclusion of high school he have appropriate plans, either to enter upon an apprenticeship in the vocational world—if this seems the most promising course for him—or to enter a college or technical school best suited to his interests and the general level of his abilities. As the Pennsylvania Study proved so conclusively, colleges differ very widely indeed in the caliber of student they attract and the standards of achievement which they attempt to maintain. As suggested in the discussion of the admission of students to college (Chap. IV), the college should not be a passive agent in determining whether it is the appropriate place for each of the students applying for admission. When a college finally accepts a student, however, a contract is made in effect: the student agrees to try to meet the standards which the college holds up for him, and the college also assumes the obligation, not only of parading knowledge before his eyes and ears, but also of continuing to study his interests and abilities and attempting to develop them to their highest possible levels.

The process of continually studying each of its students whom it has accepted, recognizing that each is possessed of individual differences important to his proper education, and the prescription of conditions under which those qualities may develop most desirably, is educational guidance. The "continual study of the student" involves the use, not only of the best standardized instruments, but also the effective mobilization of constant appraisal and suggestion on the part of the college faculty—a group of people possessed, on the whole, of extensive experience with young people—and the findings of all the various specialists (physicians, heads of residence, directors of extracurricular activities, religious counselors, and the like) who belong to the personnel staff. The director of personnel, as a routine part of the personnel program, should continuously be acquiring information about each student which can be used to help the student in formulating and modifying his immediate and long-view plans. When this routine information seems inadequate, it should be possible, without making the student feel an undue concentration of expert attention, to employ further clinical facilities to help answer problems that may have arisen concerning his educational or vocational plans.

If it becomes evident that a student has, in spite of everyone's best efforts, gotten into an institution which cannot gear its facilities to his interests, or his level or rate of development, the best possible solution may be to aid that student in finding and adjusting to another situation that is able to offer a program suited to his needs. If this measure seems unnecessary, there are other especial efforts that the college can make to help the student remedy weaknesses that may be interfering with his progress. It may be that he should change his course of study; it may be he needs special tutoring at points of deficiency in subject matter; perhaps it is a matter of poor study habits; or inadequate reading skills; or speech defects. Possibly he is distracted by worry, physical illness, competing interests, overactivity in social affairs, or by a feeling of social inadequacy. Skillful counseling, the genuine interest of an experienced person, the utilization of expert teaching at points of deficiency, can usually turn failure into success. Education properly has the dual function of remedying weaknesses and capitalizing on assets.

Many institutions are providing facilities for the clinical study of those students who need more understanding than is gained by even superior routine methods for studying students. Many are implementing this clinical study with how-to-study courses, with courses in remedial speech work, with tutorial plans, with thorough health programs, with good housing plans, with trained counselors. A well-organized program of student personnel work would provide all these facilities.

Educational guidance has received more attention in higher education, for the most part, than has vocational guidance. As a matter of fact, higher education has done little in an organized way to further vocational guidance. This may be due largely to the attitude of the traditional liberal arts colleges which do not think anything vocational is academically respectable and will not concern themselves with anything so mundane. Katz and Allport report in their study of student attitudes, however, that the majority of students at Syracuse University came to college for vocational training as well as cultural betterment; that nearly three-fourths of the students had failed to receive needed counsel on some particular problem; and almost one-fourth had desired advice regarding their vocations which they had not obtained.[1] The results of this study could probably be duplicated in other institutions, and illustrate the need for both educational and vocational guidance in colleges and universities.

Furthermore, the lack of vocational information on the part of college students is emphasized by the facts brought out in Pitkin's investigations of university students' opinions on vocations: the men interviewed expected to earn four times as much as the average annual salary in their chosen field; about 70 out of every 100 persons were trying to enter the worst-crowded professions; and women candidates for teaching expected to earn three times as much as the average salary for women teachers.[2]

Both educational and vocational guidance are indispensable functions of the college or university personnel

[1] KATZ, DANIEL, and F. H. ALLPORT, *Students' Attitudes*, Craftsman Press, Syracuse, N. Y., 1931, xxviii + 401 pp.

[2] PITKIN, WALTER B., *New Careers for Youth*, p. 15, Simon & Schuster, Inc., New York, 1934.

program. They are, in actual practice, as well as in theory, so closely related that they are often indistinguishable.

It is impossible to separate sharply the vocational aspects of guidance from the educational, moral and cultural aspects. In choosing a school or a course, the future occupation often bears a large part, but not always. Occupational choices depend frequently upon educational background and they are often concerned with health, social and cultural problems. The counselor cannot and should not try to keep the various aspects of guidance entirely distinct. That would be working directly contrary to that unity of character and personality that is essential.[1]

Educational and vocational guidance aids students to define their objectives sharply, to plan their programs in the light of their abilities, interests, and objectives, to discover inadequacies, lacks and deficiencies that may condition academic progress, to evaluate their own capacities and abilities, aptitudes and interests in the light of vocations they may be considering, and to secure full and accurate information regarding these and other vocations. Educational and vocational guidance assists students to make intelligent decisions, not only regarding their education, but also regarding their vocations.

The use of educational and occupational information cannot be effective unless this information is closely related to the individual student. It is a well-known fact that young people mature at different rates and the program of educational and occupational guidance must recognize this fact. All freshmen are not ready to choose a vocation; nor do upper classmen develop occupational interests all at once, hence the program must be largely individual rather than group.

Developments in science, engineering, production, and management have eliminated many jobs, and it is well known that the professions are overcrowded. Students in

[1] JONES, ARTHUR J., *Principles of Guidance*, p. 316, McGraw-Hill Book Company, Inc., New York, 1934.

higher education, however, go on heedlessly preparing for positions and professions in which they in all probability will find employment difficult. Williamson adds even more of a discouraging note when he says that "roughly four-fifths of the 48,000,000 workers in this country are doing work which does not require a college education."[1] Facts such as these must be given the student in order that he may face squarely the possibilities of the future. A careful study of his personal assets and liabilities and of occupational requirements and opportunities must be made by each student under the direction of staff members trained and experienced in this type of guidance.

To give students this assistance should be an important objective of the personnel program of the institution. The educational and vocational counseling program may involve a number of faculty members especially designated to act as counselors to students who are assigned to them on the basis of their expressed vocational choice or preference. This is the system in use at the University of Chicago. When a student changes his choice of a vocational field he is transferred to the appropriate counselor or adviser. The advisers assist in planning tentative programs of courses and discuss with the student any special problems he may have. Complete data regarding the student are available to the advisers: the application for admission to the university, the results of the psychological examinations, scores on personality ratings and other tests, reports from the health service, personnel reports from instructors, and a special personnel card and a self-analysis blank filled out by each student. These data are used by the adviser in encouraging the student to make intelligent progressive choices, both educationally and vocationally.

In some other institutions every member of the personnel staff is expected to serve as an educational and vocational adviser. Sometimes a vocational guidance expert is employed to direct the vocational guidance program, per-

[1] WILLIAMSON, op. cit., p. 11.

haps to serve as placement director and to be a source of information and help to all the counselors.

Often representatives of different occupational fields within the community are utilized in the counseling program. Public-spirited lawyers, doctors, engineers, store executives, advertisers, etc., are frequently willing to talk individually with interested students regarding the possibilities in their respective vocations.

The director of personnel on the campus can sometimes encourage and stimulate the different faculty members to present their courses from a vocational point of view. Vocational material can be introduced into classroom subjects even on the higher educational level. As Kitson points out, chemistry has a great many occupations related to it, English may lead to secretarial and journalistic occupations, while a general vocational view of society may be imparted in connection with history, etc.[1] Interest and ability in a certain subject may lead to an occupational choice in that general field, if practical possibilities of employment are pointed out.

Extracurricular activities may have definite relationship to vocational choices. They may be utilized for tryout experiences in the students' chosen careers. Cornell University is using such a method in having its Hotel Ezra Cornell promoted, financed, and operated by students of the Cornell School of Hotel Administration. This puts into practice the principles of hotel operation they are learning and one day a year the students play host to hotel men from all parts of the country. The Floriculture Club of Cornell has organized the Cornell House of Flowers which assembles landscape features, flower arrangement, and information on garden opportunities.[2]

The educational and vocational guidance program of the campus may include actual classes in vocations. William-

[1] KITSON, HARRY D., "Vocational Guidance through School Subjects," *Teachers College Record*, 28: 900–915, May, 1927.

[2] "Cornell Relates Events to Careers," *The New York Times*, Apr. 25, 1937.

son describes such a course in the University General College at the University of Minnesota.[1] In this course, an attempt is made to introduce students to what is known of the psychological factors involved in making a vocational choice. The students are also given a broad overview of the various occupations most appropriate to their interests with an indication of the number of workers and the trend of future employment in each. This course is a general introduction to the broad occupational fields with emphasis on the grouping of occupations, the need for versatility within groups, and the desirability of general background training rather than rigid specialization from the very beginning of training. The counseling program at this institution stresses tentative occupational choices of broad fields of work. In this way, the difficulty of placement in one narrow field is somewhat overcome.

Courses may involve educational guidance almost to a greater degree than vocational. Such courses are the exploratory courses of the junior colleges which expedite educational and vocational choices on the college level. Students, through this type of actual exploration and experience, can make more intelligent choices of their courses of study and of the vocational field for which they wish to prepare.

Stevens Institute of Technology offers summer camp exploratory courses to students who think they may want to study engineering. During this camp experience prospective students are carefully tested, not only by means of paper and pencil tests, but also by means of actual field tryouts. In this way, each boy finds out before it is too late whether he really is interested and has the aptitude for engineering.

Observational trips for the purpose of seeing the work done in factories, offices, courtrooms, etc., may afford further help in making vocational choices. The type of

[1] Williamson, E. G., "A College Class in Occupational Information," *School Review*, 45: 123–129, March, 1937.

information obtained from such observation, although better than none, is often fragmentary and meager; students should have help in critically evaluating what they have seen. These trips can often be tied up with field work in connection with such courses as sociology, economics, etc.

Freshman week or orientation week on the campus usually includes some reference to the importance of making intelligent vocational choices and the necessity of preparing for vocational competency. Such advice is now usually given in the form of lectures and is not always listened to by the somewhat surfeited freshmen. Freshman week does, however, provide an excellent opportunity for both educational and vocational guidance. Motivation and information might much more effectively be given dramatically, however, through the medium of the enacted interview or the motion picture than through mere declamation.

The entire campus may receive stimulation to vocational thinking and vocational information if an occupational conference is held on the campus. It is customary for some institutions to invite outstanding representatives of different vocations and occupational areas to visit the campus annually. These guests hold group and individual conferences about their respective occupations, their advantages and disadvantages. Not only do all the students receive a lot of needed and valuable information, but also the students' organization committees gain experience in organizing, planning, and in carrying through successfully a large campus undertaking.

Those responsible for the educational and vocational guidance program should see to it that books, periodicals, clippings, and pamphlets on vocations are easily accessible to the students. The librarian is usually glad to devote a convenient shelf in the library to this literature. Through contact with this type of information, guidance for many students will be self-inspired and self-directed. Other students will need to be directed to certain books to answer their own problems for themselves. *The Occupational Index* of the National Occupational Conference[1] is an index to all the current literature on vocations and occupations and is an invaluable tool for use in the vocational counseling program.

A number of institutions arrange for their students to have summer tryout experiences in occupations. These experiences assist the students to make choices of vocations in the light of their interests, abilities, and aptitudes and give them practical knowledge of what the occupation entails. This plan of exploration can be carried into the academic-year curriculum itself, as at Antioch and other colleges where the students study for a certain period of time and then spend a similar period in industry, or business, or in other occupational areas.

In an educational and vocational guidance program there should be some check on the subjectivity of the advice and assistance given. Objective tests and measurement are an essential supplement to the other methods used in the program. They form bases for better individual and class guidance and instruction and are a method of checking progress. As Wood points out: "Their primary purpose is to help schools ascertain in meaningful terms the achievements, effective interests, and capacities of individual pupils in order that the schools may more surely lead them to the most effective self-realization in the life they are to live."[2]

Brewer defines measurement as every attempt to secure quantitative data about the present and potential ability or knowledge of students or other individuals with a view to the use of such data for their educational or vocational progress.[3] Valid measuring instruments must be used if education is progressively to help students discover their greatest educational and vocational possibilities.

[1] National Occupational Conference, 551 Fifth Avenue, New York.
[2] WOOD, BEN D., "Coordinated Examining and Testing Programs," *Educational Record*, 15: 46–55, January, 1934.
[3] BREWER, JOHN M., *Mental Measurement in Educational and Vocational Guidance*, p. 46, Harvard University Press, Cambridge, Mass., 1924.

Even the most reliable tests cannot be substituted, however, for instruction or guidance. "The sole purpose of testing is to refine our impressions of a given individual, to make those impressions more accurate, and to permit the impressions to be passed on to other people who may serve the individual in a counseling capacity."[1]

There are those who feel that testing is the only important phase of the educational and vocational guidance program; others who would go a step further in considering testing the only important function of the entire personnel program. Testing has value only in its proper relationship to the educational and vocational guidance program, as a supplementary aid for proper and wise counseling, and is merely one phase of the services in the student personnel program on the campus.

Objective tests should always be given, scored, and interpreted by well-qualified and trained persons. If the purpose for which objective tests were designed, *i.e.*, better educational diagnosis and placement, is to be realized, the greatest possible accuracy must be insured. Even so, too much faith must not be placed in the results of any one test or one group of tests. It is fairly safe to assume that an individual could do as well on any number of other similar tests (unless he cheated) as he did on a certain one, but it is not safe to assume that the result on any one test or one group of tests is a maximum result.

Standard tests provide definite, objective, and fairly dependable information about the traits and abilities of individuals and groups. Such tests are important for comparisons and for finding elements of weakness and strength in groups and in individuals. Their use in a guidance program should provide for the comparison of an individual and a group not only with the national norms but also with local norms and should provide a means for comparing present levels of ability and achievement with past levels.

[1] WILLIAMSON, E. G., and J. G. DARLEY, *Student Personnel Work*, McGraw-Hill Book Company, Inc., New York, 1936, p. 313.

No problem has yet been solved completely by tests, but a wise use of tests has proved helpful in approaching some of the problems. It would certainly seem to be "best practice" to give tests and examinations of many kinds frequently but informally; to record the results carefully but skeptically; to study them carefully in the light of personal impressions, teachers' estimates, and all available facts pertaining to the student's background and achievement; and to base administrative decisions with respect to guidance upon the total picture of the student's abilities, aptitudes, character, and potentialities.

A personnel staff should include at least one member who is thoroughly qualified to direct a testing program: who is trained in giving tests, in scoring them, in converting scores into percentiles and other terms for interpretation, and in recording and interpreting the results. Some organization must be available for immediate and accurate scoring when large numbers of tests are given. There should be clinical provision for rechecking and supplementing test information on those individuals for whom the routine methods do not, for some reason, seem adequate.

Every member of the personnel staff should know the uses, limitations, and values of tests whether he take an active technical interest in the testing program or not, for he will always want to relate counseling to the most reasonable interpretation of a student's test results.

A list of tests for college students and adults, classified according to their use, is to be found in the Appendix.

As has been pointed out, tests and measurement may play an important role in securing information regarding individual differences which must be known in an educational and vocational guidance program. They are valuable diagnostic devices and offer useful facts regarding intelligence, aptitudes, and interests of students. But the successful guidance program must take into account as well the temperament, motivation, physical condition, attitudes, social and economic status, and educational background of the individual. Diagnostic devices which consider these factors are the interview, the cumulative record, personnel rating scales, the daily schedule, the case history, and anecdotal reports. The individual must be carefully studied, for successful educational and occupational guidance is built upon a synthesis of individual diagnosis and educational and occupational information.

Factors which contribute heavily to young people's choice of vocations in many cases are parental wishes and decisions. Parents cannot be blamed for wishing their children to achieve more than they themselves have, nor can those parents be condemned who desire their sons and daughters to carry on the family profession or business. Parents often overlook the defects and overrate the abilities of their offspring, and, unfortunately, they frequently know little of the requirements of the vocations they would choose for their children. These factors, as well as the influence of friends and the tendency to herd-mindedness, should not be underestimated, however, in an educational and vocational guidance program.

Unfortunately, the limited scope and flexibility of the curriculum in many institutions definitely restrict the effectiveness of educational and vocational counseling. The needs of many individuals are not met by existing curricula. Differential instruction such as that offered in the University General College at the University of Minnesota would do much to further educational and vocational guidance.

All of the educational and vocational guidance efforts in an institution must be coordinated by some one individual —the vice-president or dean of students or director of personnel—in a purposeful and well-organized program. Someone should be responsible for relating this program to the other personnel services of the college or university. It is particularly important that vocational and educational counseling be closely tied to the placement program of the institution.

Whatever the methods of diagnosing individual needs for educational and vocational guidance, whatever the methods of imparting essential information and stimulation to the students, it should be recognized that individual differences in native capacities and interests are great, that the curricula offered by colleges and universities are highly diversified, that there is an increasing specialization in all lines of work, that abilities, on the other hand, tend to be general rather than specific, that the period of preparation necessary for entrance upon vocational life is increasingly greater in length, that students cannot meet many important crises in their lives without expert assistance, that the college or university is in a strategic position to give this assistance, and that guidance should not be imposed but should aim at progressive ability in self-direction.

BIBLIOGRAPHY

Educational and Vocational Guidance

BOUCHER, CHAUNCEY S.: *The Chicago College Plan*, Chicago University Press, Chicago, 1935, 344 pp.

BREWER, JOHN M.: *Mental Measurement in Educational and Vocational Guidance*, Harvard University Press, Cambridge, Mass., 1924, 46 pp.

BREWER, JOHN M.: *Education as Guidance*, The Macmillan Company, New York, 1932, ix + 668 pp.

BROWN, RICHARD R.: "Multiple Skills Called Keys to Job," *The New York Times*, 6(2): 1, Apr. 25, 1937.

"Cornell Relates Events to Careers," *The New York Times* 6 (2): 1, Apr. 25, 1937.

"Faculty Adopts Plan to Modify Tutorial System," *The New York Times*, 20: 1, Mar. 29, 1937.

GARDNER, DONFRED H.: *The Evaluation of Higher Institutions*, V: "Student Personnel Service," University of Chicago Press, Chicago, 1936, xx + 235 pp.

GRAY, WILLIAM S. (Ed.): "Tests and Measurements in Higher Education," in *Proceedings of the Institute for Administrative Officers of Higher Institutions*, vol. VIII, University of Chicago Press, Chicago, 1936, 237 pp.

HEATON, K. L., and G. R. KOOPMAN: *College Curriculum Based on Functional Needs of Students*, University of Chicago Press, Chicago, 1936, 157 pp.

JONES, ARTHUR J.: *Principles of Guidance*, McGraw-Hill Book Company, Inc., New York, 1934, xxvii + 456 pp.

KATZ, DANIEL, and F. H. ALLPORT: *Students' Attitudes*, Craftsman Press, Syracuse, N. Y., 1931, xxviii + 401 pp.
KITSON, HARRY D.: *The Psychology of Vocational Adjustment*, J. B. Lippincott Company, Philadelphia, 1925, viii + 273.
———: "Vocational Guidance through School Subjects," *Teachers College Record*, 28: 900–915, May, 1927.
———: *How to Find the Right Vocation*, Harper & Brothers, New York, 1929, x + 202 pp.
———: *I Find My Vocation*, McGraw-Hill Book Company, Inc., New York, 1931, xiii + 216 pp.
KOOS, LEONARD V., and GRAYSON N. KEFAUVER: *Guidance in Secondary Schools*, The Macmillan Company, New York, 1932, xi + 640 pp.
LINGENFELTER, MARY REBECCA: *Vocations in Fiction, an Annotated Bibliography*, American Library Association, Chicago, 1932, 100 pp.
MCCONN, MAX: "Educational Guidance Is Now Possible," *Educational Record*, 14: 475–499, October, 1933.
MORRIS, E. H.: "Some Results Secured in Personnel Work in a Teachers College," *School and Society*, 39: 574–576, May 5, 1934.
MYERS, C. S.: "Some Present-day Trends in Vocational Psychology," *British Journal of Educational Psychology*, 6: 225–232, November, 1936.
"National Occupational Conference Reports on Year's Survey of 300 Occupations," *The New York Times*, 6 (2): 3, Mar. 21, 1937.
PITKIN, WALTER B.: *New Careers for Youth*, Simon & Schuster, Inc., New York, 1934, 236 pp.
RAINEY, HOMER P.: "Guidance and Placement for America's Youth," *Occupations*, 15: 838–844, June, 1937.
REYNOLDS, O. E.: *Social and Economic Background of College Students*, Teachers College, Bureau of Publications, Columbia University, New York, 1927, 57 pp.
STRANG, RUTH: *Study Types of Reading Exercises and Manual*, Teachers College, Bureau of Publications, Columbia University, New York, 1935, viii + 112 pp.
STRONG, E. K.: "Aptitudes versus Attitudes in Vocational Guidance," *Journal of Applied Psychology*, 18: 501–515, August, 1934.
"Student Failures Reduced at Yale," *The New York Times*, Apr. 5, 1937.
TEETER, VERL A.: *A Syllabus on Vocational Guidance*, The Macmillan Company, New York, 1930, xii + 217 pp.
White House Conference on Child Health and Protection, *Vocational Guidance, Report of the Sub-committee on Vocational Guidance*, D. Appleton-Century Company, Inc., New York, 1932, xxiii + 396 pp.
WILLIAMSON, E. G.: "Cooperative Guidance Movement," *School Review*, 43: 273–280, April, 1935.
———: "A College Class in Occupational Information," *School Review*, 45: 123–129, March, 1937.
———: *Students and Occupations*, Henry Holt & Company, New York, 1937, xxiv + 437 pp.
———, and J. B. DARLEY: *Student Personnel Work*, McGraw-Hill Book Company, Inc., New York, 1936, 313 pp.

WRENN, C. GILBERT, and LUELLA COLE: *How to Read Rapidly and Well: A Manual of Silent Reading*, Stanford University Press, Stanford University, 1935, 16 pp.

WRISTON, HENRY MERRITT: "Integrity of the College," *School and Society*, 43: 183–193, Feb. 8, 1936.

Tests and Measurements

ANDERSON, R. N.: "Comparative Study of Three Vocational Interest Tests," *Psychological Clinic*, 22: 117–127, June, 1933.

BAKER, J. J., and A. C. CROCKET: "Vocational Aptitudes Tests and Their Applications," *Journal Educational Research*, 2: 321–324, October, 1932.

BERGEN, G. R.: "Practical Use of Tests in Appraising Occupational Fitness," *Personnel Journal*, 13: 73–81, August, 1934.

BETTS, EVELYN W.: "Time-limit vs. Work-limit in Learning," in *Mental Measurement Monograph*, ser. 10, Williams & Wilkins Company, Baltimore, 1934, 58 pp.

BINGHAM, WALTER V.: *Aptitudes and Aptitude Testing*, Harper & Brothers, New York, 1937, viii + 390 pp.

BOYNTON, PAUL L.: *Intelligence—Its Manifestations and Measurements*, D. Appleton-Century Company, Inc., New York, 1933, 466 pp.

BRACE, DAVID, K.: *Measuring Motor Ability, a Scale of Motor Ability*, A. S. Barnes & Company, New York, 1930, xvi + 138 pp.

BRUNNER, AUGUSTA F., WILLIAM HEALY, GLADYS M. LOWE, and MYRA E. SHIMBERG: *A Manual of Individual Mental Tests and Testing*, Little, Brown & Company, Boston, 1927, 287 pp.

DICKSON, V. E.: "What Effective Guidance Techniques Are Being Administered through Tests and Measuring Devices?" *Vocational Guidance Magazine*, 6: 212 ff., February, 1928.

FREEMAN, F. S.: "On the Improper Use of Psychological Tests," *School and Society*, 37: 653–654, May 20, 1933.

FRYER, DOUGLAS: *The Measurement of Interests in Relation to Human Adjustment*, Henry Holt & Company, New York, 1931, 488 pp.

GARRETT, HENRY E., and M. R. SCHNECK: *Psychological Tests, Methods and Results*, Harper & Brothers, New York, 1933, 235 pp.

HALL, C. W.: "Test Data as Forecasts of Vocational and College Success," *Vocational Guidance Magazine*, 11: 214–217, February, 1933.

HAWKES, HERBERT E.: "The Cooperative Test Service," *Educational Record*, 12: 30–38, January, 1931.

———: "Real and Imaginary Dangers in the Testing Movement," in *Third Educational Conference of American Council on Education*, Washington, D. C., 1934, 17–37 pp.

———, E. F. LINDQUIST, and C. R. MANN: *The Construction and Use of Achievement Examinations*, Houghton Mifflin Company, Boston, 1936, 496 pp.

HULL, CLARK L.: *Aptitude Testing*, World Book Company, Yonkers-on-Hudson, N. Y., 1928, xiii + 535 pp.

JONES, EDWARD S.: *Comprehensive Examinations in American Colleges*, The Macmillan Company, New York, 1933, 436 pp.

KELLEY, TRUMAN L., and A. C. KREY: *Tests and Measurements in the Social Sciences*, Charles Scribner's Sons, New York, 1934, xiv + 635 pp.

LINCOLN, EDWARD A.: *Testing and the Uses of Test Results*, The Macmillan Company, New York, 1935, xi + 317 pp.

MCCONN, C. M.: "Measurement in Educational Experimentation," *Educational Record*, 15: 106–119, January, 1934.

MOFFATT, B. S.: "Do Preoccupational Tests Test?" *Occupations*, 13: 235–238, December, 1934.

PATERSON, D. G., G. G. SCHNEIDLER, and E. G. WILLIAMSON: *Student Guidance Techniques*, McGraw-Hill Book Company, Inc., New York 1938, xviii + 316 pp.

POND, M.: "What Is New in Employment Testing," *Personnel Journal*, 11: 10–16, June, 1932.

STRONG, E. K.: "Predictive Value of the Vocational Interest Test," *Journal Educational Psychology*, 26: 331–349, May, 1935.

TOMPKINS, RICHARD: "Tests Discover Student's Needs," *The New York Times*, 9 (6): 1, Nov. 1, 1936.

TRABUE, M. R.: "Recent Developments in Testing for Guidance," *Review of Educational Research*, 3: 41–48, February, 1933.

TRILLINGHAM, C. C.: "Philosophy of Testing," *Journal of Education*, 116: 91–92, Feb. 20, 1933.

WOOD, BEN D.: "Basic Considerations in Educational Testing," *Review of Educational Research*, 3: 5–20, February, 1933.

———: "Coordinated Examining and Testing Programs," in "Conference on Educational Measurements and Guidance, 1933," *The Educational Record*, 15: 46–55, January, 1934.

———: "The Program of the Cooperative Test Service," in *Proceedings of the Institute for Administrative Officers of Higher Institutions*, 1936, pp. 109–127, University of Chicago Press, Chicago.

CHAPTER X

HELPING STUDENTS FINANCIALLY AND HELPING THEM TO HELP THEMSELVES

FINANCIAL AID

Financial aid for students is as old as institutions of higher education themselves. There always have been individuals of ability whose personal finances were so meager as to demand support for schooling from others than the family. This problem has been accentuated by the increasingly higher cost of education beyond the secondary level. Such education would long ago have been limited to the economically privileged had not fellowships, scholarships, loans, and part-time work been made available for many students. During the recent depression years an added emphasis and stress have been put upon this phase of service to students.

The philosophy of student financial aid has not been sufficiently studied or acknowledged, but that experts do not agree in their points of view is evident from the literature in this field. There are some who feel that secondary education should be made possible for all but that only those who can themselves finance their education beyond this level should be encouraged to study in colleges or universities. Others state that higher education should be made available to all individuals who can profit by it and that systems of financial aid are not only necessary but essential in a democratic social system. Chambers[1] goes so far as to advocate a nation-wide system of college and university scholarships at public expense, aided by the

[1] CHAMBERS, M. M., "Youth Merits Educational Opportunity," *Progressive Education*, 13 (5): 364–369, May, 1936.

federal government and partly supported by the states, to be administered by state educational authorities.

At the present time, an able student who does not have the personal finances to go to college has various alternatives. He may attempt to get a job upon leaving high school, but it is only rarely that he can save enough money, should he find work at all, to finance a year in college. Or he may find a position in which, if there is a chance of permanency, he will be influenced to give up all thought of additional education. He may go to college without any finances of his own, hoping to work his way through. We only briefly point out here the risks he runs, the hardships he undergoes, the effect such an undertaking may have on his health, and what he misses in social opportunity and college life, if he can keep his academic work sufficiently high even to remain in college. He may be able to get a tuition scholarship or a loan, and honesty makes us admit that, if he is an athlete, these are not difficult to acquire. Whether he is an athlete or not, the chances are that he will shop about and choose the largest financial grant rather than the institution best fitted to his needs. If he has no personal financial backing at all, he cannot be blamed for this too severely. In all likelihood, even with a scholarship, or a loan (although these are rarely given to freshmen) the grants will be so small that this student will have to work part time as well. He may become so discouraged that he withdraws from the institution before the end of his first year. Moon[1] found that the percentage of students who permanently withdrew from the University of Chicago at the close of the first and second quarters was larger for students holding entrance scholarships than for an entire freshman class.

All institutions of higher education have some form of financial aid for students, whether it take the form of fellowships, scholarships, loans, or part-time work. The

[1] Moon, George R., "Records of Students Who Entered the University with Freshmen Scholarships," *School Review*, 38: 446, June, 1930.

majority, however, have no clearly defined policies or philosophy of student aid. That the policies of administration of loans, fellowships, and scholarships are chaotic to a degree that endangers their ultimate value is brought out in a survey of student aid by Smith.[1] Generally speaking, the systems of awards are arbitrary and opportunistic. Most institutions are not even aware that this is the case. Evaluations of current practice in other institutions, similar to that made of the student-aid situation in Teachers College, Columbia University,[2] would do much toward clarifying policies and procedures.

To illustrate the financial-aid situation as it exists in so many institutions of higher education, let us consider a rather typical system. In a college of some 4,000 students, there is no centralized program of student aid. There is an administrative office handling loans, one handling fellowships and scholarships, and another handling placement in part-time positions. A fourth office administers the National Youth Administration work when federal funds are available. Financial aid is not recognized as an important phase of the student personnel program, nor can there be said to be a real program of student aid within the college because each office operates more or less independently. As a result, some students receive all forms of financial aid, while others who merit help find the resources are too limited to include them. The student whose abilities and opportunities may permit him to earn sufficient money without his academic work's suffering may be given a scholarship, while a student whose financial difficulties are temporary may do an excessive amount of work when he could have been granted an emergency loan to meet the

[1] SMITH, MARGARET RUTH, "Student Aid: A Study of Loans, Scholarships, and Fellowships in Colleges and Universities," *Journal of Higher Education*, 7 (1): 29-35, January, 1936.

[2] SMITH, MARGARET RUTH, *Student Aid: Bases of Selection of Students to Whom Loans, Scholarships, and Fellowships Are Awarded in a Graduate School of Education*, Teachers College, Bureau of Publications, Columbia University, New York, 1937, p. 152.

situation. Nor does the college know the costs of the administration of its various financial aids or how much overlapping or inefficiency or duplication exists.

Our proposed remedy for this situation and other similar setups would be to have all student financial aid (including part-time work) centralized in one office under the direction of a person with a personnel point of view, trained in personnel techniques. This individual may be the secretary of a faculty student aid committee, or, if the program is subdivided, he may serve as a member of a faculty loan fund committee, of the college fellowship and scholarship committee, and of the advisory committee for part-time work. Or the director of student aid may also be the director of the entire personnel program of the college. Committees of faculty members are invaluable in making final decisions regarding who shall receive aid, for such decisions should not be made by any one individual, no matter how well he is trained or how capable he is.

We cannot overemphasize how important it is for any institution to have a definite philosophy of student aid and to have clear and definitely worked out policies. This should be done in terms of the objectives of the college, its resources for aid, and the percentage of the student body who need and are worthy of assistance.

With a central office, any student seeking financial help applies, either by letter or in person, first to a personnel officer. Many students asking for loans may in reality be served best by part-time work; others thinking only in terms of scholarships may find loans more satisfactory, particularly, if the competition is keen for the former. The personnel officer or administrator of financial aid has the opportunity to study the student and his financial problems and to offer expert advice in the light of his situation and the entire student aid program. He also has the opportunity to consult with students regarding their financial plans by mail and in interviews before they are admitted to the college and in some instances can dissuade them from coming for study if they have no financial resources of their own. Few colleges can undertake to finance a student completely, even through one year of college. The director of financial aid should be familiar with policies of admission and placement, for both of these services are interrelated with financial aid. Many students borrow and work their way through colleges and universities to find they are not trained or equipped for the work they want to do when they are graduated. It is practically impossible to place others who have personality or emotional difficulties, although these frequently tend to be most insistent in their demand that the college continue to look after them, as they have become accustomed to have it do.

It is the responsibility of this centralized office of financial aid to interview, investigate, and collect all data regarding applicants for various types of aid. The director of the financial-aid program should make recommendations to a committee on financial aid, but the rejection or acceptance of the applicant should rest with the committee, (except, of course, in the case of part-time work).

Fellowships and scholarships are usually outright gifts awarded to students on the basis of scholastic ability and promise for the future, as determined by reports, recommendations, and examinations. There is a tendency to weight ability against need in the granting of fellowships and scholarships. Competition for these awards is usually very keen in practically every institution offering them. Invariably almost as many worthy applicants have to be rejected as accepted, in spite of the fact that one estimate of the capital involved in these types of aid was $50,000,000 in 24 institutions surveyed.[1] The personnel officer in charge of financial aid can do much to prevent the refusal of applications for fellowships or scholarships from being too much of a blow, offering encouragement and frank advice

[1] BADGLEY, HERBERT H., "Study of Fellowships and Scholarships in Universities," M. A. thesis, Stanford University, unpublished manuscript, 1931, 106 pp.

where this is warranted. A rejection letter may include an invitation to confer with the director where this is possible.

Although most institutions limit the award of fellowships and scholarships to the "cream" of the group applying for these grants, there are a few colleges and universities which feel these awards should go to the outstanding students of the country, whether they have applied for them or not, and that these geniuses should be adequately financed throughout their entire education, or as long as high standards of work are maintained. The policy of these institutions is to seek out individuals whose ability cannot be questioned and to offer them grants covering all educational expenses. Such a practice is in accord with the philosophy of Plato who stated in his *Republic* that society should subsidize outstanding ability in the interest of social betterment.

The fellowship or scholarship application blank should ask for information in clear, concise terms. There should be plenty of room for the applicant's replies. Only information that will actually be used in evaluating the candidate should be requested. Since recommendations are one of the chief bases of selection, a carefully worked out form to be filled in by the reference, asking for explicit information is far superior to the usual very general letter of recommendation that is solicited. Questions on categorical traits such as emotional stability, creative thinking, effective energy, and leadership, enlisting specific examples from the reference is more useful than general statements. It is wise to encourage the reference to volunteer other information than that specifically asked for by including additional blank space.

The administration of loan funds received an added impetus during the depression. The trend during this period seemed to be toward loans rather than scholarships, due, no doubt, to the fact that more students could be assisted through loans. In 1933, Woellner found that in 161 colleges and universities loan funds had been increased to a greater extent than scholarship funds.[1] In spite of the pressure of the depression years which demanded that a larger number of students be financially aided, it seems safe to say that there is a growing attitude in favor of loans for students rather than gift subsidies, such as scholarships. Advocates of this plan feel that higher education is not an inherent right of the average man of adequate intelligence, but rather a valuable privilege that should be paid for by the individual and not by society at large.

There is no doubt but that some students place a higher value on a fund that must be returned, that loans give valuable financial and business training to the student, and that the obligation of repayment eliminates the idea of many students that society should "hand them" an education.

Applicants for loans are usually considered on the bases of: (1) present need, determined by the analysis of application blank, containing budgets and a clear statement of present financial circumstances, and a personal conference; (2) future ability and willingness to repay the loan, estimated by intelligence and talent as judged by scholastic standing and examinations; (3) enterprise, which may be ascertained by what he is doing to help himself; (4) health, which is rated by a physical examination and the student's present record; (5) integrity and reliability, estimated by past performance in the home community and the college or university community. These are the usual criteria on which evidence and information are sought in the loan application blank. Past performances in the home and college community are evaluated through references. The student should be asked to give the names and addresses of his banker, minister, or other citizens of his home town who are not relatives, as well as a number of the college or university group who know him well.

[1] WOELLNER, R. C., "Provisions for the Financial Support of Students," *Proceedings of the Institute for Administrative Officers of Higher Institutions*, 1933, pp. 141–155.

The administration of student loan funds has to be worked out by each institution in order best to meet the need. However, the Harmon Foundation, which has had wide experience in this field and which has made a number of studies, makes certain recommendations which they feel are generally useful for successful administration. These are: the careful selection of risks, an interest rate of 6 per cent from the date of the loan, an installment form of repayment beginning a sufficient time after graduation or leaving school for the borrower to orient himself to some form of occupation yielding a living wage, a strict and regular follow-up, the protection against loss through mutual group guarantee, and the granting of a credit recommendation when the loan is paid in full on time.

The plan of the mutual group guarantee which has served the Harmon Foundation in its administration of loan funds has not yet been adopted to any great extent by colleges and universities. This plan provides that each recipient of a loan pay into a general group fund a small additional sum which is utilized in all or in part by the Foundation if all in the group do not repay their loans in full. If the loans are all paid, the sum is not forfeited but is returned to each member of the group.

There is no doubt but that collections of loans have received too little attention in many institutions. Follow-up should be exacting, precise, and prompt, with notice before payment is due, follow-up notice if payment is not made, and a more personal handling of the case if both reminders fail. In the latter instances, fairly inexpensive investigation of whether the former student is able to pay can be made by credit agencies. This procedure of follow-up must be worked out in close cooperation between the personnel officer in charge of student aid and the business office of the institution.

All administrators of loan funds have asked themselves at some time or another: "What is the maximum amount we can safely loan a student without placing too great a burden upon him after graduation?" The Harmon Foundation answers by stating that there is no way of determining the maximum amount of an obligation that a student should assume to complete his education.[1] Smith found that it is not the size of the loan alone that influences the burdensomeness of repayment, but rather other factors, such as health, financial conditions, and family obligations.[2] The amount loaned to each student must be decided individually on the bases of the average cost at the institution, the student's health, his academic standing, his opportunities for self-help, his need, and the known employment opportunities which present themselves to each group of students after graduation according to their type of training.

There are two types of loan funds in use in colleges and universities. These are revolving and restricted funds. The revolving fund enables the institution to loan both the principal and the income, and in this way many more students can be assisted financially. The restricted fund permits only the use of the income, and the greater number of funds are administered on this basis, although many colleges and universities state that they favor the revolving method.

Each institution has its own individual practices regarding security for loans. The common practice, however, seems to be to demand a note signed by the student, and in as many instances signed by him alone as with an endorser. No doubt, security has not been deemed more important because the institutional losses have not been great. Data are not available on losses throughout the country, but it would seem safe to say that they do not exceed 3 per cent.

[1] *Student Loan Funds—A Study of Student Loan Funds and Their Administration throughout the United States*, p. 22, Harmon Foundation, Inc., New York, 1924.

[2] SMITH, MARGARET RUTH, *Student Aid: Bases of Selection of Students to Whom Loans, Scholarships, and Fellowships Are Awarded in a Graduate School of Education*, p. 124, Teachers College, Bureau of Publications, Columbia University, New York, 1937.

Those in control of student aid will find that an emergency loan fund which does not involve more than a bare minimum of "red-tape" is essential for solving certain student problems. A small loan often means the difference between triumph and defeat. These emergency loans are usually for less than $100, and it is the customary procedure to charge a smaller interest rate than upon the larger loans. At the University of Oregon, however, an expedient system of administration has been worked out. A service charge of $0.25 is demanded for each $25 or part thereof for each 30-day period until the loan is paid.[1]

Part-time work offered by many colleges and universities has contributed its share to the belief that any one of average ability and health can earn a college education. As Dean McKnight points out, however, a different attitude prevails today than formerly:[2]

"With increasing frequency college administrators are pointing out the disadvantages, and in many instances, the downright dangers, which accompany the effort to combine full time collegiate study with an extensive program of self-support. Recently President Conant of Harvard University, speaking before a large educational conference, condemned the 'work your way through college' theory as more destructive than productive. In other institutions and sections of the country similar opinions are being expressed. . . . In 1932, a group of personnel officers in a number of Eastern colleges came to the following conclusions regarding part-time work:

"1. The health hazards involved in combining a full collegiate program with sufficient outside employment to provide full support are most serious.

"2. Constant worry over financial matters and excessive time devoted to self-support produce a demoralizing effect on the student's scholastic achievement general adjustment and social contacts.

[1] ONTHANK, KARL W., "Loan Funds at the University of Oregon," *School and Society*, 42 (1073): 98, July 20, 1935.

[2] McKNIGHT, N. D., "Self-support in College," *The New York Times* (Education Section), Sunday, Mar. 15, 1936.

"3. The more numerous the self-supporting students, the thinner the available means of assistance must be spread.

"4. An excessive number of self-supporting students renders the competition for jobs so keen that employers are able to take advantage of students.

"5. A disproportionately large number of self-supporting students, being in a sense part-time students, tends to turn the college into a part-time institution.

"6. A too large proportion of self-supporting students jeopardizes the extra-curricular and social life of the institution."

What is the answer? In part, it may be to give wider publicity to the difficulties and uncertainties of part-time work. Again, there should be an admission procedure operating which will enable the director of student aid to study carefully the financial needs and purposes of many of these self-supporting individuals in coming to college. Many wish to enter college for reasons of secondary importance and because no more appealing alternatives have presented themselves. The institution's resources for part-time work should be studied and made the basis for clearly defined policies of administration which will help eliminate many students who should be diverted into other channels. Hard and fast rules cannot be laid down, of course, for decisions must be made by administrators who possess a personnel point of view, considering each case individually.

The part-time program must be well coordinated with the entire program of student aid and with admission and placement policies. Much of the present attack upon student self-support is not due to part-time work itself but rather to the amount of work permitted and the unsystematic way in which this and other forms of student aid are assigned. It is necessary that there be at the helm an individual who knows the institutional situation, not only in regard to part-time work, but also as to fellowships, scholarships, and loans, as well as the individual student's problems.

Each institution must work out standards for part-time work. There should be a maximum of hours of work permitted each week and minimum standard rates of pay for different types of work. These may vary in different parts of the country, depending upon the cost of living in the community, and the demand and supply of workers.

The director of the bureau for part-time work, the director of the placement bureau, or—in the small college—the director of personnel himself may be the director of the entire student aid program. Whoever he is, he must be a person of imagination, for it is the imaginative person who can understand people and create jobs. He should attempt to relate the employment program to the educational program in order to make self-support supplement rather than interrupt or handicap the student's scholastic pursuits. Employment in libraries, museums, on research problems, in the design and construction of laboratory apparatus, etc., are ways in which student employment can be correlated with academic work.

Careful records must be kept. It is only through records that accurate information can be made available as to the possibilities of earning in different types of work, as to the amount that can be safely counted on by a prospective student, with certain abilities and skills, and also in order that leads may be followed for additional employment situations. Carefully kept records demand a sufficient office staff to enable the director to spend his time with students and employers rather than with records.

The logical place for the administration of federal funds under the National Youth Administration is in the part-time office, for National Youth Administration work is part-time work. There is no need here to go into the controversy as to whether the federal government should make available funds for this purpose. That these funds have possibilities for great harm as well as good can be readily acknowledged.

One of the chief difficulties in the administration of the National Youth Administration work is to determine true need. Since the cost of administration must be borne by the institution concerned, few can afford extensive investigation of applicants. Under the circumstances, an application blank demanding complete information, as well as a budget, and a personal interview are the best means of determining need. As in other part-time work, the National Youth Administration work should supplement rather than handicap the educational program of the student. Careful assignments should be worked out. This alleviates innumerable changes in assignments which have irritating effects upon both student and employer.

The student applicant for National Youth Administration work should be made to feel that such work is as much of an employment situation as any other form of part-time work. The institution should maintain a constant check on the student's dependability, the quality and quantity of his work, and his attitude. Too many have the idea that National Youth Administration funds do not need to be earned. Reports should be made by the campus National Youth Administration Office to the college placement bureau indicating how the student measured up in this tryout employment situation, and these reports should have some effect upon his recommendations for placement following graduation.

Funds for fellowships and scholarships have, for the most part, been gifts to the institutions from wealthy persons who wished to establish memorials. These donors often make restrictions stating that the award must go to students of a certain nationality or race, have a certain name, attend a certain undergraduate school, are from a certain state, or are studying in a certain field. A number of institutions no longer will accept restricted funds, for experience has proved that it may be difficult to carry out the requirements. An increasing number of colleges and universities are appropriating funds from their own budgets for fellowships and scholarships. This may in part be due to the fact that since the depression large privately granted gifts of money have decreased in number.

The sources of loan funds have been much the same as those of fellowships and scholarships. Wealthy individuals have contributed sums to institutions to be loaned to students. The colleges and universities themselves have designated certain school funds to be used for this purpose. Institutional clubs and organizations also have made many gifts to loan funds. At times, these organizational sums are turned over to a personnel officer with the instruction that they be used where they will do the most good, not as a loan but as an outright gift. Personnel officers who have this money at their disposal have been grateful more than once for such a resource.

The recommendation has been made that all financial aid in an institution be centered in one administrative office under the direction of a personnel officer. This office will need a centralized student aid record form in order to operate efficiently and to have the necessary information for instant use. A record should be kept for each student applying for, receiving, or refused aid, for the duration of his stay in college. A suggested form for this purpose is herewith presented. This should be modified to meet the especial needs of any institution. The purpose of this form is to supply information as to the number applying for aid, the number receiving aid, and the number refused. A study of this card will tell how much aid any individual student receives during his stay in college, the type and the amount. It is our plan that the part-time office be a section of the central financial-aid office, and an application for part-time employment should be entered on this central card. It may be that under "decision" may be entered merely "registered in the part-time bureau" (reg. p.t.b.) or it may be possible to enter "cafeteria job"—and, under "amount," "$_____ per month." Under "comment," numerous data would be available: the reason the application was refused, for instance, or if a student applied for a scholarship and was advised to apply for a loan, this information would be entered. The file number is suggested so that currently used cards may be kept in the front of the file. A cross index in the form of an alphabetized card index file will permit this.

Last name	First name	Middle name				File Number
Date of application	Type of aid	Decision	Date of decision	If aid, amount	Number of references on file	Comment

Financial Aid
Name of Institution

Financial aid for students is a student personnel service. The personnel point of view and personnel techniques should play primary roles in its administration. Too long have institutions thought of loans, scholarships, fellowships, and part-time work as merely something to be administered in the easiest and most expedient way, with too little consideration for those refused aid. Instead, its philosophy, policies, and administration must be established in terms of admissions and placement policies, in terms of the individual student—his abilities, needs, and hopes, his life in college, and his vocational future following graduation—as well as in the light of the objectives of the institution and its resources for financial aid.

BIBLIOGRAPHY

ARCHER, JOHN K.: "University Scholarships," *New York State Education*, 22 (4): 313, January, 1935.

———: "Achievement of Scholars," *New York State Education*, 22 (5): 375, 414–416, February, 1935.

BADGLEY, HERBERT H.: "Study of Fellowships and Scholarships in Universities," M. A. thesis, Stanford University, unpublished manuscript, 1931, 106 pp.

BETTS, G. H.: "Subsidizing Graduate Study," *Journal of Higher Education*, 3: 415–418, November, 1932.

BILDERSEE, ADELE: *State Scholarship Students at Hunter College of the City of New York*, Teachers College, Bureau of Publications, Columbia University, New York, 1932, iii + 138 pp.

BOATWRIGHT, F. W.: "Scholarship and Loan Funds," *Association of Universities and College Business Officers of the Eastern States, Proceedings of the Thirteenth Annual Meeting*, 1932, pp. 64–68.

BRIGHAM, CARL C.: "Examining Fellowship Applicants," *Social Science Research Council Bulletin* 23, Princeton University Press, Princeton, N. J., 1935, 58 pp.

CHAMBERS, M. M.: "Youth Merits Educational Opportunity," *Progressive Education*, 13: 364–369, May, 1936.

CHASSEE, L. J.: "A Study of Student Loans and Their Relation to Higher Educational Finance," *Harmon Foundation Monograph* 1, Harmon Foundation, Inc., New York, 1925, 170 pp.

CRAWFORD, ALBERT B.: "The Scholarship Racket," *The Saturday Evening Post*, Apr. 6, 1935, pp. 27, 103–104, 106, 109–110.

———: "A New Deal for Needy Students?" *Educational Record*, 17: 227–247, April, 1936.

FERNBERGER, SAMUEL W.: "Objective Control of One Factor in the Granting of Post-graduate Fellowships and Scholarships," *School and Society*, 37: 787–792, June 17, 1933.

FOERSTER, NORMAN: "Lowering Higher Education" *Scribner's Magazine*, 99: 368–370, June, 1936.

JOSTEN, MARGARET H.: "An Investment in Youth," *Wisconsin Journal of Education*, 68: 397–398, April, 1936.

MCKNIGHT, N. D.: "Self-support in College," *The New York Times* (Education Section), Sunday, Mar. 15, 1937.
MALLER, J. B.: "Personality of the Candidates for the Edison Scholarship," *School and Society*, 35: 438–442, Mar. 26, 1932.
MOON, GEORGE R.: "Records of Students Who Entered the University with Freshman Scholarships," *School Review*, 38: 443–449, June, 1930.
ONTHANK, KARL W.: "Who Pays for Administration of Student Loan Funds?" *School and Society*, 41: 733–735, June, 1, 1935.
———: "Loan Funds at the University of Oregon," *School and Society*, 42 (1073): 97–98, July 20, 1935.
PULLIAS, EARL VIVON: "The Qualifications and Achievements of the Henry Strong Foundation Scholars," M.A. thesis, University of Chicago, unpublished manuscript, 1931, vii + 97 pp.
RATCLIFFE, E. B.: "Scholarships and Fellowships Available at Institutions of Higher Education," U. S. Office of Education, *Bulletin* 19, 1936, 117 pp.
REEVES, FLOYD W., and JOHN DALE RUSSELL: "Some University Student Problems," *University of Chicago Survey*, vol. X, University of Chicago Press, Chicago, 1933, xix + 194 pp.
REYNOLDS, O. EDGAR: *The Social and Economic Status of College Students*, Teachers College, Bureau of Publications, Columbia University, New York, 1927, v + 58 pp.
RIPPERGER, HENRIETTA: "The Kept Student," *Atlantic Monthly*, 153: 449–454, April, 1934.
Seven Years' Experience with Student Loans, Harmon Foundation, Inc., New York, 1929, 23 pp.
SMITH, MARGARET RUTH: "Student Aid: A Study of Loans, Scholarships, and Fellowships in Colleges and Universities," *Journal of Higher Education*, 7: 29–35, January, 1936.
———: *Student Aid: Bases of Selection of Students to Whom Loans, Scholarships, and Fellowships Are Awarded in a Graduate School of Education*, Teachers College, Bureau of Publications, Columbia University, New York, 1937, 152 pp.
STALNAKER, J. M., and M. W. RICHARDSON: "Scholarship Examinations," *Journal of Higher Education*, 5: 305–313, June, 1934.
State-aided Colleges and Scholarships in Maryland, Maryland League of Women Voters, Baltimore, 1932, mimeographed, 10 pp.
STONE, H. E.: "Analysis of the Results of the Survey of Loan Fund Administration in the United States," *School and Society*, 36: 538–540, Oct. 22, 1932.
STROMBERG, EDWARD H.: "Student Loan Fund Survey," *Educational Record*, 14: 516–521, October, 1933.
Student Loan Funds—A Study of Student Loan Funds and Their Administration throughout the United States, Harmon Foundation, Inc., New York, 1924, 40 pp.
Survey of Student Aid Sources in New Jersey, D. Appleton-Century Company, Inc., New York, 1932, 121 pp.

"Trends and Procedure in Student Loans," *Harmon Foundation Monograph* 4, Harmon Foundation, Inc., New York, 1932, 150 pp.

UMSTATTD, JAMES G.: *Student Self-support at the University of Minnesota*, University of Minnesota Press, Minneapolis, 1932, xii + 205 pp.

WAKEQUIST, JOHN T.: "An Evaluation of the New Deal in Education," *School and Society*, 42: 859–863, Dec. 21, 1935.

WALTERS, RAYMOND: "The Academic Record of Rhodes Scholars," *School and Society*, 36: 340–343, Sept. 10, 1932.

WOELLNER, R. C.: "Provisions for the Financial Support of Students," in *Proceedings of the Institute for Administrative Officers of Higher Institutions*, pp. 141–155, University of Chicago Press, Chicago, 1933.

Year Book, American Students Foundation, Inc., New York, 1934–1935.

CHAPTER XI

FACILITATING AND DIRECTING THE ORGANIZED EXTRACLASS LIFE OF STUDENTS

Extracurricular Activities

"Educators must come more definitely to recognize that to the average undergraduate, student life constitutes the real life of the college."[1] It is safe to assume that the writers of these words and the undergraduates concerned mean by student life that which exists outside the classroom. That this student life is made up largely of "extracurricular activities" and social activities is another safe assumption. "Broadly speaking, faculties tend to think in terms of a subject-centered world, and undergraduates in terms of student activities."[2]

Extracurricular activities take care of those normal, wholesome student interests for which the curriculum in most colleges and universities does not adequately provide. Brewer goes so far as to say that

... the very use of the word 'extra' spells defeat for the guidance point of view if guidance is to be education, and if it is to be put into the agency which educators use to educate, namely, the curriculum. If well established subjects are still to absorb the chief effort of teachers, to be carefully taught and marked, and to receive 'credit,' and if real living is to be called 'extra,' we cannot hope to proceed very far in turning education into guidance.[3]

[1] Cowley, W. H., and W. Waller, "A Study of Student Life," *Journal of Higher Education*, 6 (3): 141, March, 1935.

[2] Edwards, Artman, and Fisher, *Undergraduates*, p. 91, Doubleday, Doran & Company, Inc., Garden City, N. Y., 1928.

[3] Brewer, John M., *Education as Guidance*, p. 74, The Macmillan Company, New York, 1932.

Some institutions will not agree with Brewer that the so-called extracurricular activities should be a part of the curriculum, while others have already given these activities a recognized place in the curriculum. The latter is the case at Stephens College and at Sarah Lawrence College. In 1931 Stephens College made extracurricular activities one of its five major divisions.

This division is headed by an instructor or 'Adviser on Social Adjustment' who ranks equally with other divisional heads. Since junior college years are years when social adjustment is of paramount importance, this Extra-Curricular Division sees that an individual program of development is mapped out for every girl who needs it and administers the organized group activities of the general student body . . . The general type of organization that is evolving is a type of decentralized co-ordinated personnel service in which all faculty members participate, certain specialists render individual service and all services are coordinated through the Extra-Curricular Division office.[1]

At Sarah Lawrence College, the setup is somewhat different, but the student activities are definitely within the curriculum. The activities are group enterprises, each with its own officers and dues, but the work is highly individualized. A girl works in publications, social service, dramatics, arts and crafts, orchestra, chorus, health activity, or business activity, or in two of these. The responsibility for the work and the organization of the activity rest upon the students who consult with an adviser, who is not a member of the faculty but an expert, someone with experience in this field outside of the college. The adviser is chosen by the faculty to give the most educational value possible to the activity. In publications, for instance, John Bakeless, a former member of the *Atlantic Monthly* staff and author of a recent book on journalism, is the adviser. The activity chosen by the students counts as one-quarter of the year's work, requiring, as a rule, 10 to

[1] PRICE, LOUISE, "Social Adjustments in the Junior College," *Junior College Journal* 3: 456–461, May, 1933.

12 hours a week. "In addition to the element of cooperative work and the development of responsibility for organization of one's own work, we feel that these activities develop a sense of service to the community, and bring out the educational value of practical work," states President Warren.[1]

In the majority of institutions of higher education, however, extracurricular activities are "extra" curricular. They are not part of the curriculum and, moreover, in a few colleges have even very little supervision from the faculty or the personnel staff. In these instances the student world is practically separate and distinct from that of the administration or of the faculty. The students, administration, and faculty should, however, make up a community of three interrelated elements, bound closely together by mutual interests and objectives. The administration and faculty should be as much interested in the values of student activities and affairs as the students are interested in them, for these activities have a greater value than merely taking care of the natural exuberance of youth. They can be truly educational and can serve a purpose that subject matter and classroom-taught subjects do not.

Leadership drives of individuals have a normal place on the campus as they do in the world proper. What is leadership? Bogardus defines it as personality in action under group conditions.[2] If a person is individual enough, he may be able to perform in ways sufficiently different and superior to his fellows to qualify for leadership. But this individuality must be expressed in attitudes and directions favorable to the social group, or he will not become a leader. From Moore's study of leadership traits of college women, we learn that democratic attitudes, vitality, positiveness,

[1] WARREN, CONSTANCE, "Activities at Sarah Lawrence College," *Association of American Colleges Bulletin* 18: 205–208, May, 1932.

[2] BOGARDUS, EMORY S., *Leaders and Leadership*, Chap. I, D. Appleton-Century & Company, Inc., New York, 1934.

friendliness, enthusiasm, sympathy, trustworthiness, and perseverance are the outstanding traits of women who ranked highest as leaders, while those preventing leadership include narrowness, timidity, affectation, egotism, silliness, fickleness, and stubbornness.[1] Leadership on the campus may be of different types: the social climber who is mostly interested in popularity, the athlete who is admired for his physical achievements alone, the "Phi Bete" intellectual who has more admirers than followers, the "big shot" who is in close contact with several social groups, and the athletic big shot who is a combination of the athlete and the social climber, the pseudo-intellectual who sells his ideas to followers who are interested in "reforms," and the combination of the intellectual and social success who is primarily interested in service to his college.

All leaders have followship traits as well, for what may be leadership characteristics in one social situation may be followship traits in another situation. It is as important to develop good followers as it is to develop good leaders. The majority of our students and our citizens have to be followers much of the time, and educators are interested that they should be intelligent followers. Extracurricular activities can provide the best possible means for developing fine leaders and followers, but this development can be very haphazard and unsatisfactory unless the extracurricular program is recognized as an important part of the total educational program of the institution and placed under the direction of someone who is competent to cultivate its potentialities. The person in charge of the extracurricular program should understand thoroughly the principles and methods which will best ensure that the extracurricular program provide all students with valuable experiences.

Student activities should be democratic. There should be a sufficient range and variety of activities on the campus to permit all who are interested from seniors down to

[1] MOORE, L. H., "Leadership Traits of College Women," *Sociology and Social Research*, 17: 44–54, May, 1933.

freshmen to participate in some form of activity. They should have worth while purposes from the standpoint of meeting student needs and interests. There should be homogeneous as well as heterogeneous groupings in extracurricular activities. Some groupings should be cross sections of the student body including all racial and age groups of the college or university. Others may profitably be narrowly exclusive in membership. The objectives of the organizations should be those of the student members rather than those of the faculty or administration. In the majority, dues should be nominal. All members of each organization should participate in some way in its activities.

Extracurricular activities on the campus may take many different forms. The most democratic is the student-government organization through which students participate in the government of the campus. All the students are usually members of this organization and are privileged to take part in its program. Many of the oldest organizations are honorary societies or fraternities, such as Phi Beta Kappa and a number of others based on high scholarship and achievement in specialized fields, such as chemistry, engineering, education, journalism, dramatics, and sociology. There may be religious organizations, the Y. M. C. A., the Y. W. C. A., the Newman Club, and others originated upon the basis of a religious homogeneity. The activity may take the form of a purely social club, such as a sorority or fraternity, or it may be an outgrowth of the curriculum, such as the many departmental clubs, English, psychology, social science, physical education, dramatic and musical associations, etc. The organization may have the purpose of service to the college or community. Student publications, a daily or weekly newspaper, the college or university annual, literary, humorous, and departmental magazines play an important part in the student activities program. Some of the activities, such as intercollegiate athletics and debating, extend beyond campus walls. Class organizations on large campuses are dying a natural death due to their size and the fact that their purposes are met by many other group activities, but on the small campus the class may still be a democratic outlet for many activities. The intramural sports program may function largely on class lines, while, even on the large campus, class elections may revive class spirit and loyalties for a brief time. Campus elections of all types are frequently occasions for intense political rivalry, and campaign methods, if not guided, can at times equal the most evil of the city political machines.

Most colleges and universities publish a student handbook which outlines and catalogues the different student activities on the campus. Herein are given brief histories of organizations, their purposes, eligibility requirements for membership, dues, officers, time and place of meeting, etc. This handbook may be used extensively in an orientation program. On some campuses, it is published by the student-government organization, while in other instances the institution's Y. M. C. A. or Y. W. C. A. is responsible for its publication. The handbook has a value, but its contents all too easily become obsolete. Many handbooks every year contain data pertaining to organizations long since nonexistent. A great deal of organization and hard work is required each year if the handbook is to contain a complete index of student organizations with accurate information regarding each. The editors of such a book should check carefully every year with every organization. This may be done easily if there is a personnel office on the campus which files all records of students' activities.

In any institution where there is a wide program of extracurricular activities, there is need for limiting participation on the part of some students and for stimulating others to become active. Many sorts of systems are in use with the general aim of distributing more widely the opportunities for participation than would be possible without some control. Johnston[1] describes the different systems: the simplest is merely limitation, setting two, three, or four as a limiting number of activities in which any one student may engage at any one time; "the major and minor" system holds a student to one major, *i.e.*, more important and time consuming, and to one or two minor activities; a third sort of system is the point scale where a number of points is assigned to each office and activity, and no student may exceed a certain number of points during a year; and the group system in which activities are classed as social, artistic, athletic, academic, and general, no student participating outside one of these groups. The system most frequently used in colleges and universities is the point scale which is flexible and adaptable. The installation of a point system, however, should be based upon the situation at the particular institution, and the actual situation on any campus can be determined only by periodic surveys of the opportunities for participation in activities and the extent of the distribution of students among them.

Whatever point system is used, there must be some provision for recording and checking upon the activities of each student. A student is usually elected or appointed to do this work, and, if the campus is large enough, he or she may have a staff of assistants. His or her best sources of acquiring the necessary information are the college or university newspaper and the bulletin boards.

Another method of limiting participation in student activities is the requirement of a certain grade point average for those permitted to participate. This method is more universally used in athletics than in other forms of extracurricular activities, but it has desirable features for all activities. Certain health standards might operate in the same way, but their need has evidently not yet been thought to be so great, since few institutions demand them.

[1] JOHNSTON, EDGAR G., *Point Systems and Awards*, A. S. Barnes & Company, New York, 1930, xiv + 160 pp.

The two aims, that of limiting participation of some students and that of stimulating participation of others, can conflict. Requiring some form of participation by each student is a means of stimulation which is somewhat artificial. Middlebury College has a policy of granting points for participation in activities including athletics and requires a certain number of these points for graduation. But the best method of stimulation is to make participation attractive.

Sad experience has made it necessary in many institutions to have all financial accounts of every student organization that handles money audited by a member of the faculty or business staff. This insures careful keeping of financial records and accurate accounts. Learning proper business methods is an educational value of student activities. This value is achieved more readily by the decentralized control of funds where an accounting must be made to an auditor at the end of each quarter or semester. In instances, where a faculty representative, or committee, or administrator has absolute control of all activities' funds, of preparing budgets for organizations, investigating requests for funds, and approving requisitions, the students gain little financial experience. Collecting dues, or raising money, bookkeeping, banking money, writing checks, and maintaining accounts in a businesslike way are educative experiences which even students on the college and university level woefully need.

Meetings of student organizations should be held in campus buildings wherever possible. Adequate physical space for organizations is not only desirable but essential. College or university union or league buildings on some campuses take care of this need efficiently, while on others classrooms have to be utilized for meeting purposes. In order to prevent conflicts in use of space and also in time of meetings, a student activity calendar should be maintained by some member of the personnel staff. All events and meetings should be properly scheduled with this office, recording the time, place, and approximate number expected to attend. The personnel office then makes the necessary arrangements for the building to be open, lighted, etc.

The same member of the personnel staff may be responsible for seeing that reports are filed in his or her office before student affairs are held. These reports help insure careful planning sufficiently in advance of the event. Information asked for may include: name of the organization sponsoring the affair, officer or chairman in charge, other committees, (chairmen and members), time and place, chaperons (when required), a financial budget if money is to be expended, and the purpose of the event. With such reports filed in a central office, college newspaper reporters may be sure of reliable advance notice of coming events and of learning the names of those responsible. After the event has taken place, another report should be filed in the personnel office, giving details of the number who actually attended, the exact financial outcome, and recommendations to improve a similar affair that may be held the following year. Such a plan of reporting not only provides a means of control for the personnel office and assists the students in an orderly efficient carrying out of their activities, but also provides some basis for improving affairs from year to year on the basis of previous experience carefully transmitted in written reports.

Some institutions have developed a control of all student activities centered in a faculty-student committee which has final authority in all extracurricular activities. This committee may be responsible for limiting participation, stimulating participation, controlling finances, chartering new organizations, etc. In the opinion of the authors of this book, such a committee would serve better in an advisory rather than a regulatory capacity. Students should be permitted the experience of regulating their own affairs and activities with advice and tactful supervision cooperatively given by such a committee.

It is the opinion of many educators that most colleges and universities have too many extracurricular activities and that the campuses are overorganized. Too great a number of extracurricular activities and overorganization constitute a real danger, but action in regard to these problems should be based on well-organized information pertaining to the distribution and concentration of student activities. A survey to obtain this information can be truly educative for both faculty and students. The survey might be made in this way: if the point scale system is used, it is fairly simple to determine the percentage of the entire student body carrying the maximum number of points permitted, and the distribution of students from this maximum number down to none at all. From this can also be ascertained the percentage of active participation and the percentage of inactive participation in activities, as well as the percentage of the student body which is not entering into any activity, even as inactive members. If a point scale is not in use, the same facts can be procured, but it will be necessary to check the complete rosters of all activities.

Many personnel officers have experienced the difficulty of keeping track of the activities and memberships of the great number of student organizations. This problem arises particularly where student activities are really *student* activities and are not imposed or too heavily regulated by the administration or faculty. It is highly desirable, however, that a personnel officer know what is happening in student affairs. One means of accomplishing this is to check the college or university newspaper carefully each day for the announcement of new organizations and all other data regarding extracurricular affairs. It is expedient for the personnel officer concerned to send a form to all organizations once a quarter or semester asking for a complete report of the officers, committees, membership, dues, budget, time and place of meetings, the name of the faculty adviser (if there is one), as well as a copy of the constitution. A copy of the latter insures some check on whether the organization is abiding by its constitution, on whether it has been or should be revised, etc. The personnel officer can keep himself informed of the foci of student leadership better through these reports than in any other way.

Student organizations should have a permanent filing place for their records and reports. It is important that a group have some means of transmitting its heritage to the group that follows, particularly since the turnover in student activities is so great. There is no need for the same mistakes to be made year after year, and this can be prevented by having complete reports and recommendations filed under the supervision of a personnel officer. A brief résumé of the activities of the year, semester, or quarter can be made with suggestions incorporated for the students who follow.

In spite of methods of limitation and stimulation of participation in student activities on many campuses, studies show that a large group of students do not participate in any form of student organization.

Of one hundred students (at the University of Chicago), thirteen are neither interested nor participants in student activity; thirty-eight are interested but do not engage in activities because of lack of opportunity; forty-three engage in activities but not sufficiently to affect time given to regular work; while five have assumed a heavy activity program.[1]

At the University of Minnesota, one-third of the students reported that they did not participate in any activity on the campus and, according to Chapin, "this suggests a need of providing guidance on extracurricular activities to students, especially since about forty per cent report engaging in two or more activities."[2] Chapin also found that upper-

[1] SCOTT, WILLIAM E., "The Individual and Student Activities," in W. S. Gray (Ed.) *Provision for the Individual*, pp. 235–237, University of Chicago Press, Chicago, 1932.

[2] CHAPIN, F. STUART, *Extra-curricular Activities at the University of Minnesota*, pp. 102–118, University of Minnesota Press, Minneapolis, 1929.

classmen are more active than underclassmen, and women in general are more active than men; that more than one-third of the students attend church or do religious work off the campus; that there is a steady increase in the number of men who participate in religious organizations from the freshmen to the senior year; and that the period of greatest concentration of activities is the senior year.

If the extracurricular activities are excellent training for future responsibilities, these facts raise certain questions. Could not a sufficiently well-organized personnel program provide guidance on student activities for the many students who seem to miss the opportunity of participation? Such guidance would have to come from counselors well aware of all the possibilities that inhere in student activities, and there would probably need to be a constant program of education for counselors as well as for the students. Yet, much could be done in this direction.

Is the fact that women participate to a greater degree than men due perhaps to the more carefully organized personnel programs for women on most coeducational campuses? It would seem that better housing facilities and supervision for women may have something to do with this. However, a more carefully directed personnel program for men might improve the situation greatly.

Do seniors and upperclassmen gain facility in group participation through the years on the campus, or is it that the greatest concentration in activities comes during these years due to established precedents that only the older and more experienced students should hold the most important positions? Election to many of these positions is a form of recognition and rightly so. Throughout the years of college life, a natural selection also operates, leaving the most capable students as upperclassmen.

Some of the individuals who argue against extracurricular activities plead that scholastic standing suffers at the hands of the activities. Chapin[1] reports that none of the data of

[1] *Ibid.*, pp. 115–118.

his survey shows finally that students do or do not sacrifice academic attainment to prominence in activities. Chapin also found that the active undergraduates show a more substantial carry-over into adult activity, particularly alumni-community activity, than the less active students.

No attempt will be made here to discuss in detail most of the extracurricular activities, their individual purposes and problems. Student government, student publications, and sororities and fraternities are so significant in the college experience of many students, however, that they cannot be passed over without some further discussion.

A campus community is made up of administration, faculty, and students. None of these can function properly in college or university life without the others. Satisfactory government of campus life cannot be carried on by administration or faculty or students alone. Certainly, the term "student government" is misleading. Administration and faculty cannot legally delegate to students the right to govern themselves independent of faculty and administration. But there must be student participation in government to insure the richest community living among the students, faculty, and administration. The ideal of campus government should be a shared campus living, with all contributing to the administration's, faculty's, and students' interests and advantages. Students will learn the art of government only through actual responsibility and practice in it. Democratic ideals demand participation by the students, and both students and faculty will learn much through mutual counsel and cooperation.

The organization by means of which students participate in campus government is usually called the "students' organization." In the majority of institutions, all members of the student body automatically become members of this organization upon admission to the college or university. All theoretically have an opportunity to participate in its program, but, unfortunately, in the larger number of institutions, the bulk of the members are inactive. One of the reasons for this is that many students' organizations have deteriorated into purely disciplinary boards whose one function seems to be to punish cheating. Amos found that "the mass of students insist that student government is a kind of Paul-Pry organization that enjoys meddling; and as a consequence they do not wish to be connected with it."[1] The responsibility for the students' organization and its share in disciplinary action is discussed in Chap. VIII on Discipline. It is maintained, however, that the organization can and should have many purposes and objectives other than discipline.

One of the first and most important of these objectives is the general welfare of all students. Another is purposeful and worth-while activity which permits a large number of students to learn the nature of responsibility and how to cooperate with their elders and with each other. The students' organization also serves as a mouth-piece for the student body as well as for the administration and faculty. It should not serve in this capacity to the detriment of one group or the other but should act in the interests of all. It should provide many demonstrations of how majorities may avoid abridging the rights of minority groups.

Officers democratically elected by the student body and a council composed of these officers and delegates elected by the classes of the college or university head the organization and should be representative of the best minds and finest character among the students on the campus. It should be an honor and a privilege to serve the institution in this way. The council may act as the executive branch of the organization, while the legislative body may be composed of elected students, representatives of the alumni and of the faculty. Most students' organizations also have a judiciary body composed of junior, senior, and faculty representatives. This judiciary body,

[1] AMOS, THYRSA, "Student Government," *National Education Association Addresses and Proceedings*, 63: 444, 1925.

in our opinion, can serve more valuably as a consultative council for the head counselor of the personnel staff than it can as a student court (see Chap. VIII). It is essential that the organization have a simple yet efficient constitution carefully outlining the duties of the branches of the organization and accurately declaring the sources of its power.

In many instances, student participation in government is a farce and a sham. It is frequently used merely to voice the decrees and wishes of the administration. This is because neither the administration nor the faculty nor the students have definite concepts of the ideals or philosophy of student participation in government. The philosophy should be based upon cooperation, mutual interests, and the welfare of the entire campus community. It should hold the definite concept of all working together for mutually advantageous objectives and interests. The students should not have the idea that they can run the whole show; nor should the administration and faculty have that idea. Unless both factions can work together for desirable and socially productive ends, there should be no pretense of student participation in government.

In a number of coeducational institutions, the women and men have separate and distinct student organizations. In other cases, the women's organization is the only organization of its kind functioning, with the men of the campus taking no part in campus government. Women students have for many years had better personnel supervision than men and in many cases are more ready to profit by participation in government. Perhaps their housing experiences help to place women students ahead of men in the art of cooperative government of campus living. It is an established precedent on any number of coeducational campuses that men must be elected to all the important positions, so that if a college attempted one organization which included both men and women there would probably still be a tendency for the chief offices to be monopolized by men. Then, too, the mores and traditions for men and women tend to be different and should probably not be artificially coerced into similarity in one such organization.

The director of personnel on the campus or a member of his staff should be vitally interested in the students' organization or organizations, for many reasons, but particularly from the standpoint of the development of all student members of the institution. Campus-wide activities under the direction of the students' organization offer many opportunities for a large number of students to serve the institution or community and to develop in so doing. The program of work may include committees on community chest, traditions, honors and awards, publications, publicity, occupational and vocational studies, social affairs, student activity point scale, interorganization activity and relations, and other matters pertaining to the welfare and interests of the college and community. The personnel officer who knows the student body and the needs of individuals can work closely with the officers of the organization in order to include as many students as possible in the program. This personnel officer should be one who respects and enjoys student projects. Frequent conferences with the organization's officers and a genuine interest in their problems can do much to further the program.

Any student organization program entails the expenditure of money, and no program can be successful unless it has an adequate budget. One of the simplest and most efficient means of securing the required funds, and at the same time providing that each student feel a sense of responsibility in the organization is for every student to pay a fee which may cover, not only membership in this organization, but also subscriptions to the campus publications and admission to athletic events.

Wells and McCalister have summarized well the different ways student publications serve the college or university:

School publications serve the students by training those interested in journalism, by encouraging the use of good English, by developing a desire for creative literature, by furnishing information about the school, by giving authentic school news and by making growth possible through purposeful activity. . . . They serve the school by unifying it, by encouraging desirable enterprises or activities, by influencing public opinion, by keeping other schools in touch with the progress obtained, and by recording the school history.[1]

These are desirable criteria to use in evaluating the college or university newspaper, the annual, the literary or humorous magazine, and any departmental magazines. These are the purposes the publications should serve.

In some instances where students have been in entire control of publications, they have used them for personal ends. This does not always result in benefits to the whole campus community. Most institutions have found some control of publications necessary and the control is usually centered in a student-faculty committee with power to set policies and to supervise finances. The latter task is made easier where a student fee covers the cost of subscriptions to student publications. It is desirable to have faculty advisers who are trained in journalism or magazine techniques for the different publications. These individuals are helpful in maintaining high standards of make-up, high quality of material, efficient distribution of work to be done, and conformity to established policy.

Edwards, Artman, and Fisher found that from 50 to 300 students were employed voluntarily in getting out the student publications in each college they studied.[2] Many institutions have evolved apprenticeship systems for publication staff members. Students undergo a tryout period before a definite appointment is made. Usually, the posi-

---

[1] WELLS, GEORGE C., and W. H. McCALISTER, *Student Publications*, p. 1, A. S. Barnes & Company, New York, 1930.

[2] EDWARDS, R. H., J. M. ARTMAN, and GALEN M. FISHER, *Undergraduates*, p. 91, Doubleday, Doran & Company, Inc., Garden City, N. Y., 1928.

tions of responsibility go to those who merit them through a year or more of service as assistants or in minor capacities. The selections may be made by the student-faculty publications committee. In some colleges, editors, business managers, etc., are still elected by the student body with too little regard for their qualifications. Since work on publications involves a high degree of craftsmanship, only students who demonstrate their ability and interest should fill the various positions. A plan for this end gives the positions prestige and makes them worth working for.

Fraternities and sororities undoubtedly originated out of the psychological and sociological desires of the adolescent for a small, intimate group of contemporaries who were as much like himself as possible. Ever since their inception the pros and cons of these organizations have been frequently reviewed by concerned administration and faculty. The arguments in favor of sororities and fraternities may be summarized as follows:

1. They provide the student with the experience of cooperation within a tightly knit group, with the institution, and with the alumni.
2. They encourage self-discipline in some respects to a high extent.
3. They give experience in group discussion.
4. They offer social training through activities.
5. They encourage service to the group and the institution.
6. They give training in student management.
7. They are an excellent medium for the establishment of intimate and lasting friendships.
8. They encourage mutual appreciation of others' interests and accomplishments.
9. They offer frequent opportunities for creative activity.
10. They constitute ideal counseling units through which personnel officers and various student and faculty groups on the campus may work.
11. They provide ideal housing units, as to size, with excellent possibilities for education in social attitudes and behavior, and the improvement of health attitudes and habits.

12. They encourage scholarship through:
    a. Group loyalty
    b. Interfraternity competition
    c. Maintaining study hall and tutors within the group.
13. They tend to perpetuate college spirit and campus mores.
14. They serve as a medium for administrative reforms, experiments, and enterprises.
15. They encourage individual participation in campus activities through group incentive.
16. They act as a stabilizing force in guiding freshmen and transfers (a device for orientation).
17. They aid in rule enforcement and discipline.
18. They provide loans and scholarships for their own members, and sometimes for nonmembers.
19. They maintain altruistic programs and encourage the participation of their members in these programs.

The objections to fraternities and sororities are based on the following grounds:

1. They tend to exclusiveness and even snobbishness.
2. Their members tend to place fraternity interests before college interests.
3. They tend to the cultivation of taste in dress and standards of living which may not be satisfied later.
4. The members may in effect receive training in habits not conducive to good health.
5. Members are often forced to sacrifice desirable independence.
6. Fraternities and sororities discriminate unjustly in rushing and pledging.
7. Every group has periods of poor leadership; at such times instability of scholarship and morals frequently occurs.
8. They tend to become arbiters of social life on a discriminating and artificial basis.
9. They tend to increase the cost of college life.
10. They usually create a real problem for those students who are not invited to join any groups or who are not invited to join the group of their choice.

In those institutions where fraternities and sororities do exist, the job of the personnel officer is to maximize the possible assets and minimize the possible liabilities of these groups in the corporate life of the campus. A well-organized interfraternity council and Panhellenic control of the appointment and the dismissal of the heads of houses,[1] an effective plan for the supervision of finances and management, a cooperative association of the individual house councils through the students' organization, reasonable, well-observed rushing rules, cooperation with the national officers and alumni in the maintenance of standards, and occasional "all-college" projects are all ways whereby the personnel officer successfully gears fraternities and sororities into the constructive forces on the campus.

Frequent drives to raise money for different purposes constitute a real problem on many campuses. The basketball team may need new uniforms, the "annual" may have a deficit, etc. But at the same time pocketbooks suffer and many persons are annoyed. Often the same group of students is exploited, being utilized over and over to solicit funds. Some institutions have attempted to solve the problem by laying down a hard and fast rule that students may not solicit money for any undertaking. Yet there are values in the experience of raising money for a worthy purpose. A clearinghouse for these projects should exist on the campus. This may be a student-faculty committee of the students' organization which should investigate the object, the methods, and all details of the project before granting permission to solicit funds. A student fee collected at the beginning of each session covering students' organization dues, subscriptions to

[1] On some campuses the chief personnel officer has a good deal to say about the hiring of the heads of houses for sororities and fraternities, but the group of students and alumni are left entirely free to dismiss the appointee at will, even without conference with the personnel director. This is a poor policy. Incumbents of such positions should be both hired and fired after a consultative process involving personnel officials, alumni, and student representatives.

publications, and admission to athletic events alleviates to a great degree the necessity for students to raise money.

Frequent mention has been made in this chapter of the part a director of personnel or a member of his staff may play in the student activity program. This individual can assist in many ways the success of the program. His or her function is to advise, counsel, and steer. He should not coerce the students or impose his ideas upon them. He should not be domineering or take his duties too seriously. He should be on good terms with the leaders of the campus but should have no favorites. Nor is it wise for him to "be one of the boys." In some institutions there is too much paternalism in regard to extracurricular activities, and in others there is not enough supervision to insure that values are received by each student. The successful personnel officer finds a course between these two extremes.

He is aware of the possibilities for growth and development in the different organizations and is interested in the guidance of individual students toward the opportunities best meeting their needs. He has the opportunity of educating all the counselors to this point of view, as well as of giving them the necessary information regarding the many activities. Counselors too often do not have the interest or the time to acquire such information for themselves.

Faculty advisers are important to departmental clubs but in some other organizations are not needed, since a member of the central personnel staff may serve as general adviser.

The member of the central personnel staff who acts as group adviser should be available to help solve the problems of newly elected officers, the problems of framing and drawing up constitutions, of working out budgets, of learning parliamentary procedure. His library should contain material on these points which should be accessible to students but not forced upon them. He may give each committee chairman hints on how to handle his duties, helping him to select persons for responsibilities from a wide range of students rather than from among his own limited circle of friends. He should understand the problem of committee efficiency: that size is important and should vary for different kinds of committees. South has found that groups of three perform better than groups of six on certain projects; that on concrete problems, large committees do as well as small groups.[1] The group adviser should be familiar with the processes of group thinking and of group leadership[2] and should give students who are responsible for large group discussions, training in techniques which will enable every individual to participate actively up to the limit of his capacity and will enable the group as a whole to decide and plan as a group.

Extracurricular activities offer the opportunity for students to develop good qualities of leadership and followership. They offer the opportunity to serve the institution; to experience and to help create good fellowship and social goodwill; they further self-realization, and all-round growth. They assist students in adjusting to their student world and in learning the qualities of good citizenship. That they have a constructive effect upon students is shown by Angell who reports that at the University of Michigan there is positive correlation between social adjustments and the number of extracurricular activities in which a student engages.[3]

BIBLIOGRAPHY

Student Organizations

Amos, Thyrsa: "Student Government," *National Education Association Addresses and Proceedings*, 63: 440–449, 1925.
Angell, Robert C.: *Study in Undergraduate Adjustment*, University of Chicago Press, Chicago, 1930, ix + 164 pp.

[1] South, E. B., "Some Psychological Aspects of Committee Work," *Journal of Applied Psychology*, 11: 348–368, 1927.

[2] Books which explain these techniques and are of invaluable help are: Harrison S. Elliot, *The Process of Group Thinking*, Association Press, New York, 1928, x + 229 pp. Henry M. Busch, *Leadership in Group Work*, pp. vi + 305, Association Press, New York, 1934.

[3] Angell, R. C., *A Study in Undergraduate Adjustment*, p. 122, University of Chicago Press, Chicago, 1930.

ATKINSON, H. M., and C. W. FLEMMING: *Education for Constructive Social Influence through Student Organizations*, Teachers College, Bureau of Publications, Columbia University, New York, 1933, 31 pp.
BOGARDUS, EMORY S.: *Leaders and Leadership*, D. Appleton-Century Company, Inc., New York, 1934, viii + 319 pp.
BOUCHER, CHAUNCEY S.: *The Chicago College Plan*, University of Chicago Press, Chicago, 1935, xi + 344.
BREWER, JOHN M.: *Education as Guidance*. The Macmillan Company, New York, 1932, ix + 668 pp.
BREWSTER, ETHEL: "Social Life as An Academic Problem," *National Association of Deans of Women, Yearbook*, 1924, pp. 67–72.
BUSCH, HENRY M.: *Leadership in Group Work*, Association Press, New York, 1934, vi + 305 pp.
CHAPIN, F. STUART: *Extra-curricular Activities at the University of Minnesota*, University of Minnesota Press, Minneapolis, 1929, iv + 126 pp.
COWLEY, W. H., and W. WALLER: "A Study of Student Life," *Journal of Higher Education*, 6 (3): 132–142, March, 1935.
EDWARDS, R. H., J. M. ARTMAN, and G. M. FISHER: *Undergraduates*, Doubleday, Doran & Company, Inc., Garden City, N. Y., 1928, 376 pp.
ELLIOT, HARRISON S.: *The Process of Group Thinking*, Association Press, New York, 1928, x + 229 pp.
HAND, HAROLD C.: *Campus Activities*, McGraw-Hill Book Company, Inc., New York, 1938, xvi + 357 pp.
HUDELSON, EARL (Ed.): *Problems of College Education*, University of Minnesota Press, Minneapolis, 1928, xvi + 449 pp.
JOHNSTON, EDGAR G.: *Point Systems and Awards*, A. S. Barnes & Company, New York, 1930, xiv + 160 pp.
KEFAUVER, G. N., and C. BULLARD: "Student Activities in Junior Colleges," *Teachers College Record*, 32: 445–456, February, 1931.
MCKOWN, HARRY C.: *School Clubs*, The Macmillan Company, New York, 1929, xviii + 498 pp.
———: *Assembly and Auditorium Activities*, The Macmillan Company, New York, 1930, 462 pp.
MEYER, HAROLD D., and SAMUEL EDDLEMAN: *Financing Extra-curricular Activities*, A. S. Barnes & Company, New York, 1929, xii + 129 pp.
MOORE, L. H.: "Leadership Traits of College Women," *Sociology and Social Research*, 17 (1): 44–54, September–October, 1932.
National Education Association Department of Superintendence, Sixth Yearbook, N. E. A., Washington, D. C., 1928, pp. 230–242.
PIGORS, PAUL: *Leadership or Domination*, Houghton Mifflin Company, Boston, 1935, xiii + 354 pp.
PRICE, LOUISE: "Social Adjustments in the Junior College," *Junior College Journal*, 3: 456–461, May, 1933.
REYNOLDS, O. EDGAR: *The Social and Economic Status of College Students*, Teachers College, Bureau of Publications, Columbia University, New York, 1927, v + 57 pp.
RYAN, W. CARSON JR.: "The Literature of American School and College Athletics," *Carnegie Foundation for the Advancement of Teaching, Bulletin* 24, 1929, xiv + 305 pp.

SAVAGE, HOWARD J., HAROLD W. BENTLEY, JOHN T. MCGOVERN, and F. M. D. SMILEY: "American College Athletics," *Carnegie Foundation for the Advancement of Teaching, Bulletin* 23, 1929, xxii + 383 pp.

SCOTT, WILLIAM E.: "The Individual and Student Activities," in W. S. Gray (Ed.) *Provision for the Individual*, pp. 234–245, University of Chicago Press, Chicago, 1932.

SHEFFIELD, ALFRED D.: *Training for Group Experience*, Association Press, New York, 1929, 56 pp.

———: *Creative Discussion*, Association Press, New York, 1931, 63 pp.

SOUTH, E. B.: "Some Psychological Aspects of Committee Work," *Journal of Applied Psychology*, 11: 348–368, September, 1927.

"Survey of Land-grant Colleges and Universities," *U. S. Office of Education, Bulletin* 9 (1): 403–568, 1930.

TEAD, ORDWAY: *The Art of Leadership*, Whittlesey House, McGraw-Hill Book Company, Inc., New York, 1935, xi + 308 pp.

VAN WAGENEN, BEULAH CLARK: *Extra-curricular Activities in the Colleges of United Lutheran Church of America*, Teachers College, Bureau of Publications, Columbia University, New York, 1929, 153 pp.

VINEYARD, JERRY J., and C. F. POOLE: *Student Participation in School Government*, A. S. Barnes & Company, New York, 1930, xiv + 104 pp.

WARREN, CONSTANCE: "Activities at Sarah Lawrence College," *Association of American Colleges Bulletin* 18: 205–208, May, 1932.

WELLS, GEORGE C., and W. H. MCCALISTER: *Student Publications*, A. S. Barnes & Company, New York, 1930, x + 180 pp.

Y. W. C. A. National Board, *The New Leadership, a Handbook for Adults Working with Girls*, Woman's Press, New York, 1930, 109 pp.

YOUNGER, JOHN: "Student Self Government," *Journal of Higher Education*, 2: 204–206, April, 1931.

Sororities and Fraternities

ANGELL, R. C.: *The Campus*, D. Appleton-Century Company, Inc., New York, 1928, 139 pp.

———: *Study in Undergraduate Adjustment*, pp. 112–118, University of Chicago Press, Chicago, 1930.

BAIRD, W. R.: *Manual of American College Fraternities*, George Banta Publishing Company, Menasha, Wis., 1935, xxii + 803 pp.

BALLOU, FRANK W.: "High School Fraternities and Sororities," *School Life*, 7: 47–48, October, 1921.

Banta's Greek Exchange (a Panhellenic journal published monthly in the interest of the college fraternity world), George Banta Publishing Company, Menasha, Wis.

BROOKS, RUTH C.: "College and Sorority," *School and Society*, 14: 199–205, September, 1921.

CONSTANCE, C. L.: "Greeks of the Campus," *School and Society*, 30: 409–414, September, 1929.

CRAWFORD, N. A.: "Nobility of the Campus," *American Mercury*, 21: 184–192, October, 1930.

DEALEY, H. L.: "Problem of College Sororities," *School and Society*, 4: 735–740, November, 1916.

EDWARDS, R. H., J. M. ARTMAN, and G. M. FISHER: *Undergraduates*, pp. 49–90, Doubleday, Doran & Company, Inc., New York, 1928.

EURICH, A. C.: "Relationship of Achievement between College Fraternity and Non-fraternity Groups," *School and Society*, 26: 624–630, Nov. 12, 1937.

FRETWELL, E. K.: "Extra-curricular Activities in Secondary Schools," Houghton Mifflin Company, Boston, 1931, xix + 552 pp.

GRANT, DANIEL L.: "Social Fraternity," *School and Society*, 33: 229–233, Feb. 14, 1931.

———: "Leadership in the Fraternity," *Journal of Higher Education*, 3: 257–261, May, 1932.

KEMP, MRS. FRANK A.: "The Chaperon," in *National Association of Deans of Women, Fifteenth Yearbook*, 1928, pp. 179–188.

LEONARD, LOUISE: "Sororities," in *National Association of Deans of Women, Twelfth Yearbook*, Cincinnati, Ohio, 1925, pp. 130–133.

LEONARD, MARIA, and M. F. PALMER: *Building and Balancing Budgets for Men's and Women's Fraternities*, L. G. Balfour Co., Attleboro, Mass., 1934, 82 pp.

"Living Costs of Fraternities and Sororities at Oregon State College," *School and Society*, 32: 220–225, Aug. 16, 1930.

National Association of Deans of Women Yearbook, 12: 130, 1925; 15: 173–203, 1928; 17: 188–189, 1930; 18: 49–50, 1931.

"Penn. State College Tries House Counselors," *The New York Times*, 4 (2): 3, May 2, 1937.

PRUNTY, MERLE: "National High School Honor Society versus High School Fraternities," *Junior-senior High School Clearing House*, 4: 263, January, 1930.

RANDALL, OTIS E.: *The Dean's Window, a Portrayal of College Life*, Stratford Co., Boston, 1934, viii + 320 pp.

ROBNETT, FLORENCE: "Campus Activities for Women's Fraternity Chapters," *Arrow of Pi Beta Phi*, February, 1932, pp. 441–442.

ROBSON, BARBARA REID: *House Management Problems of Fraternities and Sororities*, Teachers College, Bureau of Publications, Columbia University, New York, 1933, 93 pp.

SPEER, J. B.: "College Fraternities and Their Money Matters," *School and Society*, 36: 517–524, Oct. 22, 1932.

STONE, H. E.: "Fraternities, Are They Good or Bad?" *Educational Review*, 74: 146–147, March, 1927.

VAN WAGENAN, B. C.: *Extra-curricular Activities in Lutheran Colleges*, Teachers College, Bureau of Publications, Columbia University, New York, 1928, 114 pp.

WAUGH, F. A.: "College Fraternity," *Review of Reviews*, 74: 641–646, December, 1926.

WELLS, AGNES E.: "Sorority Standards," in *National Association of Deans of Women, Fifteenth Yearbook*, Washington, D. C., 1928, pp. 173–188.

WERNER, O. H.: *Every College Students' Problems*, pp. 11–13, 68–69, Silver, Burdett & Company, New York, 1929.

Chapter XII
EDUCATING STUDENTS THROUGH HOUSING ENVIRONMENT

Housing

Most educators hope that maximum physical, emotional, moral, and social development—as well as mental—will take place in young people while they are students in colleges and universities. Such educators are increasingly recognizing the opportunities that a good housing program affords for realizing their hope. Through the housing program the college or university has a method for controlling experiences and influences that affect all phases of students' development and that can be so well controlled by no other method.

Some institutions of higher education are not yet consciously attempting to utilize their housing units for educational purposes. It is probable that there is no institution that consciously attempts to so use housing units that could not do a better job in this respect. There is still too much of mere "landlord-and-tenant" relationship between colleges and dormitory students and a feeling that obligation ends when a safe shelter and three meals a day are provided.

The authors of this book take the point of view that housing units are subpersonnel divisions of the larger campus personnel program. Dormitories for both men and women, private homes in the community which house students, and cooperative houses are all units in this program. Group living can have much the same values that family life offers and an institution that neglects its opportunities in this direction does not offer a complete educational program.

The dormitory movement for women students grew out of the desire to protect the women on the campus. The protection motive became well established before other values of dormitory living were also recognized. Protection is still a part of the picture, but now it assumes a less conspicuous role. This early idea of protection may explain in part, however, why college-controlled dormitories for men have only fairly recently become a concern on many campuses. For the most part at the present time men are still "chucked together" in a dormitory and are permitted to evolve any kind of a corporate living they can. There are still far fewer college-operated dormitories for men than for women. When dormitories were thought of primarily as a means of physical protection, men were left to fend for themselves. They tended to find bed and board any place in the community that they could, usually at a price as low as possible. Colleges are slowly recognizing that the social and educational values that are being discovered in housing programs apply as surely to men as to women. It is interesting to note that a good many of the suggestions offered in this chapter are being increasingly applied in men's dormitories as well as in women's. It is coming to be believed that standards of health and living—for men as well as for women—can be maintained more easily and naturally and at far less cost in dormitories, controlled by competent people, than by any other means.

The administration of dormitories plays a dominant role in the success of the housing program. Every house should have a head, and this head should be trained in personnel work. If all the values of dormitory life are to be realized the leadership certainly cannot be entrusted to a person who does not know what these values are. The head of the dormitory may be a social director, a head of residence, the dean of women or of men, or the director of personnel, or a member of his or her staff. If the campus is sufficiently large and there are a number of dormitories, there may be a separate member of the staff of the personnel director who has jurisdiction over the personnel programs in dormitories, as well as in private homes where students live, cooperative houses, and sorority and fraternity houses.

This assistant dean in charge of housing or this assistant director of personnel may have a staff composed of those individuals who are in charge of the respective housing units, that is, the various Heads of Residence.

Whatever system of organization is used, there must be a direct tie-up with the personnel program of the entire campus. The individual responsible for the college or university personnel program, whether it be a vice-president or a director of personnel, should have the final responsibility for hiring and firing heads of residences. Each head of residence should be chosen with a great deal of care and should be a person who has the personnel point of view, who is adept at dealing with students, who has intellectual interests, is a gracious, attractive person, and who is in sympathy with the objectives of the college or university. Many institutions make the mistake of hiring as heads of residence women who "just love girls or boys," who have had no training in personnel techniques, and in many instances are not even college graduates. These women may have not the slightest inkling of personnel possibilities and are primarily interested in being "glorified hostesses."

Should the head of residence be responsible for the hiring and supervision of the house staff, the maids, cooks, etc., for the planning of meals, the purchasing and care of equipment, etc., and for the finances of the dormitory? It would be a rare individual who could efficiently and capably carry out a personnel program in a dormitory and manage all of the above as well. It seems a better plan to hire someone else for these duties, someone in many instances called a house manager.

The house manager should be responsible to the business manager of the institution, for it is in the business office that the responsibility for finances usually is centered. At this point, it is wise to admit that the business point of view (maintained by the house manager and the business office) and the personnel point of view (maintained by the head of residence and the director of personnel on the campus) do not always coincide. It is necessary that the director of personnel and the business manager educate each other to the desirability of certain policies. Just as the business office cannot operate efficiently unless the officers of the university follow a good business practice as outlined by the business office, similarly the director of personnel and the head of residence cannot accomplish their purposes unless the business officials understand and are in sympathy with personnel objectives. There must be close cooperation and planning between the chief personnel and business officers on the campus. It is their problem to work out and solve difficulties which may arise between their subordinates in the respective dormitories.

It is well to state at this point that no dormitory in an educational institution should be maintained for the purpose of making money. Each dormitory should, however, be entirely self-supporting, maintaining all upkeep costs, and retiring original building costs.

The administration of the dormitory cannot be successful unless the students play a part in the administration. Student participation in house government is both desirable and essential. It is the students living in the house that make "the house," and it is only to the degree that they feel that the different house programs are *their* programs and to the degree that the head of residence realizes the students' interests that these programs accomplish their real educational and social purposes.

There should be an organization of students in each house which works in close harmony with its head of residence. This is usually a student council or executive board composed of house officers and representatives of the classes residing in the dormitory. The head of residence must work very intimately with this group, and he or she must respect the personalities of the students and place trust and confidence in them. These students can be educated to the personnel point of view and can form a small personnel staff directed and supervised by the head of residence. Discussions of all problems involving group welfare in frequent house meetings, which are well planned and do not waste the members' time, do much to instill a sense of responsibility for the house good in each resident.

Group living demands certain standards and at least a minimum of rules and regulations. These should not be imposed by college authorities, but should be the outgrowth of discussions, with students really understanding their purposes and the philosophy out of which they have come to be. Rules and regulations should be frequently reviewed and revised by the student executive board and the head of residence, and then presented to the entire house for discussion and action.

If the campus has more than one dormitory, rules, practices, and regulations developed in the various dormitories should come to a central housing executive council composed of student representatives of each unit, the heads of residences, and the director of personnel, for discussion and final review.

Traditions of the house are well worth establishing, for students respond to these, and unwritten laws are usually better foundations than written laws for high standards of conduct and social behavior. Such traditions, however, must have whole-hearted acceptance by the students. "Old" students and the head of residence should unite to see that new residents get adequate education in house traditions as well as in the various house rules and regulations that have served former students well. Placing the responsibility for this education upon old student residents gives the latter a sense of belonging and of responsibility that is beneficial. A practical procedure for this is for two old residents to entertain not more than ten new residents in one of the old residents' rooms early in the year. Many questions can be answered and a congenial understanding of rules, regulations, and traditions can result. In some setups old residents begin the contact with new students in the summer through letter writing.

The head of the student executive board of the dormitory can often handle minor cases of house discipline with the approval and supervision of the head of residence. Major and serious infractions of group standards should be reported to the educational officer in charge of discipline to insure an outcome most beneficial to the transgressor and the group.

Authorities do not agree on the distribution of classes within dormitories. It is the policy on some campuses to house in upperclass dormitories the sophomores, juniors, and seniors, while the freshmen are housed in a freshman dormitory. Other institutions favor placing a proportion of all four classes in each dormitory. If there is only one dormitory, still another plan is to house in that dormitory all freshmen, permitting the other classes to live in private homes, and in sorority and fraternity houses.

There are advantages and disadvantages to each of these methods of distribution. Where the freshmen are housed without the upper classes, they establish a solidarity of group that is beneficial, and they tend not to be so overcome by the sophistication of the upper classes. Living regulations, also, can be worked out by and for freshmen alone. The personnel head of a freshman unit has an excellent opportunity to carry on an orientation program. Yet, upperclassmen feel that freshmen who live separately from the other classes "get too cocky"—and there may be a tendency in this direction. Another disadvantage is that upperclassmen feel less responsibility for the new students when they live apart. Guidance supplied within a group of students, through group mores, guidance given by one student to another, is a spontaneous and a natural orientation that has benefits worth considering. Freshmen living apart from the other classes do not get to know the upperclassmen as well as they would living in housing units with them. To secure the advantages of freshman segregation without its attendant disadvantages, some institutions select a few upperclassmen to live in the freshman dormitory, but this plan more or less isolates these upperclass students and prevents them from participating in the leadership of their own classes.

Although there is no agreement on the distribution of classes within the dormitories, it is generally agreed that the total number of students residing in one unit should be from 100 to 200. A group as small as 50 has definite social and educational advantages but is prohibitively expensive for most institutions. A larger number than 100 to 200 loses much in the way of house spirit and solidarity, nor is it possible to work out an effective personnel and social program for too large a group. The nearer to 100 the group is, the more effective the program can be. Advocates of larger groups have in mind resultant financial advantages: the fact that one large building costs less to build than three one-third as large; and the fact that substantial management economies result where operating units are large.

Since an important part of education may be the socializing effect of living with other people, the assignment of rooms for new residents is important. Room assigning may be done in a haphazard or mechanical manner, or it may be done with care because it is seen to possess personnel values. In some instances, the assigning is done by a group composed of the heads of residences, the director of admissions, and a representative from the campus personnel office. In a few instances, dormitory student presidents join in the task of room assignment. The room-assignment committee should have as much information as possible about the new resident's background, experiences, and interests. This committee may also have some idea of the needs of the individual, and these may be the bases of the room assignment. Placing students as roommates or suitemates who will develop each other and contribute to each other's education can frequently be done by a wise committee.

It is a custom for old residents to choose their rooms in the spring for the coming academic year. One practice which adds to the prestige of the dormitory president and vice-president is that of permitting them to have first choice of rooms. Usually the remainder of the old residents choose rooms in order of seniority, seniors, juniors, and sophomores. This is done by number drawing, and experience has taught us that it is wise to keep a careful record of the name of the student and the number drawn.

The head of residence will need certain records. The system evolved should be based on principles of simplicity and consideration of the purposes to which they are to be put. Card files of names, home addresses, parents' names and occupations, telephone numbers, students' secondary schools, interests and skills, as well as date of birth, are useful. A card file of class schedules is necessary, for the head of residence may need to send to class for a student, should some sort of crisis occur. A folder should be set up for each resident containing his application for the dormitory and any confidential information the head of residence may wish to add (pertaining to important incidents, behavior, interviews or conferences, etc.). Late and special permissions should be filed in students' folders throughout each academic year. The system of records maintained in the dormitory should not duplicate any more than is necessary the records kept in the central personnel office of the institution. The director of personnel will wish to work out with the heads of residences the type of information he will want added to the records in the central office.

A graduate student is often employed in dormitories to act as "night chaperon" and her or his duties are to close the house, admit those with late or special permissions, and to take night telephone calls. This individual should be hired by the head of residence after consultation with the house manager, and should be educated to the point of view that she or he is a member of the personnel staff, not merely a machine to carry on routine duties. It is well to have this staff member attend student house executive committee meetings, either with or without power of vote; also, as a house member, this person should attend all house meetings.

The social and recreational program of the dormitory is of outstanding importance, for it is through it that development of social standards can be achieved. The social program should supplement and in no way compete with the scholastic efforts of the residents. The program of social affairs for each house should be carefully planned in connection with the social program of the campus. Formal as well as informal affairs are desirable. Many students need to learn to feel comfortable and at ease in evening clothes, and wearing them frequently helps achieve this end. One of the early events of the year may be a formal dinner for the house alone, so that a certain familiarity with procedures and formal clothes may be acquired before guests are entertained. Whether the affair be formal or informal, careful planning will do much to make it a success. The house chairman of the occasion and the head of residence should pick their committees not only for the greatest immediate efficiency but also on the basis of the experience needed by members of the house. One individual may need practice in introducing guests, another who is shy needs to feel the responsibility of being a host or hostess. Whatever the need, the head of residence must approach the assignment in a way that will stimulate interest and a desire on the part of each individual to perform his duty not only to his own credit but also to the credit of the house. A head of residence who knows his or her students can, through the social program, develop their social ease and poise. Having each resident feel some responsibility for the event, even though a very small duty, gives the affair an atmosphere which it otherwise cannot have. The student chairman must be made to feel responsible—with advice, suggestions, and supervision tactfully coming from the head of the residence. These two must work out their plans together and have a mutual understanding of the purpose of the affair.

One way of attempting to integrate the student's social and intellectual life is to bring groups of faculty members and interesting persons from outside the campus circle into the dormitories. As Cheek points out:[1]

... the contacts in these gatherings differ from those in department clubs because they assemble groups having diverse rather than similar interests. Is it too much to hope that these contacts and the play of the mind on mind should not only be stimulating but eventually prove to be a real aid in fostering that general education which is the goal of most institutions?

In some institutions such as at Bennington, Harvard, and Yale, the entire housing system is based upon the principle of a close contact between faculty and students. The Bennington plan involves 12 houses accommodating 20 students each and a faculty apartment attached to each set of four houses. Both faculty and students have separate entrances. The faculty are members of the house but are in no sense custodians or disciplinarians. The few regulations are enforced by student organizations and, when necessary, by members of the college administrative staff. The Harvard and Yale house plans, modeled somewhat on the plan of Oxford University, bring together in one house groups of men approximating in number the size of a small college. These men live together under the supervision of especially selected faculty co-residents for the 4 years of their college life.

Through participation in house sports and house activities of various kinds, each resident can be made to feel a sense of belonging to "his house." Each student has some contribution to make and each has possibilities for development. The head of residence should be aware of the opportunities for leisure-time activity and for informal,

[1] CHEEK, MARY ASHBY, "Reorganized Residence Halls," *Journal of Higher Education*, 7: 375, October, 1936.

spontaneous gatherings. A keen interest in young people will stimulate ideas along these lines.

Financing the social program is often a problem. A plan frequently used is to have residents pay house dues each quarter or semester. A budget can be worked out carefully on the basis of these dues. It is often necessary, in addition, to have a certain sum allotted by the business office from the financial budget for the house. Large amounts of money do not need to be spent on social affairs but certainly enough should be available to "do the affair" nicely. Many times, half the fun for the students is in having only a certain amount of money for an event so that their ingenuity and cleverness may be challenged. Students respond to the problem, particularly if the head of residence is enthusiastic and lavish in his or her praise of good ideas; he or she can often subtly suggest ways and means that are more heartily received than the traditional methods of entertaining. A good rule for any house is that house funds are to be utilized only when the whole house is entertaining. It has sometimes been found best, for instance, for those house dances which are attended only by those members who care to invite partners, to be financed entirely by those who attend.

The dormitory head must be in close touch with the health program and health facilities on the campus. In women's dormitories, it is often the practice to have a registered nurse, who may also be a part-time student, live in the dormitory. She, as a member of the house staff, can help maintain standards of cleanliness, good sleep and study habits, as well as take an interest in the health of each individual student.

Good standards of health, living, and study can be stimulated indirectly through the environment of the house. Adequate bathroom facilities, laundry and pressing rooms conveniently accessible, and clean, sufficiently heated and lighted rooms stimulate proper habits of living. Surveys show that the majority of rooms in dormitories are doubles, although three- and four-occupant rooms can still be found.[1] Fortunately, single beds are the rule. A few dormitories have regular inspection of rooms to encourage neatness and orderly living. Taking visitors on tours of the building is considered by others an effective and subtle method of inspecting rooms. This practice may provide embarrassment at times, but, if it does, it gives the head of residence a talking point.

Most dormitories find it advantageous to have an upstairs lounge room which is cheerfully and comfortably furnished. This may be used for small group parties and for study purposes when roommates wish to sleep. Kitchenettes on each floor may be a means of happy times for the residents. A library, where interesting books and magazines as well as daily papers are available, is certainly desirable.

Men frequently call in a women's dormitory, and the same good standards should prevail as would in the girls' own homes. The dormitory is the girls' home on the campus and the head of residence is the official hostess. Introduction of guests to the head of residence should take place as naturally and informally as in homes when introductions are made to mothers. A dormitory is well equipped which has an informal recreation room accessible to men or women guests where bridge, ping-pong, and other games may be played. A small kitchenette off this recreation room is a desirable feature, for here fudge and other concoctions can be made by the men and women. These facilities can help make the dormitory a really popular, happy place. Students who have a kitchenette and interesting games available do not feel the same need to resort prematurely to a program of "petting" and thus are apt to learn more diversified social skills!

Many dormitories have one large living room which is about as homelike as a railway station waiting room. A

[1] HAYES, HARRIET, *College-operated Residence Halls for Women Students in 125 Colleges and Universities*, p. 11, Teachers College, Bureau of Publications, Columbia University, New York, 1932.

head of residence who has sympathy with the resulting problems for girls and their dates can see to it that the furniture is arranged attractively and in small, comfortable groupings so that dates may have some degree of privacy—at least for their conversation. A cloakroom for guests' wraps should be near the main entrance of the building and living room.

Most dormitories of 100 to 200 students have dining facilities within the building. The smaller the number to be taken care of, the easier it is to utilize the dining room for social purposes and for standards of good taste. Although Bennington College has a central commons building, it contains five dining rooms opening from a central kitchen, 40 students eating in each dining room.[1] The goals of a well-run dining room are "adequacy of diet for the age, palatable food, table service to satisfy the most discriminating, and dining as a social technique in the education for social standards."[2]

It has been found satisfactory in a number of colleges to have breakfast and lunch served in the cafeteria manner in order that students may eat as hurriedly as they like and with whom they choose, but dinner in the evening should be a more formal meal with the students changing their clothes for dinner and taking sufficient time to make this meal leisurely and conversational. Here it is possible to stress manners which are learned far more effectively by imitation than by description. In the hurried life of the present-day college, too few opportunities permit the practice of good manners. It is desirable to have a student host or hostess for each table selected from the old residents, or upperclassmen, or by careful choice of freshmen in a freshman dormitory. Added prestige is given the house president and vice-president if they are given tables of their own throughout the year. Rotating table assignments for

[1] "Housing College Students," in *American Association of University Women Bulletin*, p. 54,
[2] *Ibid.*, p. IX.

all residents for the dinner meal is a means of all in the house knowing each other and broadening their interests. These assignments may be changed a number of times during the year, but a period of not less than 2 weeks for each assignment has been found advisable. Each resident should be assigned to the director's table for some time during the year.

Singing in the dining room builds house spirit and shortens the wait between courses. A house chorister may be chosen whose duties are to start the songs and the grace, if grace is sung. This person may act as host or hostess at an advantageously placed table throughout the year, as do the president and vice-president.

Residents should be proud and pleased to entertain their own personal guests at dinner. It is a good plan to have one night a week set apart as "guest night." On this night, individuals make reservations for their guests knowing that a particularly good meal will be served and that the entire house will dress for dinner with guests in mind.

There is no need of going into detail here regarding the many opportunities a dining room provides for the cultivation of habits of good taste and for good standards of social usage. It is also a place where the social program of the house can be developed, where house ceremonies can be held, and holidays celebrated. Many students will long remember Christmas breakfasts and the junior dinner in honor of the seniors, etc. An imaginative head of residence can use the dining room to excellent advantage to add to the pleasure and experience of the residents.

The dormitory can become the hearthstone of the entire campus. "School life should provide a time and place for acquiring self-development, self-enrichment, and self-control. To the extent that supervision of the dormitory helps in the attainment of these ends, the dormitory may be regarded as an important factor in school life."[1]

[1] LYFORD, CARRIE ALBERTA, *The School Dormitory*, pp. 8–9, M. Barrows & Company, Boston, 1932.

Walker has found that dormitories influence the scholastic success of students:

> A definite relation exists between student academic success and the place of dwelling during attendance at college. Residence halls had the most successful students, students living at home ranked second, students living at fraternity houses third, and students living in rooming houses fourth. . . . Students living at residence halls made grades higher than those predicted for University students. Home groups approximated predicted grades and chapter houses and rooming house groups made grades below predicted grades. . . . If a person holds that higher education is democratic in aim and directed toward social development of the many, he will recognize student housing as a vital factor. He will hold that the college has a custodial function and is as responsible for securing proper student housing as for providing proper classroom instruction.[1]

Owing to the lack of dormitory facilities, a great number of colleges find it necessary to house some students in private homes out in town. The women who rent the rooms in their homes to students are usually called housemothers. That these rooms may offer the right kind of living conditions, it is considered good practice for members of the personnel staff of the campus to inspect them, placing those which meet the required standards on an approved list which is available to students at the central personnel office. These standards prescribe adequate bathing and toilet facilities, sufficient heat, light, ventilation, adequate closet space and desk space, cleanliness, and, if girls are to live in the rooms, occasional use of the living room. On the majority of campuses, those students who do not live in residence halls are permitted to live only in those town houses that have been approved. Three-girl or three-boy rooms are generally frowned upon, and it is only where

---

[1] WALKER, ERNEST TIMOTHY, *The Relation of the Housing of Students to Success in a University*, University of Chicago Press, Chicago, 1935, vii + 76 pp.

living quarters are at a premium that these are permitted. Single beds are the objective toward which every house inspector and standards committee is working, but double beds are still very frequently found in town houses.

"Since the housemother (in town houses) has such an important part in the life of the student . . . it is a self evident truth that the living conditions and their effects on the character and morals are centered largely in the type of housemother."[1] Brogdon names the traits of a good housemother: "irreproachable character; good health; motherly interest; sympathy; humor; flexibility; love for young people; fair-mindedness; self-control; kindly aloofness; sincere firmness; intelligent interest; tact; good judgment; ability to make the home attractive; and knowledge of well-balanced meals,"[2] (if board is supplied as well as room).

If the institution is to have a successful housing program, there must be close cooperation between housemothers and the personnel staff of the college. One means for bringing this about is an organization of housemothers called "housemothers' association" or something similar. Regular meetings with the personnel staff to discuss and solve common problems, the establishment of standing committees such as standards, social, etc., go far toward bringing about desired cooperation. Such an organization can make the householders feel that the institution's problems of "outside" housing are their own, and the college can through discussion also understand the problems of the housemothers.

It is important that the students who live in these homes off-campus should not feel cut off from the campus life and activities. On one Middle Western campus all students

[1] MINROW, MAUDE E., "How Housemothers May Aid in the Betterment of Living Conditions of Students, and Their Effect upon Character and Morals," *National Association of Deans of Women, Thirteenth Yearbook*, 1926, p. 156.

[2] BROGDON, MARY C., "Better Housing through Better Householders," *National Association of Deans of Women, Fourteenth Year Book*, 1927, p. 153.

who live in private homes or in their own homes are joined together in an organization called Varsity Villagers. They have the usual officers and committees and a well-planned social program under the supervision of a member of the college personnel staff. Through this program they are given needed experience in social affairs, and, since all the students are members, all have access to some participation in some affairs on the campus. Then, too, their complaints and problems can be discussed with the proper college authority through their officers.

Hayes found in her study of 125 colleges and universities that 14 of these institutions operate cooperative halls.[1] The purpose of these halls is to supply board and room at less cost than it can be had otherwise. The students for the most part do their own marketing, their own cooking, cleaning, and care of the house. Hayes reports that the savings involved equal one-fourth to one-half that of other residence halls and that the supervision seems to be the same as that given in other dormitories. Students are often selected for residence in cooperative houses on the bases of financial need, good scholarship, good health, and cooperative spirit. Membership in a cooperative house at Smith College is regarded as a form of scholarship, for only students of very high scholastic standing as well as financial need are chosen for this type of living. The amount of work each student does each day varies on different campuses but the minimum seems to be 1 hour a day.

Cooperative housing offers a practical situation and can involve social and educational experiences for its residents. A danger arises, however, when the purpose is merely to reduce living expenses and educational values are lost sight of. Black Mountain College in North Carolina functions on the philosophy that all in the college community, both faculty and students, should carry their own

[1] HAYES, HARRIET, *College-operated Residence Halls for Women Students in 125 Colleges and Universities*, pp. 35–36, Teachers College, Bureau of Publications, Columbia University, New York, 1932.

weight in daily, self-maintenance duties, and the venture may be regarded as an experiment not only in cooperative housing but also in cooperative living.

BIBLIOGRAPHY

BROGDON, MARY C.: "Better Housing through Better Householders," *National Association of Deans of Women, Fourteenth Yearbook*, 1927, pp. 149–160.

CHANEY, MARGARET S., and ELIZABETH ROGGE: "The First Year of a College Cooperative House," *Journal of Home Economics*, 27: 166–168, March, 1935.

CHASE, H. W.: "Financing and Operating Dormitories," *National Association of State Universities*, 26: 50–59, 1928.

CHEEK, MARY ASHBY: "Reorganized Residence Halls," *Journal of Higher Education*, 7: 371–376, October, 1936.

DIRKS, L. H.: "Operation of Dormitories," *National Association of Deans and Advisers of Men, Thirteenth Annual Conference*, 1931, pp. 125–133.

DOHL, CRETE M.: *Housekeeping Management in Hotels and Institutions*, Harper & Brothers, New York, 1931, xv + 447 pp.

FITZGERALD, RUFUS H.: "Personal Adjustments in Relation to Living Conditions," in W. S. Gray, *Provision for the Individual*, 189–198, University of Chicago Press, Chicago, 1932.

FRANKLIN, JENKINS LUCY: "Cooperative Housing," *Journal of Higher Education*, 2: 35–36, January, 1931.

HAYES, HARRIET: *College-operated Residence Halls for Women Students in 125 Colleges and Universities*, pp. 1–35, Teachers College, Bureau of Publications, Columbia University, New York, 1932.

————: *Planning Residence Halls*, Teachers College, Bureau of Publications, Columbia University, New York, 1932, v + 247 pp.

"Housing College Students" in *American Association of University Women Bulletin*, 1934, x + 96 pp.

JONES, I. HOWLAND: "Planning of Girls' Dormitories," *Association of American College Bulletin*, 18: 242–245, May, 1932.

KLAUDER, CHARLES Z., and HERBERT C. WISE: *College Architecture in America*, Charles Scribner's Sons, New York, 1929, xix + 301 pp.

LYFORD, CARRIE ALBERTA: *The School Dormitory*, M. Barrows & Company, Boston, 1932, vi + 200 pp.

MATHEWS, LOIS: *The Dean of Women*, Houghton Mifflin Company, Boston, 1915, vii + 275 pp.

MINROW, MAUDE E.: "How Housemothers May Aid in the Betterment of Living Conditions of Students and Their Effect upon Character and Morals," *National Association of Deans of Women, Thirteenth Yearbook*, 1926, pp. 156–158.

NEWMAN, A. EVELYN: "Student Living Conditions and Their Effect on Character and Morals," *National Association of Deans of Women, Thirteenth Yearbook*, 1927, pp. 143–151.

SCALES, LAURA WOOLSEY: "The Operation of College Houses at Smith College," *American School and University Yearbook*, 1933–1934, pp. 279–281.

SOUTHARD, LYDIA: *Institutional Household Administration*, J. B. Lippincott Company, Philadelphia, 1923, 214 pp.

WALKER, ERNEST TIMOTHY: *The Relation of the Housing of Students to Success in a University*, University of Chicago Press, Chicago, 1935, vii + 76 pp.

Chapter XIII

EDUCATING STUDENTS TO LIVE HEALTHFULLY

Health

For the better part of a century scholarship was held to be the sole obligation of the American college or university, but newer standards for students have included health, character, conduct, and manners. Health has become one of the major objectives of education.

Just what is meant by health? Most persons think of it as meaning "not ill," but this negative definition is without much practical usefulness. The concept of health should rather connote personal well-being, including not only bodily and mental vigor and soundness, but also generally adequate living. Health is not an aim in life that can be achieved directly, but rather it is the result of the way one lives and cares for one's body and mind. Health is an outcome, a resultant, of the interplay of factors of environment and heredity.

Educators have realized that the hygiene and habits of students eventually become those of the public, for it is reasonable to suppose that many college students will become the leaders of the future. The need for such leadership is great since the public is not eager to change traditional health habits. People have not been taught to live healthfully or to use their own initiative in securing either corrective or prophylactic medical care, nor, for the most part, are they even acquainted with medical facilities and practices or how to use them to their best advantage.

Institutions of higher education are interested not only in the health of future citizens but in the health and well-being of the students who are spending years in their care, that these students may profit by their education to the fullest possible extent. Colleges and universities pretty generally have assumed a responsibility for the health of students; they have come to realize the importance of supervision of the environment, of health instruction, and of health service. The programs of health have taken on educational and preventative aspects as well as clinical.

The objectives of a good health program in colleges and universities are many. Hughes lists them as: safeguarding sick students, faculty, and other employees, protecting the well from the sick, detecting and investigating structural and functional defects of the individual, securing treatment of remediable physical and mental defects, discovering illogical or defective habits and attitudes and supplying appropriate scientific information and advice for their correction, establishing habits of periodic health examinations, training that will enable the student to select scientific health service with intelligent discrimination, and teaching hygiene by means of pertinent scientific information and advice given the student concerning the nature and importance of health needs as shown by his health examinations, consultations, and conferences.[1]

The successful health program will also provide for first aid or emergency treatment for any student, faculty member, or employee of the institution who needs it, cooperation with city, state, and national health agencies; advisement and reference to specialized care of those students needing such attention; the correlation of the program for health education with personal health service; and the inspection, supervision, and maintenance of general sanitation and safety.

In most institutions of higher education, the health program is under the supervision of a full-time doctor of medicine who is a member of the student personnel staff. He is also often a member of the instructional staff and

[1] HUGHES, WILLIAM LEONARD, *Administration of Health and Physical Education in Colleges*, p. 53, A. S. Barnes & Company, New York, 1935.

teaches some courses. In some coeducational institutions, it has been found desirable to have both a man and a woman physician because some students are reluctant to go to physicians of the opposite sex. The health staff is usually composed of one or more registered nurses (it has been suggested that there should be one full-time nurse for every 1,000 students) and, if the institution is large enough, additional physicians who may be on the staff full time or who may act as consultants, giving part time to the college or university and carrying on their own private practices in the community. It is suggested in the chapter on Housing that each dormitory should have a registered nurse in residence. These nurses are an integral part of the institutional health staff. If the college is small, they may combine dormitory duties with general campus health functions.

The responsibility for health is not limited exclusively to the health or medical office of the college, however. It is an important responsibility of the entire personnel staff and faculty of the institution. All who work with students will come in contact with health problems and will need to understand the part these problems play in effective student living. In addition, these individuals will have the opportunity to direct students with difficulties to the health service for proper attention. The personnel staff and faculty of the institution should know the objectives and procedures of the health program in order that all efforts may be directed into the right channels.

Some method should be found to coordinate the efforts of the institution in behalf of student health. This may take the form of a health council with the director of personnel and the director of health as cochairmen. Other members on the health council may include representatives of the medical staff, faculty representatives, representatives from the physical education department, the director of admissions, and other personnel officers, such as the director of the part-time employment bureau and the heads of residences. There must be a close tie-up between the health program and that of the program of admissions, for standards of health should be included among criteria for admission. Since the program of physical education is closely concerned with health, this department becomes an important factor in the health program. The director of the health program will be vitally interested in the social and recreational program of the college or university, for social adjustment plays an important role in mental health. The director of personnel will have an active interest in coordinating all of these programs into a purposeful institutional program for health.

The college infirmary or health service must be accessible to students and should be located near the center of student life on the campus. The infirmary in many colleges and universities is in the nature of a small hospital and medical laboratory, having sufficient beds and nursing staff for cases needing expert care and, in some instances, a surgery. It has been found in many instances, however, that it is foolish to equip an infirmary for surgery if there is a well-equipped and well-staffed hospital in the community. The doctor or doctors on the health staff must have consultation hours convenient for all students and staff.

It is customary to demand complete physical examinations of all entering students. These may reveal defects that can be corrected, or they may result in the recommendation that a student withdraw from the institution. It may be found that a student cannot carry a full-time schedule of classes or that he should not carry on certain activities that may impair his health. Suitable physical exercise or courses in physical education may be recommended as a result of these examinations. The invaluable opportunities that the physical examination affords for individualized education on physical and mental health problems are as yet recognized, apparently, in only a few college health programs.

Students need to be taught the benefits of periodic examinations by physicians and dentists. In many institutions, freshmen and seniors are compelled to have these examinations, while sophomores and juniors may come voluntarily. It has been found in a number of institutions that the health habits of students become progressively worse during their four years in college, that students sleep less, smoke more, exercise less, and use more coffee in college than they have previously.[1] Surveys such as these show only too convincingly the need of vigorous collegiate health programs. Individual conferences and recommendations by experts, based upon scientific information gained through thorough examinations each year that a student is in college, may do much to alleviate this situation.

The health service should maintain a close relationship with parents of students. Parents should be kept informed as to their son's or daughter's health status. The health service may sometimes find it necessary to carry on a program of parental education along health lines.

The director of the health program should work closely and carefully with the heads of residences and nurses in the housing units on the campus. He will find that these comparatively small units are excellent situations for education in health habits, good habits of eating, bathing, sleeping, playing, and exercising. Here it is possible to put into practice a knowledge of normal health conditions and of how to keep well.

The director of the health program should also work closely with the personnel staff in maintaining sanitary and healthful living conditions in private homes where students are living off the campus. He or some other member of the personnel staff will wish to inspect the rooms in which these students live and the facilities available for their comfort and health. He is also interested in students procuring

[1] "Student Health Program at Cornell University," *School and Society*, 43: 146–147, Feb. 1, 1936.

good food at reasonable prices and in their having adequate and healthful classroom conditions.

A number of collegiate institutions have on their health staff a trained and competent psychiatrist, who works under the direction of the director of health. Since mental health and hygiene are important elements in the health program, it has been found advisable to provide an expert in this field for consultation concerning the health program and to care for cases needing psychiatric attention. The psychiatrist's place on the medical staff should not be overemphasized, however, because most students are reluctant to report to a psychiatrist or to anyone specializing in mental difficulties. His place on the staff should not be stressed any more than that of the dentist or the surgeon. It is well, also, for students not to be sent directly to the psychiatrist but to clear first through a conference with the doctor who is in charge of the health program.

Some colleges and universities have access to competent psychiatrists in near-by cities or within the community itself. In these instances, the psychiatrist is not a member of the health staff of the institution, but it is possible to refer cases needing this highly specialized type of attention to this expert.

Almost all institutions of higher education have access to a well-equipped and well-staffed hospital within the community or in a near-by town. Students demanding surgical treatment or prolonged medical and nursing care are usually sent to the hospital.

The cost of health service for students is usually divided between the students and the college or university, since the function of the health service is personal as well as institutional. The student's share is in the nature of a student fee—a sort of insurance payment which is required of all students whether they use the health service or not. The plan of periodic health examinations for all insures that all students will receive some value for the fees paid.

A financial arrangement is often made with the community or near-by hospital for the student health fee to cover hospitalization (with the exception of medicines, nurse's or doctor's charges where these are above a certain amount). The fee usually provides hospitalization for only a certain number of days, the student or his family being responsible for charges after this time.

Where the number of students on the campus demands a large health service staff, it has been found successful to appoint a health adviser for each incoming class. The same man physician looks after the men, the same woman physician looks after the women of the class for the entire 4 years. In this way the adviser takes on the nature of the family physician and may well become the student's personal friend as well as his physician during the 4 years.

Where the health staff is large enough to make the plan feasible, it is wise to carry on a follow-up program of individual students. Assuming that each student in the institution is thoroughly examined early in each year of his residence, a good "tickler file" will remind the director of health to call the various students in for checkups on individual health programs. A follow-up program must be individual to be successful.

Most medical men do not need to be convinced of the necessity for careful and accurate records. All will agree that these records are confidential; and some even take the attitude that they are so confidential that no one but the physician concerned should know their contents. This latter point of view defeats many of the aims of a student personnel program. The personnel staff and student counselors, to work intelligently with students and their problems, must know and understand individual health liabilities and assets. It is an easy matter for clerks in the health service to send daily explicit but simple memos or carbon copies of records to the central personnel office. A second carbon or set of memos may also be sent to the personnel officer in charge of the housing unit in which the student lives. Even though it may not be an institutional regulation that absences from classes must be excused, individual faculty members may require excuses for absences from their classes. In instances where these are demanded, the daily report from the health service makes it possible for the personnel office to write the excuse. It is well to mention here the illnesses that do not require a visit to the health service but that keep a student in his dormitory or room temporarily. These should be reported by the house head to the personnel office, to expedite excuses if they are necessary and to inform the personnel staff when such indispositions occur.

The health reports will also assist the personnel office to supervise and advise those students whose health is such that they should not carry heavy part-time work schedules, or class schedules, or an overload of extracurricular activities. The personnel office should confer frequently with the medical staff about individual cases, should carry out the recommendations of the director of health, and should aid the students in every way possible.

Campus health programs usually include required courses in physiology and hygiene for sophomores or freshmen or both. These are usually taught by members of the health staff, and it has frequently been thought by students that the courses are a waste of time and energy. This is no doubt true where the courses are carried on in a routine, uninteresting manner. No one doubts, however, that it is quite possible for these courses to have value in teaching students an appreciation of the necessity and importance of early medical advice, the dangers of self-medication, and of over-the-counter drug-store prescribing; they can impart information concerning transmission of communicable diseases, the methods of protection and the proper health behavior relative to their control, principles of sex, family, and mental hygiene. But, most important, they can present standards of wholesome living so concretely and attractively as to make students intelligent concerning the laws of health and to make them want to practice healthful living persistently. Even with the best of courses, however, the teaching of health principles and standards cannot all be done by the group method. Health is, in the final analysis, a very individual matter, and a group educational program should be augmented with individual tutoring which renders abstract health principles more specific and personal.

In one institution with which the authors are familiar, living, vital, purposeful lectures and discussions compose these required courses. The courses are the responsibility of the physician who heads the health service and who personally and completely examines each student each year. The lectures are based upon experiences personally applicable to the group; the examinations given the students are the bases of the material presented and illustrations have to do with the health deficiencies of the group itself. The course is not filled with textbook material or statistics but is composed of personal experiences (disguised, of course) that may be those of any student present. Moving pictures and slides are also utilized.

The director of health may find it possible to participate in other courses than the hygiene courses. He can frequently make a valuable contribution to courses in psychology, sociology, chemistry, etc. A close coordination of knowledge gained in these courses with health knowledge is certainly desirable.

The director of the college health program will in all probability be quite active in the health affairs of the community. He may serve as a member of the community health board, and, certainly, he will wish to cooperate with local and state health agencies in the control of, and education pertaining to, communicable and venereal diseases. He will be interested in local control and regulations regarding supplies of milk and water and sanitary conditions. Epidemics either on the campus or in the community or both will necessitate close cooperation between the college health authorities and those of the town or city.

The health program on the campus must be headed by a very superior man or woman. The success of the program will largely depend upon this one individual. We would have this person be an individual with many years of experience, well trained, and certainly up to date in his profession. He must be an educator above all and wise in the knowledge of how to handle people of all ages. He should be calm, and deliberate and intelligent, a person in whom confidence is freely and unquestionably placed, concerning whose personal and professional integrity there can be no question. He is counselor and friend as well as physician.

The success of the health program on the campus also depends upon a carefully selected congenial staff who are competent and well trained. They also must have the educational point of view. These individuals and the director must have the confidence of the students both as to their skill and knowledge, and as to their integrity. No program of health in institutions of higher education will function as such unless it is preventative and educational rather than merely remedial.

BIBLIOGRAPHY

BROWN B.: "New Deal in Health Education," *American Journal of Public Health*, 24: 743–748, July, 1934.

CHAYER, MARY ELLA: *Bibliography in Health Education for Schools and Colleges*, G. P. Putnam's Sons, New York, 1936, 100 pp.

GUDAKUNST, D. W.: "School Health Program as an Educational Activity," *American Journal of Public Health*, 25: 463–468, April, 1935.

———: "Aims of School Health Service," *American Journal of Public Health*, 25: 1135–1139, October, 1935.

HOLMAN, M. E.: "Health Service in a State Normal School," *Public Health Nursing*, 27: 205–208, May, 1935.

HUGHES, WILLIAM LEONARD: *Administration of Health and Physical Education in Colleges*, A. S. Barnes & Company, New York, 1935, 368 pp.

LEWIS, E. M.: "University Health Service," *National Association of State Universities, Transactions and Proceedings*, 33: 223–229, 1935.

LIPPERT, J.: "Health Comes First," *Scholastic*, 27: 27, Oct. 5, 1935.

"New Obligations Met by Colleges, Hawkes Citing Health and Conduct," *The New York Times*, Oct. 25, 1936.

PALMER, G. T., and M. DERRYBERRY: "Appraising the Educational Content of a Health Service Program," *American Journal of Public Health*, 27: 476–480, May, 1937.

RADL, ROBERT B.: "The Students Health Service of University of Minnesota," *American School and University Yearbook*, 1936, pp. 341–346.

ROGERS, J. F.: "Student Health Service in Institutions of Higher Education," *U. S. Office of Education Bulletin* 7, 1937.

"The School Health Program," *White House Conference*, D. Appleton-Century Company, Inc., New York, 1932, xx + 400 pp.

SHEPARD, W. P.: "Recent Progress in Health Education," *American Journal of Public Health*, 27: 454–463, May, 1937.

SMILEY, DEAN F.: "Provisions for the Health of Students," in *Proceedings of the Institute for Administrative Officers of Higher Institutions*, vol. IV, pp. 177–188, University of Chicago Press, Chicago, 1932.

STOREY, THOMAS A.: "The Status of Hygiene Programs in Institutions of Higher Learning," *Stanford University Publications, Medical Sciences*, vol. 1, no. 1, 1927.

"Student Health Program at Cornell University," *School and Society*, 43: 146–147, Feb. 1, 1936.

WINSLOW, C. E. A.: "Cultural Objectives of Health Education," *School and Society*, 40: 1–5, July 7, 1934.

Chapter XIV

HELPING STUDENTS TO DISCOVER VALUES

Religion

Religion in higher education is time-honored. Our colonial colleges were established to educate religious people and all through our history churches have been active in founding colleges and universities to educate their members. There is no doubt but that much of our progress in education beyond the secondary level has been due to the activity of religious agencies interested in education. But little by little religion in education has been crowded out due to the pressure of formulated knowledge, to the growth of scientific knowledge, and to the changes in modern thought and living.

The need for religious education and for collegiate programs of religion is still great, however. Eminent psychologists tell us that each individual must work out his own system of values during adolescence if he is to grow up. "A specific religion becomes a technique by which persons and groups represent to themselves the total meaning and worth of reality in its cosmic aspects and by which they seek to utilize the cosmic resources for the furthering of the valued ends of living."[1] "Religion is the attempt to find self-realization in terms of those things to which are attached universal and absolute values."[2] "Religion is the revelation to the human spirit of an interpretation of

[1] Definition given by William Clayton Bower in *Character through Creative Experience*, Chap. XIV, University of Chicago Press, Chicago, 1930.

[2] A definition worked out and used in the interpretation of a syllabus on religion prepared and followed by the Springfield, Ill., Branch of the American Association of University Women under the direction of Elizabeth Conner Lindsay.

life that puts into living sense and reason, worth and dignity, joy and satisfaction."[1] Most students can profitably use assistance and help in working out such techniques and systems of values for themselves in order that they may become truly mature.

While there is much informal discussion of, and argument about, religion, values in life, and philosophies of living among students in spontaneous and informal gatherings, for the great majority of undergraduates the attitude toward *organized* religion is one of indifference. A study of undergraduate adjustment at the University of Michigan showed that about one-third of the group studied were seriously and actively interested in formalized religious matters, and the remainder showed varying degrees of indifference and dislike.[2] It is further reported that familiarity with the Bible and a belief in an institutionalized creed are unusual among undergraduates.[3] Some students are completely indifferent to religion in its institutional aspect while others are willing docilely to accept some authority on religion without achieving maturity of thought individually. According to a responsible official at Harvard, it is surprising how many really able students prefer to find some authority on religion rather than to work the thing out for themselves.[4]

The indifference toward formalized or orthodox religion on the part of so large a number of students on our campuses may be attributed in varying degrees to many factors. Many students do not make any distinction between religion and theology. Many who do not understand or who cannot accept the teachings of theology turn aside from "religion" on this basis. Many intelligent students revolt against what they consider to be "religious authority and

[1] FOSDICK, HARRY EMERSON, From a sermon preached May 9, 1937.
[2] ANGELL, ROBERT COOLEY, *A Study in Undergraduate Adjustment*, Chap. VII, University of Chicago Press, Chicago, 1930.
[3] ANGELL, ROBERT COOLEY, *The Campus*, Chap. IX, D. Appleton-Century Company, Inc., New York, 1928.
[4] GRAY, GEORGE W., "The Student Gropes for a Faith," *The New York Times Magazine*, Feb. 5, 1933, pp. 10–11, 15.

tradition." To quote a student, "Religion must not insult intelligence and experience." Preceding generations failed to keep thinking in the religious field apace with that in the fields of science and philosophy and students do not yet generally realize the degree of harmony that now prevails between religion and science, and they fail (largely because they do not have expert assistance) to integrate these lines of knowledge. Abbé Lemaître, the famous physicist who is also a priest, has said that once one realizes that the Bible does not purport to be a textbook of science, the old controversy between religion and science vanishes; that the real conflict between science and religion is to be found in men and not in the Bible or the findings of physicists.[1]

Other factors which have contributed to students' attitudes and perplexities concerning what they believe to be religion are: a confusion of religion with sectarianism and an acceptance of inherited religion which often leads to a loss of faith in the church and what it has stood for in the past as a basis of authority; the indications that preaching and precept are frequently at variance; the lack of opportunity for reflection since materialistic society does not encourage reflection and reflection is necessary to religious interpretation; and the fact that religion and religious activity suffer from competition with other interests not only on the campus but in life off the campus.

The separation of church and state has placed emphasis on secular education to the neglect of religious education. Many colleges have taken no responsibility for a program of religion except to permit the organization of various church clubs on the campuses, yet they are concerned with the growing indifference of their students toward overt systems of individual values and with the religious conflicts and perplexities which many of their students display. Some educators are recognizing the need for reappraising and

[1] "Lemaitre Follows Two Paths to Truth," *The New York Times Magazine*, Feb. 19, 1933, pp. 3 *ff.*

reaffirming the intellectual and philosophical bases of religion, for emphasizing the relation of religion to ethical action (since many feel that religion is not a true religion until it expands into ethical action), for emphasizing the place of religion in government, citizenship, and education, and for worship and disciplines expressive of new concepts and new social practices in religion.

These educators are also realizing that students desire some resources to which, when they need it, they can look for help, that students need assistance in making religious syntheses and constructive proposals for action, and that they need a stable group to give them added security in a period in which religious resources are relatively disorganized and inarticulate.

Some students are displaying a complacency toward religion which may be the result of innocence or ignorance, or of indifference, or of dogmatism. Others are clearly bewildered; while still others are in conflict with the religious points of view in which they have been trained. Said a student at Harvard, editor of one of the undergraduate publications: "Among my associates, the literary group, I haven't met a student who is an atheist. They all believe in God, but the problem is the approach to God. We don't find it in the existing churches, and we want it. If some man would show us the way, we'd run to him."[1]

Colleges and universities cannot alone be blamed for destroying or neglecting faith and participation in religion. The present situation is instead the result of the interplay of many factors and a world of constant change.

Critics to whom changes are distressing never tire of telling us that colleges have destroyed the undergraduate's religion. This is nonsense; for if there is one set of problems more earnestly discussed in college bickers than any other, it is these very problems of God, freedom, and immortality which have constituted the fundamentals of religion in every age. . . . It is the forms

[1] GRAY, *loc. cit.*

and the character of the appeal, but not the substance of religion, that have changed.[1]

There seems to be little doubt in the minds of a number of personnel officers but that a great number of students are groping for a religion that will satisfy individual needs. The gropings may be informal, unorganized, and largely manifested in spontaneous student groups where for the most part adults are not present, but the desire, covered very frequently by a noninterest and indifference to organized church and other religious organizational activities, is present. As Gauss has pointed out, the forms and character of the religious appeal have failed students in the past but many are deeply interested, although most often not overtly, in discovering the resources which religion, in one form or another, has offered mankind since time immemorial.

There also seems to be little doubt in the minds of many personnel officers but that a campus program of religion is worth while, and, although no program yet has solved all of the difficulties it meets, a well-thought-out and planned institutional program in which students play an important participant role may assist students in discovering the values which religion has to offer.

The director of personnel in an institution of higher education who is interested in establishing or developing a program of religion on his campus inevitably finds himself facing certain practical issues. In the first place, he finds himself concerned as to whether the college program of religion should be locally controlled or whether to some extent the local program should be dictated by a national organization interested in collegiate programs of religion. A purely local program may meet the needs of his particular group more advantageously than one of national scope. On the other hand, those participating in a local program

[1] GAUSS, CHRISTIAN, *Life in College*, p. 95, Charles Scribner's Sons, New York, 1930.

may miss the stimulation of intercollegiate conferences and the interchange of ideas which frequently have great suggestive value to a campus. Students often return from the intercollegiate religious conferences "bursting" with ideas and with enough momentum to sweep an ineffective program of religion off its base. Some personnel officers disapprove of these conferences because, they say, students who attend such intercollegiate meetings often come back with uncontrollable and illogical proposals for their individual campuses. Then, too, some colleges and universities feel that national student religious organizations impose standards difficult to meet or not important to local institutions. One of these standards may be the employment of a professionally trained worker for the religious program at a minimum salary named by the national organization, although the college may be able to procure a local person with the necessary personality and interests—but not professionally trained—at a much lower salary. On the whole, however, there seems to be some merit in the contention that the national organizations are tending to advocate educational method and programs closely related to students' religious experience and needs and do, therefore, tend to prevent domination of the local program by faculty who may (usually with the best of intentions) attempt to control the religious program in terms of their own mature religious experience and beliefs, to some extent thereby denying students the opportunity to work out their own systems of values in terms of their own experience.

Another practical issue which the director of personnel will also have to consider is whether the religious program should be dominated by churches of different denominations or, perhaps, by an interdenominational church organization, or whether the college administration itself should keep close control of its own program. If the religious program is in the control of the different churches, it is believed by many that students will find less difficulty in making satisfactory church connections when they are out of college. This, the protagonists claim, is important, not only to the students as individuals, but also to the leadership and vitality of the churches themselves. The disadvantage with having the religious program in the college in the control of the separate churches is that false distinctions between sects and different denominations are preserved and crippling rivalries are often developed. A program which is interdenominational does not have these disadvantages. It has also been said that students who participate in the interdenominational program of religion incline to withdraw from denominational churches when they return to their respective communities upon graduation. A point in favor of the college's controlling its own program is that it may choose its own purposes and educational methods.

Another problem confronting the personnel official who attempts to foster a program of religion is whether this type of program should include the consideration of social and economic justice as an important part of its program. Some personnel officers boldly demand that no controversial social questions shall be included in the campus program of religion, while others welcome the consideration of these topics as educative and fundamental to a vital religious program.

The director of personnel may have to answer the question of whether there should be a distinction between the programs of religion for men and for women. In the past, because men's and women's organizations were started separately, vested interests have tended to keep the programs for men and women separate. Should this be continued? It is claimed by some as an argument against the merging of the men's and women's movements that the two programs are not at an equal stage of development and that the stronger program would tend to be held back to a level of mediocrity by fusion with the weaker. Men and women, others contend, are required to work together in all sorts of social, community, and religious work after college, so why not begin in college?

Those wisest in building religious programs for college students have consistently stressed the values of student autonomy. The director of personnel in contemplating his program of religion, or in building one anew, must face the fact that there may be a tendency for vested interests to take over the program and to run it *for* the students rather than permitting the students to share actively in its direction and leadership.

The difficulties in putting a religious program into effect on a campus loom large. The director of personnel must realize that there is a wide diversity of maturity of thought on religious questions among students, that most adolescents are not very articulate about spiritual values, that the institution has a rapidly changing student personnel, that the religious program must compete with many student interests, and that many group attitudes and traditions are both hostile and indifferent to religion. The organization of a religious program is difficult because of the personal nature of the problem and the variety of approaches that can be made to it. It is often difficult to finance religious projects, and it may be even more difficult to find the right sort of voluntary or paid leadership.

Certainly, there are some elements which seem basic, however, and which, taken altogether, should furnish a program of religion which holds values for college students.

The campus religious program should provide the opportunity for students to enjoy the fellowship of persons who care about religious values; to discuss value concepts with interested contemporaries and with thoughtful adults; to worship and meditate; to participate in religious activity, expression, and leadership; to solve individual religious problems in an individual manner if desired; and to learn the different systems, principles, and philosophies of religion.

The faculty of the institution should afford students contact with people who have an attractive, joyous, useful religious faith and who may offer this type of fellowship to students. Students need to know individuals who have sources of power that lend meaning and purpose to life and who will furnish them general leadership in building their own systems of values. Such individuals may be found in the community as well as on the faculty; they are frequently interested in assisting in the religious program of the college even to the extent of being willing to entertain small groups of students in their homes. The personnel director who does not utilize these persons, whether they be on the college staff or off the campus, is missing a real opportunity to display to students a living sort of religion which is felt rather than taught.

The institution may or may not have a chapel or a student church upon its campus. Students should, however, have some place where they can go for private and corporate worship and for meditation. Many of us have seen, on a number of campuses, beautiful chapels where the atmosphere is peaceful, quiet, and reverent. These should be open to students to drop in at any hour of the day or evening. If there is no campus chapel or church, the community churches may be so utilized, particularly if they are participants in the campus program. In this busy world of ours, too few pause to meditate. Colleges all the more, therefore, have a responsibility for making the opportunity available.

On many campuses, unfortunately, there is no distinction between chapel programs and assemblies. The purposes of the two are not even remotely related. There is no need to go into detail here regarding the purposes of the various assemblies regularly held throughout our colleges and universities. The chapel program, however, should be for the purpose of worship and should be devoted to religious considerations. It should be a service of unity and dignity. It should not be held oftener than such a program can be provided. Many institutions feel that attendance should be compulsory while others maintain it should be voluntary. It is the opinion of many that students will come of their own free will if the programs are of sufficient worth. Others believe that valuable habits are often based on coercion. The chapel program may include a vesper service at twilight on Sunday evening, with lovely music, and speakers who talk briefly but to the point. These speakers may be the outstanding ministers representing all sects and denominations within a radius of 100 miles.

There should be student participation in planning the chapel programs and in the actual services themselves. If students are consulted as to what they want, what type of services will best meet their interests and needs, and if they actually take part in the affair, they will make the venture a success. Student choirs, soloists, and ushers add much to the occasion, while the student who is chosen to introduce the speaker should feel it an honor and a privilege.

Students dislike to be talked at and prayed for (as do most adults). The reasons so many chapel services are so poorly attended by students are that the subjects treated in the service are remote from student life, students have small opportunity to exercise their initiative and ideas in planning the services, and their part in executing the plans is kept at a minimum.

Many students should and will want to worship in the community churches as well as in the college chapel. The religious programs of the community churches may be printed in the campus newspaper each week. It is well, too, to invite the community pastors to appear on the chapel programs of the campus early in the academic year, so that the students may early have a contact with the ministers of their respective denominations.

A religious program is not fulfilling its purpose unless it is providing opportunities for student participation in religious activity, expression, and leadership. The chapel programs just discussed may offer some of these opportunities. Reading clubs on religious subjects also may be organized, but it is wise to keep the membership in any one club small in order that there may be informal exchange of ideas and discussion. Interested faculty may assist with student-faculty seminars in which religious topics and problems are freely discussed. The faculty must be chosen carefully on the bases of their sympathy and understanding of the student point of view, a wholesome regard for religion and student religious problems, and their realization of the value of the seminar techniques. The seminar must not deteriorate into a faculty lecture course.

Student leadership and expression may be developed through week-end conferences of foreign and American students in which are provided material for new judgments and new actions. These conferences may supply the opportunity for clarifying religious thought, for developing tolerances, for the consideration of social questions in the light of religious values, and for wider contacts.

Denominational sororities and fraternities are another means of developing student leadership and activity. A program of religion on the campus of broad scope may well include them. They must be motivated, however, in such a way that denominational cleavages and cliques will not be a result of their presence on the campus.

Each campus will find that religious organizations of various types will meet some of its needs. The initiative and control (with some degree of supervision), however, should be in the hands of students. It is only in this way that students will gain training in leadership and that the program can be sure of meeting their needs. Passive participation is almost worse than none and to it is due much of the indifference evidenced by students toward religious activities. Students must have a sphere of service in which they find activity and expression.

The program of religion should include opportunities for individual religious counseling. Religious consultants and advisers are important in order that students may be able personally and individually to find help with religious problems and perplexities. The counselors must be carefully selected for their scholarship in religion, their personality, sympathy, understanding, and faith in a living and vital system of values. They should have a background in modern psychology and sociology, as well as in the historic contributions of religion. They may be members of the faculty, or members of the personnel staff specifically trained for this purpose, or ministers or workers in the churches of the community, or university or college pastors.

Many religious authorities advocate courses in religion in the college curriculum on an equal par with other subjects. They support courses in historical religious facts, literature, and thought. They feel that only through actual courses for credit will students realize that religion has played a major role in the history of the race and that it deserves an honorable place in one's thinking. If these courses are given on the campus, they should involve living issues instead of merely stressing a scholarly treatment of subject matter. One institution offers such courses and employs instructors of Jewish, Catholic, and Protestant faiths. An attempt is made to break down denominationalism and to place religion on a higher level than mere sectarianism.

The library of the institution should contain easily accessible reading matter on religion. A good collection of religious material may assist students to solve some of their own religious perplexities.

The churches in the community may serve many of the purposes of the college religious program. They should certainly be accorded an active part in the total campus program if they so desire. Their services, Sunday-school classes, young people's organizations, and social hours may become a vital element in the campus program of religion. Often their ministers are vital forces in the individual religious counseling program, and town members of the churches serve a real function in entertaining students in their homes.

A number of churches have specially appointed and selected ministers who act as full-time or part-time pastors on campuses of colleges or universities. This university or college pastor may also represent an interdenominational church organization. Such a man's success depends largely upon his personality, training, his ability to understand the students' points of view and needs, and his ability to cooperate with others in a broad program. He may provide a well-planned and very beneficial religious program of activity and counsel for students of his denominational faith but any denominational program should desirably be coordinated with the whole program of religion on the campus.

The Y. W. C. A. and Y. M. C. A. may also share in the campus religious program. These organizations have programs of national scope; they have long experience in working with college students; they are able to provide interchange of ideas between colleges, and they maintain a staff of specially trained workers who are usually well-equipped with educational methods in religion. The programs of these organizations, too, must be coordinated with that of the institution.

It is essential that the efforts of all agencies and persons participating in the religious program of the campus be integrated and coordinated if they are to function to their fullest efficiency. The coordinator may be the director of personnel or a member of the director's staff who acts as the dean of religion. The latter on some university campuses is a professionally trained psychologist and religious worker. In one institution he is called "dean of the chapel." Whether the program is under the direction of the director of personnel or a member of his staff, it is well for the one who heads up the program to work closely and carefully with a joint student-faculty committee or council on religion. It has been found most successful to have representatives of community churches and religious agencies on this council, in order that all efforts in behalf of students may be focused and coordinated. Such a council will assist in preventing overlapping in cases where more than one agency is caring for some function of the religious program.

The director of the program of religion may wish to evaluate the program by applying the following criteria:[1]

1. Is there accuracy in diagnosing and interpreting the needs and aspirations of the students?
2. Is adequate consideration given to initiative, participation, leadership, and control by students?
3. Do the agencies cooperate in a cordial spirit? Is there coordination of all efforts?
4. Do the number and variety of students influenced show that the program is inclusive and effective?
5. Is the program educative and cumulative in its effects on participants?

BIBLIOGRAPHY

ANGELL, ROBERT COOLEY: *The Campus*, D. Appleton-Century Company, Inc., New York, 1928, xii + 239 pp.

———: *A Study in Undergraduate Adjustment*, University of Chicago Press, Chicago, 1930, ix + 164 pp.

BOWER, WILLIAM CLAYTON: *Character through Creative Experience*, University of Chicago Press, Chicago, 1930, xiii + 276 pp.

BOYER, EDWARD STERLING: *Religion in the American College*, Abingdon Press, New York, 1930, 105 pp.

BRAUNSTEIN, BARUCH: "Religion at Columbia University," *Religious Education Magazine*, 25: 669–673, September, 1930.

CHAMBERLIN, ROY BULLARD: "Can Religion Recapture the Campus?" *Christian Century Magazine*, 47: 1310–1313, July–December, 1930.

"Character Education," *National Education Association Department of Superintendence, Tenth Yearbook*, 1932, 535 pp.

CHARTERS, JESSIE (Mrs. W. W. Charters): *College Student Thinking It Through*, Abingdon Press, New York, 1930, 166 pp.

COE, GEORGE A.: *What Is Christian Education?* Charles Scribner's Sons, New York, 1929, xii + 300 pp.

[1] These criteria are adapted from R. H. Edwards, J. M. Artman, and G. M. Fisher, *Undergraduates*, p. 293, Doubleday, Doran, & Company, Inc., New York, 1928.

DUDYCHA, GEORGE J.: "The Religious Beliefs of College Freshmen," *School and Society*, 31: 206–208, February, 1930.

EDDINGTON, A. S.: *Science and the Unseen World*, The Macmillan Company, New York, 1929, 91 pp.

EDWARDS, R. H., J. M. ARTMAN, and G. M. FISHER: *Undergraduates*, Doubleday, Doran & Company, Inc., New York, 1928, x + 366 pp.

EINSTEIN, A., JOHN DEWEY, SIR JAMES JEAN, et al.: *Living Philosophies*, Simon & Schuster, Inc., New York, 1931, 334 pp.

FOSDICK, HARRY E.: *The Modern Use of the Bible*, The Macmillan Company, New York, 1924, 9 + 291 pp.

———: *As I See Religion*, Harper & Brothers, New York, 1932, 201 pp.

GAUSS, CHRISTIAN: *Life in College*, Charles Scribner's Sons, New York, 1930, xv + 271 pp.

HARKNESS, GEORGIA: *The Recovery of Ideals*, Charles Scribner's Sons, New York, 1937, 237 pp.

HAWKES, HERBERT E.: "Religion in a Liberal Education," *Educational Record*, 8: 28–39, January, 1927.

HYDE, W. D.: *Five Great Philosophies of Life*, The Macmillan Company, New York, 1913, 296 pp.

JACKS, LAWRENCE: *Religious Perplexities*, Doubleday, Doran & Company, Inc., New York, 1923, 107 pp.

JAMES, WILLIAM: *On Vital Reserves*, Henry Holt & Company, New York, 1916, 78 pp.

JONES, RUFUS: *The Fundamental Ends of Life*, The Macmillan Company, New York, 1924, 76 pp.

———: *A Preface to Christian Faith in a New Age*, The Macmillan Company, New York, 1932, 206 pp.

KATZ, DANIEL, and F. H. ALLPORT: *Students' Attitudes*, Craftsman Press, Syracuse, N. Y., 1931, xxviii + 401.

LAMPE, MATHEW: "What is a Complete Religious Program at a University," *Christian Education Magazine*, 14: 1931.

MILLIKAN, R. A.: *Evolution in Science and Religion*, Yale University Press, New Haven, 1927, 4 + 95 pp.

———: *Science and the New Civilization*, Charles Scribner's Sons, New York, 1930, 5 + 194 pp.

OTTO, M. C.: "Changes in the Theory of Religion," *Mental Hygiene*, 14: 258–279, April, 1930.

PURINTON, CASE EVERETT: "Can Religion Be Taught Effectively in the College?" *Christian Education*, 14: 54–62, October, 1930.

RUGH, C. E.: "Social Standards," *School and Society*, 20: 351–361, Sept. 20, 1924.

SHAW, AVERY ALBERT, et al.: "Place of Religion in Higher Education," *Christian Education*, 13: 615–626, June, 1930.

TOWNER, MILTON: *Religion in Higher Education*, University of Chicago Press, Chicago, 1931, 327 pp.

Chapter XV

HELPING ALUMNI TO GET JOBS

Placement

College and university students are, for the most part, a highly endowed portion of the eighteen- to twenty-two-year-olds, and, in normal economic times, business, industrial, and professional employers are eager to employ them upon graduation. Students in higher education are just as eager to get into activities which are economically productive. The placement office in institutions of higher education is a means of bringing about employer-employee contacts easily and efficiently. This is the most obvious purpose of a college placement office—to serve as a complicated switchboard which connects individuals and jobs—but a placement office has other duties as well. The placement office should offer guidance as well as employment to its clientele. Through counseling, the staff of this office has an opportunity to assist students in clarifying their objectives in such ways that they may see and understand their social-economic value and in mapping programs which will prepare them for economic self-sufficiency as soon as necessary after leaving the institution. The advice and counsel of the placement office can probably be counted on not to be too theoretical; it is apt to be very practical, even, sometimes, to be based too rigidly and unimaginatively upon employment conditions as they have been found to be in the past.

It is another duty of this office to construct true pictures of the students and graduates and to transmit them to prospective employers. Many employers wish to be protected against direct personal applications and the placement office offers this protection, culling out from a large number of possible applicants a few likely candidates for each position.

The placement office can also build good will for its institution among students, alumni, and employers—either actual or probable. This office can develop into a public relations bureau for its institution, establishing confidence and good will in its relations with students, alumni, and the public at large.

Colleges and universities assume many responsibilities for their students upon admitting them to the institution. Among these responsibilities should be included assistance in working out their plans and methods for achieving economic productivity and of making a contribution to society.

The first obligation of the placement office, however, is to society rather than to student job hunters. It should not be the purpose of this office to place as many students in employment as possible, regardless of whether the students are fitted for the employment. Since placement takes place upon graduation in most cases, progressive selection which operates during the 4 years of college tends to eliminate many students who might become problems for a placement office interested in acquiring positions for able students. Yet, a certain number of students difficult to place and to fit into society will continue to be graduated, and, although the college or university accepted a certain responsibility for these students in admitting them to higher education, the placement office should not place consideration for such individuals ahead of its obligation to society at large.

The placement office should not force its services upon students; registration with this office should be voluntary on the part of the student and after consultation with its staff. Registration for placement services should be offered to all students and alumni of the institution and should, desirably, involve no charge to registrants. A policy of free registration leaves the placement office in a more favorable position to practice a policy of selective placement.

The placement office must collect much information regarding employers and positions if it is to work effectively. Specific requirements of each position, its probable future, the nature of the firm or institution, its personnel, its standing, its size, its history, its employment policies, and detailed information regarding the particular employer are of value to the applicant and to the staff member who must think in terms of the opportunities the position seems to offer as well as in terms of individuals who may best meet the needs of the position. Methods of acquiring such information are varied, but much of it comes through experience with employers and situations and through making the most of every opportunity to increase the fund of information. The placement officer who knows the conditions in business, industry, and education through actual personal experience is invaluable as a source of information and advice. If placement possibilities include educational positions in higher institutions and private schools, a library of institutional bulletins and catalogues systematically kept up to date is of great assistance. A similar collection of information about public-school requirements for employees in various states and cities and about business and industrial firms is also of help.

The successful placement officer needs a large amount of information regarding registrants. Much of this information is procured through forms and blanks which the individual student fills out. These records may ask for name, place, and date of birth; permanent and local address; educational history; all types of experience, including nature, name of employer, and title; details of training; the types of positions the candidate feels he could fill; information regarding travel, experiences in extracurricular activities, and other experiences which may make an applicant valuable to a prospective employer. An additional confidential office form may be filled out which gives a record of salary received in previous positions. Such records and forms are not sufficient, however, for satisfactory estimates of individuals' capacities, abilities, and personalities. Interviews and personal acquaintance are necessary, as well as a wise use of information contained in central personnel record files. References, although not always entirely satisfactory, play a significant part in the credentials of employment seekers. These are usually requested from former employers and faculty members of the institution named by registrants upon forms provided by the placement office. Handling students who are recommended unfavorably is sometimes a problem which can best be met by frankly but discreetly telling the student concerned the difficulties involved. No placement office can safely assume the responsibility of recommending everyone who wishes a position.

The placement office should have access to other student records, scholastic, health, extracurricular, part-time employment (or other remunerative work), on file in the institution. Access to these records is made simple in colleges and universities where there is a bureau of central records. The utmost discretion must, of course, be exercised by the placement office in the use of these records.

In graduate institutions where many of the men students may be married, it is important to know the wife of the candidate. In many instances, wives make or break the man, and, no doubt, many readers can recall cases where a man would have become a leader in his field if it were not for his wife. Reynolds goes so far as to advocate the wife's registering with the placement office too.[1]

Skillful placement officers can effectively evaluate and present the qualifications of candidates to prospective employers. Evaluations of strong and weak points of applicants, objectively and fairly made, is necessary, not only in making a choice of individuals to suggest to

[1] REYNOLDS, R. G., "The Human Side of Placement," *Report of the National Association of Appointment Secretaries*, 1924–1928, p. 5.

employers, but also in saving an employer's time and energy. Most employers wish to state the qualifications and type of person they desire, leaving the weeding out of possibilities to the placement officer, often not interviewing more than five or six applicants for any one position.

The relationships existing between the placement office and its registrants should be mutually sympathetic, constructive, cooperative, and based upon a knowledge and understanding of each other's problems. Such relationships will be achieved largely through the counseling or guidance program of the placement office. Such counseling may be given from the point of view of placement. It should be a continuous process beginning with selection for and admission to the college or university and continuing as long as the individual has need for the placement office after graduation. Most counseling programs of this type are inadequate and this inadequacy may be due to the lack of close tie-up of placement policies with admission and educational policies. The difficulties of and demands upon the placement office should be understood by those responsible for admission and educational policies in the institution. It is important that the general counseling program of the institution include vocational guidance from the placement point of view. The placement office can disseminate frank and accurate information that is very valuable to the student.

The placement officers are important members of the counseling program of the college. Students need and appreciate assistance with letters of application, with interviews, and with professional ethics. They need to learn that each interview or application for a position may actually develop into a position, and that whether it does or not depends largely upon the candidate. They need to realize the importance of personal appearance and of personality assets and liabilities. They need to understand the part religious and racial characteristics may play in employment, as well as the provincial features of positions in certain localities. Students need to plan their training in such a way that they will qualify for the type of positions in which they are interested, and they need to realize that a liberal arts education does not prepare directly for jobs. Boring's employment survey of 1931–1934 supports this fact: many more graduates of engineering and business are placed just out of college than are graduates of arts and sciences.[1]

The placement office needs to develop techniques for compiling many different types of information which are essential if the office is to function to the highest degree of efficiency and productiveness. Accurate information regarding opportunities for employment in business, industry, and the professions is important. Successful vocational guidance is based upon such facts. Most placement offices find that their employment constituency is centered in certain geographical areas and much valuable information can be gathered if representatives of the placement office visit employment centers throughout these areas. Not only is this a method of collecting information, but it is also a means of making new contacts for employment. Employers may be asked to outline the qualifications of employees they need, the training they should have, the vocational ladders employees will have to climb, the range of salaries, and the personnel policies of the firm or institution. This plan may prove to be educational for the employers as well as for the college placement officer, for employers can be encouraged to think farther than mere *status quo* in regard to their policies of employment and promotion, clarifying their own purposes and goals. The placement officer who learns what employers in the business, industrial, and professional fields expect of graduates of colleges and universities is then able to determine in what way his institution is meeting these needs and in what way

[1] BORING, M. M., "Employment Data for Recent College Graduates; College Graduate Placement as of November 1934," *American College Personnel Association Yearbook*, 1935, p. 34.

the educational program of the college or university is failing to accomplish what it might.

Whitney tells us that industry wants men who have shown well-directed purpose in their training, who are well oriented in the world in which they live, who have integrated personalities, and who are not handicapped by damaging viewpoints.[1] Whitney believes colleges and universities may well question how satisfactorily their product is meeting these standards.

Other types of information of value to the placement office require a system of running tabulation and interpretation. Statistical facts often show trends that indicate the necessity for new policies and new emphases. Up-to-date knowledge of the total number of registrants, the number on the active list (by "active" is meant those who wish to be placed in positions, being either unemployed or wishing to leave the position held), the number of inquiries, the number of placements, etc., is invaluable in indicating the desirable extent and direction of placement activity. Such information and additional facts may be ascertained by categories and classifications of different types, as well as by monthly and yearly surveys. To gain this information careful records must be kept by a clerical staff which understands the value and importance of careful and accurate records.

Records not only should provide data regarding any individual registrant or employer but also should provide group statistics by which the entire placement situation can be quickly summarized and evaluated from many points of view. Use of the Findex system; visible filing with a plentiful use of tabs; or, if possible, a Hollerith machine, all make for quick, constant, and accurate appreciation and control of the situation.

Each placement office will no doubt work out its own methods for securing contacts with vacancies in the

[1] WHITNEY, R. E., "What Does Industry Want from the University?" *American College Personnel Association Yearbook*, 1936, pp. 51–53.

employment field. Some offices do not contact vacancies of which they learn indirectly but wait until the employer asks for nominations for the position. Others make no aggressive efforts to secure new employer contacts, while still others have representatives in the field for this specific purpose. Perhaps the best means of securing openings in employment and new employer clients is the publicity that comes from work well done. Efficient, dependable service and placement of candidates of high caliber who become successful in the field are the best and most lasting recommendations of a placement office.

Any successful placement officer will say that follow-up is one of the most important angles of a placement program. After a certain length of time has elapsed from the time a student or graduate has been placed in a position, it is often desirable for the college placement director to write the employer asking for details of the student's strong and weak points in the particular position. The employer then knows that the institution is still interested in the employee and has a genuine desire that the needs of the position should be satisfactorily met. Information given by the employer is invaluable when the registrant desires to be placed again. Such a letter may also elicit information concerning other vacancies in the firm or institution. The correspondence may also bring to light certain problems the employee must face in that particular job and may increase the sympathy and understanding with which he is handled by the placement office.

Although it is expensive to send a representative of the placement office into the field actually to visit employers and employees on the office lists, yet this method often bears fruits which correspondence cannot. Talking situations over in person, particularly if the representative is tactful and wise, may result in excellent cooperation among all concerned. We have already suggested that a placement office representative may visit employment areas making new contacts and studying employment conditions. This representative may advantageously combine these functions with the follow-up of those already placed. This same individual may likewise be utilized simultaneously in developing alumni relationships of the institution, through personal calls upon alumni and appearances at alumni club meetings in the districts which he visits.

The follow-up program of the placement office should be based upon the ideal of a continuing spirit of cooperation with its clients. Students should not feel that once they have been placed, the placement office is no longer interested in them. Their success in the vocational world brings credit not only to them but to the institution, and whatever help and service the placement office can give them rebounds to its benefit and to that of the college or university.

In many institutions, the different departments and schools operate separate placement bureaus for their own specialized students. This is particularly true in many large universities. This type of placement has its advantages, for the faculty in these smaller placement units know their students well and often are personally acquainted with the employers who rely and depend upon the judgment of individual faculty members. Decentralized placement has its merits, but there should always be some coordination through a central placement office. The latter can keep in touch with the activities of the smaller decentralized units, maintain a close contact with their problems, in many ways coordinate their efforts, and help bring about a consistent, sound university placement policy.

There should be some coordination of the placement office with the part-time employment office. The establishment of definite policies and occasional conferences between the respective heads of these two offices will do much to bring about desirable cooperation. Their problems are closely related; many part-time positions may develop into full-time positions, and each of these separate offices may acquire leads on employment, either part-time or full-time, for the other.

It is absolutely essential for a placement office to maintain a high degree of office promptness and efficiency. These qualities are of supreme importance in placement and demand an office staff painstakingly careful with detail and routines.

The size of the placement office staff will depend, of course, upon the extent of the placement program. The office should be headed by a person who is trained in personnel work with as many assistants as are necessary to handle the program of placement. The qualifications necessary for the head of the office are also important for members of his staff, with the exception, of course, of the clerical staff. A placement director must know personnel techniques and research techniques. He must be a good executive, the sort, furthermore, who never loses sight of the fact that he is dealing with human beings. He is not a salesman but an educator who must find a proper balance between educational and business policies. He is a better placement officer if he has had vocational experience outside as well as in educational fields. He should preferably have a teaching relationship to students and should, if possible, teach a class or two. The director of the placement office should desirably have faculty rank and sit on faculty committees, particularly the admissions and student financial-aid committees. He must be the sort of person who easily establishes relations with faculty members and must maintain a close friendly contact with them, especially with those who are most interested in placing their major students. He should combine information, understanding, sympathy, and good judgment in his dealings with the many students with whom he comes in contact.

The expense of operating a placement office is often so great that it is questioned by the institution because of the drain that it makes upon the instructional budget. Accurate estimates of the actual cost of the placement service per registrant should be computed by each institution. Over against this cost must be weighed the value of the placement office in terms of service given students, faculty, alumni, and society in general.

BIBLIOGRAPHY

BARBOUR, LILLIAN M.: "A Diagnosis of Teacher Placement and Need for Educational Guidance," *American College Personnel Association Yearbook*, 1935, pp. 53–57.

BORING, M. M.: "Employment Data for Recent College Graduates; College Graduate Placement as of November 1934," *American College Personnel Association Yearbook*, 1935, pp. 34–36.

BRIDGMAN, DONALD S.: "Advice Given by Employers to Those Coming to Them for Help," *American College Personnel Association Yearbook*, 1933–1934, p. 41.

"Committee on General Placement Report," *American College Personnel Association Yearbook*, 1933–1934, pp. 31–38.

"Committee on Teacher Placement Report," *American College Personnel Association Yearbook*, 1933–1934, pp. 39–48.

DAVIS, VICTOR M.: "Factors Involved in Effective Teacher Placement," *American College Personnel Association Yearbook*, 1936, pp. 71–75.

FISHER, CHARLES A.: "Teacher Placement Guidance," *American College Personnel Association Yearbook*, 1935, pp. 51–53.

FRASIER, GEORGE WILLARD: "Teacher Placement Selection of Students for Teacher Education Institutions," *American College Personnel Association Yearbook*, 1936, pp. 65–68.

GARDNER, D. H.: "Placement Service," in *Evaluation of Higher Institutions*, vol. 5, pp. 182–191, University of Chicago Press, Chicago, 1936.

GOETCH, E. W.: "Predictive Ratings on Teaching Success vs. Actual Ratings on Teaching Success," *American College Personnel Association Yearbook*, 1935, pp. 45–51.

LINHART, E. A.: "How Educational Institutions Can Cooperate with Industry," *American College Personnel Association Yearbook*, 1936, pp. 54–58.

MILLER, CLYDE R.: "Publicity for a College Placement Bureau," *American College Personnel Association Yearbook*, 1933–1934, p. 43.

NIELD, MARJORY P.: "Summary of the Discussion on Placement of the College Graduate after College," *American College Personnel Association Yearbook*, 1931–1932, pp. 79–82.

PURDOM, T. LUTHER: "Guidance Function and Service of the Teacher's Placement Bureau," *American College Personnel Association Yearbook*, 1933–1934, p. 42.

REED, ANNA Y.: "Teacher Placement—Personnel Characteristics of Effective and Ineffective College Teachers," *American College Personnel Association Yearbook*, 1935, pp. 43–44.

REYNOLDS, R. G.: "The Human Side of Placement," *Report of National Association of Appointment Secretaries*, 1924–1928, pp. 1–5.

ROBERTS, E. B.: "Position Analysis and Classification in Industry," *American College Personnel Association Yearbook*, 1935, pp. 37–42.

WHITE, LEONARD D.: "Opportunities in the Government Service," *American College Personnel Association Yearbook*, 1935, p. 37.

WHITNEY, R. E.: "What does Industry Want from the University?" *American College Personnel Association Yearbook*, 1936, pp. 49–54.

WILLIAMS, LEWIS L.: "Relations of Teacher Placement Services with Registrants," *American College Personnel Association Yearbook*, 1933–1934, p. 40.

Chapter XVI

KEEPING ACCOUNT OF EDUCATIONAL ASSETS AND LIABILITIES, EFFORTS AND RESULTS

Student Personnel Records

The business of recording, filing, and indexing reaches back to the time when people had to chisel data on rocks instead of using paper. The day of hit-or-miss recording, however, is past. We are moving into an age of scientific management in education as well as in business.

Records afford us the best method yet devised for discovering exactly what it is with which we have to deal, enable us to plan and control more carefully the direction our efforts should take, and make it possible for us to evaluate the results of those efforts.

There are two general types of records with which personnel experts are concerned: (1) there are the records that facilitate the administration of the office, that make it possible to give an accurate accounting of one's stewardship, and that serve as legal protection; and (2) there are the personnel records that give, in related form, cumulative data on the development of each student. The first general type of record we shall discuss in Chap. XVII on Office Administration. In this chapter we shall give our attention to cumulative personnel records, their possible contribution to education, difficulties in introducing them, and how to go about setting up a system of cumulative personnel records.

There are many college administrators who have seen enough of the way in which business is willing to modify its practices, ever improving its methods for the sake of financial gain, to believe that education could profitably do the same, even though the reward be merely human development instead of financial profit!

① But there are four reasons that seem to make it difficult for even such college administrators to introduce into their institutions the use of adequate personnel records. In the first place, the weight of inertia in a college faculty tends to be very great. Tenure of office in the faculty group tends so to entrench the *status quo* that change is accomplished with difficulty. The faculty groups are not the only ones, moreover, who resist change in routine; some office clerks, kept on because of the policy of protracted employment in higher education, are willing to spend almost as much effort resisting any change in routine as they would need to spend to learn a new system. Their resistance is often an effective brake on the imagination of their superiors.

In the second place, it is difficult for college administrators ② to do anything about improving their personnel records because a change radical enough to be satisfactory usually involves an initial budget outlay for new forms, new filing cabinets, and the rearrangement of offices. It is often difficult to justify these expenditures to a faculty strongly concerned with propagating its subject-matter fields. The head of a business operated for financial profit, on the other hand, is under the necessity merely of justifying the change in terms of his ultimate objective—financial profit—in order to receive a powerful impetus in the direction of making the initial investment.

In the third place, individuals seem to be either fascinated by records and record keeping, or repelled. Those who ③ enjoy keeping records and who understand the values they possess frequently tend to make the means an end. Those who have never come to appreciate the possibilities which records possess, tend to consider those who enthuse about them to be uninspired, tiresome, mechanistic, entirely without perspective. These two groups, because they tend at the present to be too far apart, create misunderstanding. The first group does not sufficiently understand how to convert records into educational values for individual students; the second group is unwilling to divert any of its energies—even temporarily—from personal work with students and resists records because of the fear that attention to records will mean less direct attention to the individual needs of students and because it does not understand that this temporary diversion might make counseling efforts even more successful. In such a situation, unless strong direction is provided by someone of understanding and vision, a stalemate persists.

In the fourth place, the planning and putting into operation of a good system of cumulative personnel records have come to be a rather complicated job. Only those who have had either sound training or experience in the principles and methods of personnel records are competent to do it. A commercial organization, under similar conditions, would import an expert to study its situation, and to devise and put into operation records that would forward its objectives. Often, when colleges and universities have brought in an "outsider" to provide this service, the interests and receptivity of the faculty are further lowered and resistance to the new ideas effectually raised.

The best method for accomplishing the introduction of a satisfactory system of cumulative personnel records in a college or university seems to consist in getting a committee of alert, influential faculty to study the problem. They should have as their chairman someone who already knows something about cumulative records, or who at least has a good background for quickly acquiring some of the principles—perhaps with the counsel of an outside expert on records.

Such a committee would begin, probably, by attempting to discover what, if any, educational and administrative values a good system of cumulative personnel records possesses. They may find the following to be true:

1. Cumulative personnel records place at the disposal of those who are entitled to it, information about students that is

reliable, accurate, and concise, thus aiding inestimably the process of counseling.

Dean Hawkes has said: "Only by the intelligent use of a cumulative record extending from an early age through adolescence, filled out by a person who knows the difference between the trivial and the significant, and employing all the personnel measurements that are fit to record, can the adviser do his best work."[1]

2. They give information quickly, eliminating the necessity of an undue number of emergency interviews, telephone calls, and the slow process of letter writing.

3. The information they contain is relatively unbiased by subsequent events, having been recorded as soon as it was ascertained. All too frequently memory tends to distort earlier occurrences in the light of later ones.

4. They serve the purpose of coordination by bringing into relationship in one place at one time information that takes on added significance by being related.

5. They serve the purpose of articulation by helping to preserve the essential continuity of processes.

6. They are an indispensable aid to counseling because they describe all the significant experiences of each individual, suggest new possibilities for his growth, and chart the route to new goals.

7. They serve the purpose of evaluation. They afford the only evidence other than snap judgment of the extent to which an institution is actually accomplishing its purposes.

8. They afford a useful basis for placement of the student after college.

Many experts agree that a system of cumulative personnel records, well devised, can, as can nothing else, give an accurate appraisal of the student, both as to what he is, and what he is capable of becoming. They describe growth and achievement in terms of the student's special phase of work. They enable the counselor or instructor to evaluate accomplishment in terms of definite criteria held by the

[1] GRAY, W. S. (Ed.), "Provision for the Individual in College Education," in *Proceedings of the Institute for Administrative Officers of Higher Institutions*, vol. IV, pp. 23–24, University of Chicago Press, Chicago, 1932.

college. They bring all the pertinent information about each individual—his health, his emotional development, his achievement, his intellectual equipment, his interests, his vocational plans, his social experiences, his family background—into relationship and into units that are usable in counseling.

A faculty committee in setting up a system of records might, furthermore, follow some such plan as this:

1. Make an inventory of the information which the institution now has concerning its students. What information, for example, is asked of the high school? What information is obtained from the students when they apply for admission? What accessory information is secured from references, family physician, parents, etc.? What, if any, entering tests are given students and just what do the results of these tests tell about each student? Who of the college staff sees the student early in his college career? What sort of information does each discover and what use is made of it? What insight and other significant information do the teaching faculty, heads of residences, and other personnel officers gain, and what use is made of this? Is there any way of knowing currently what extracurricular activities each student engages in? What are his vocational interests and plans? What is his present economic situation? What provision is there for making a frequent checkup on his health?

This inventory will almost surely reveal how disjointed the educational efforts of the institution are: one officer will possess certain information concerning a student and will be attempting to bring about certain developments based on it, while another officer at the same time may possess unrelated information on which he is attempting to base another plan, in some respects antagonistic to the first.

2. What kind of information is pertinent to the educational aims of the institution? If the aims of the college are narrowly intellectual, if, as certain prominent educators would have it, the college has no concern for character

development, health, vocational future, or social adjustments of the student, then the records should be consistent with this philosophy and should not concern themselves with many of the data which are of great importance to the college which is concerned with the all-round development of the student.

3. Make an inventory of the information which is not now available but which is important to the educational aims of the institution.

4. Consider from what sources this supplementary information can best be secured. From objective tests? From the student directly? From the high school? From the parents? From instructors? From the physician? From other personnel officers? Information is never any better than its source, and records should consist merely of pertinent information in organized form.

5. What methods can best be employed to secure this information? Can questionnaires best be used, the anecdotal method, objective tests, or interviews, physical examinations, autobiography, rating scales? Or can the information desired be best secured by cooperating with the Aiken Commission of the Progressive Education Association, for example?[1]

6. When can the information desired best be secured? Some things can best be asked before a student comes to college. It is possible that the student will write a more illuminating autobiography before he begins to identify himself with the college community. On the other hand, the comprehensive physical examination may best be given as early as possible after the student arrives at college.

7. To whom in the present setup should be delegated the responsibility for "learning" the student in each of the important ways agreed upon?

8. What accessory records should these "primary sources" have and just how can these accessory records best feed into the central cumulative record?

[1] See discussion in Chap. IV.

9. Out of their study this faculty committee might formulate a plan of the various "record areas," such, for example, as health area, scholastic area, social area, etc. Each of these areas can be further analyzed to indicate the persons who can be expected to contribute regularly to them, and the methods that they may employ. The area of health, for example, might perhaps be covered in some such way as this:

Health Record (The following code may be used to indicate persons contributing to the several parts of the students' cumulative record: * specialists, † staff members, ‡ students)
  *A. Medical Examination Record—duplicate copies of form used for admission to the institution to be used at each examination.
  *B. Health Record—cumulative form to be filled in at entrance and at stated intervals during student's college life; e.g.,
    1. Mental health
    2. Emotional health
    3. Physical health—disease record, vaccination, immunization records, height and weight records, etc.
  *†C. Case History Record—"follow-up" of record of "weakness" indicated in B above
  †D. Staff Recommendation Record—cumulative form to be filled in by staff to record reactions observed or to call needs to attention of specialists; e.g.,
    1. Posture
    2. Emotional stability
    3. Speech problems, etc.

10. From this sort of analysis, it is quite possible to begin the actual formulation of "feeding records" to be used by the various contributors to the central record, and the organization of the central cumulative personnel record itself.

There are other considerations, however, that such a faculty committee on records should have in mind:

Should the record system be centralized? Records are probably the best technique available for accomplishing centralization of control, if this is desired. Many personnel experts feel that with sufficient ethical safeguard and with a professional personnel officer in charge, there is no serious drawback and there are many important educational advantages in centralizing records. <u>Coordination, with the consequent elimination</u> of many <u>weaknesses and inconsistencies of educational effort, can be greatly facilitated by the centralization of records.</u>

Should records be decentralized in order that control and responsibility should not become highly centralized? There are a few experts who feel that the centralization of records is very dangerous indeed, that it is undesirable to have personal information about an individual accessible to anyone but the person who originally learned about it. These individuals would have each professor or personnel officer keep a running, written case history of every student with whom he confers. They feel that the counseling process is better if case histories are scrupulously kept. A central office should, they contend, merely have a note from that counselor to the effect that he is keeping a record for a certain student. The professor or personnel officer should then, theoretically, be willing to confer with anyone else who is especially interested in the student with respect to his welfare. In one college which has a psychiatrist in general charge of its counseling, and where every instructor is a "don" to a certain number of students, the instructors are all expected to keep elaborate case histories on their advisees. These the psychiatrist discusses with each instructor periodically, but the case histories are the direct responsibility of the instructor who writes them and are in his personal charge. Insofar as this system operates to develop in the whole instructional staff a personnel point of view, it seems excellent. Insofar as the instructors are given and accept expert help in their counseling, the scheme has great merit. The weakness of the plan lies, of course, in the fact that all instructors are not equally qualified or interested to become counselors as well as scholars, and many of those instructors who are challenged by their counseling relationship with students are not willing to spend the hours necessary to keep careful written records of this relationship. There is the additional disadvantage that some others legitimately concerned with the student's development may not have sufficient access to his records.

Should records contribute to coordination of effort with decentralization of responsibility? This would seem a desirable compromise between a high degree of centralization and complete decentralization. It may even prove desirable to apportion the complete cumulative record among several offices with a clear allocation of responsibility related to each section. These various sections should supplement each other, forming a complete system when coordinated into a functional whole. The difference between this sort of plan and the usual one, where each office on a campus has its own records without any unified plan of records, is that, in the plan here suggested, the various sections are all drawn up with reference to the whole and the whole is planned with reference to the student and the educational aims of the institution; whereas in the usual situation, the records from office to office are planned quite independently of each other, with reference merely to the separate task of each particular office, and the larger aims of the institution and the best interests of the-student-in-all-his-aspects are lost sight of.

Even though records be highly centralized for the sake of coordination and efficiency, there is no reason in that fact alone why counseling should not still very desirably be decentralized. It would, in fact, seem highly desirable for the counseling program to utilize the efforts of all interested, qualified instructors to the utmost limit possible. But instructors will be more apt to continue an active interest if they are given some assistance with recording, as they are also apt to be more amenable to expert help if their work is not carried on in too complete isolation from the efforts of others of the college staff who, whether assigned especially as advisers or not, do learn the student to some extent and do inevitably contribute to his development.

Many institutions which attempt to formulate cumulative records are satisfied to resort ultimately to a form that can be described only as "patchwork." They think through carefully the items that should be included, they even consider carefully many of the principles which should govern the kind of record system they wish to put into operation. But, having done this, they regard the various "record areas" as though they were nothing but little squares and oblongs to be fitted together into the desired dimensions of the card. This sort of method was outmoded in 1928 by the invention of the American Council on Education Committee[1] of its now-famous cumulative personnel record folder. That card made three very valuable contributions: (1) it listed the most significant items of information about a student from the standpoint of a progressive philosophy of education; (2) it took account in its form of every worth-while method of objective measurement; and (3) it very cleverly utilized the dimensions of the card in a way that is significant for counseling. The vertical dimensions of the American Council on Education card are used to portray relationships existing between the various aspects of a student's life at any one time; and the horizontal dimensions indicate the trend that each of those elements is taking week by week. After one fully understands the principle of identifying the dimensions of the card with the time element, he can no longer be satisfied with records that merely throw together squares and oblongs into patchwork form.

The question of how and to whom records of students are to be made available causes concern to a good many institutions. A survey recently made[2] shows the widest possible divergence of opinion among psychiatrists, medical and psychological clinicians, social workers, and educators concerning the ethical use of records. An examination of legal pronouncements on the use of intimate, personal information offers no direct answers. Various professional

[1] American Council on Education, 744 Jackson Place, Washington, D. C.
[2] LLOYD-JONES, ESTHER, "The Ethical Use of Case Records," unpublished manuscript.

codes of ethics afford some general guides but are not very helpful when one examines their application by the professions in various concrete situations. There are some counselors in colleges who refuse to write down most of what students tell them because they feel that it is told to them personally and it would be a breach of confidence to put it into written form. Other counselors feel that it is a part of their professional duty to record everything of significance in order better to understand the problem, in order also to determine what effect their agency should have in the continuing relationship, and in order to have a basis for the improvement of their counseling techniques in general.

There would seem to be ample justification for every counselor to record significant points that occur in his counseling. Certainly a physician is to be commended rather than criticized if his interest in his patients and his scientific interest in improving his own methods lead him to keep careful notes on every patient. The point, it seems to us, is not whether or not to keep careful records concerning students but rather to whom those records should be available and how they should be used.

Good practice would seem to dictate, on our present professional level in education, that there be someone who has had thorough professional personnel training in control of all student personnel records. This person could well be the director of personnel. It should be his responsibility to determine safe local policy with respect to the availability and general use of records. It should be his responsibility to select the clerks to work on the records and to set the standards they should maintain in relation to the records. It would, furthermore, seem to be good policy not to let any records leave the record office except in the hands of someone who thoroughly understands the seriousness of having one mislaid or of carelessly letting one slip out of its folder while passing through a hallway.

Certainly, all instructors and all administrative officers should be encouraged to take a personal interest in students and should be encouraged in any desire they may have for better understanding of the students in whom they are interested. It is a fact, however, that not all instructors and not all administrative officers are professionally equipped to understand cumulative personnel records. It is also a fact that most instructors and administrative officers are eager to discuss students in whom they are interested with someone who may be able to contribute significantly to their better understanding. It would, therefore, seem to be good policy for the director of personnel to rule that student personnel records should be freely available to any member of the instructional or administrative staff, *but always in the hands of some member of the personnel staff who thoroughly understands the relative reliability and significance of the various items recorded and can be trusted to make true and helpful interpretations of the records data.* Under such a policy the personal interest of the instructional staff in students may be increased, mutual understanding of a student and his problems can usually be augmented, better coordination of educational effort can be brought about, and all the evils of unsupervised availability of records can be avoided. The one disadvantage, of course, is that, especially at first, the personnel staff is required to give a generous amount of time to the discussion of each record with each staff member who is interested. If there is any evidence of impatience on the part of the personnel worker, the instructor will not be apt to return. It is essential that the personnel worker, with the student records in his hands, feel a real interest in discussing them with the faculty member. The time consumed, even though it be considerable, could not be spent to the better advantage of the personnel program as a whole.

It is probably desirable, even under the above policy, to have a separate file of information concerning students that is strictly confidential. There are often items of information that it were best even for the student himself to forget.

Certainly such information should not be recorded where it will be frequently brought to view. And yet there is unquestioned value often, if such information can be rigidly protected, in having a written record of it. The file where such information is kept should be a strong one with safe locks and should be in the private office of the ✓ director of personnel. It is probably wise to label it as his personal property, to be destroyed in case his connection with the institution is broken, since it is possible that no one who does not have an intimate understanding of all the conditions surrounding it should be responsible for its use.

The placement of the regular files of personnel records should also be carefully thought out. They should obviously not be easily accessible to anyone who enters the records office, but should be conveniently located for the clerks who will record on them and for others who will resort to them most frequently.

The form in which to keep the record: cards filed inside a manila folder, a card that is itself a folder within which accessory data can be kept, a loose-leaf book for each student which grows sectionally as information accumulates concerning each of the sections of the booklet (health, academic, social, extracurricular, emotional, etc.) or visible filing—all have advantages which should be carefully weighed before final decision is made.

The question of a filing system for the cumulative personnel records must be answered. Should the cards be filed alphabetically for every student in school? Should there be an active file consisting of the folders or cards of every student who is enrolled for the present college session, and an inactive file to which are removed the cards of students who are not matriculated during a given session? Should the files be arranged by classes, or should the whole student body be filed as one large group? Is there any advantage in filing the men and the women students separately for easier location of a card? There is some advantage in being able to begin building up files as applicants for admission are accepted. Some personnel offices assign numbers as each folder is made up. The number 42,001, for example, would be given the first girl accepted as a member of the class of 1942. Girls subsequently accepted as members of the class of 1942 would be given succeeding odd numbers: 42,003, 42,005, etc. Boys of the class of '42 are given even numbers, such as 42,002, 42,004, etc. Files are then divided by classes, as to men and women, and must, of necessity, have a card index file which is arranged alphabetically. It is somewhat clumsy to have to refer first to a card index and then to the main file, but there are compensating values in having each student assigned a case number which can, on occasion, be used without the name.

If it is decided to organize a central system of records, it is probable that the offices that make most frequent use of the records should be brought together in close geographical proximity. It may be necessary to establish offices in vertical as well as horizontal relationship to the office of central records. In this case, the temptation will be to make use of buzzer systems and dumb-waiters in transporting the records back and forth. Libraries have discovered that horizontal transportation is more efficient than vertical and that transportation by tubes is to be preferred to transportation by dumb-waiters or messenger.

The desirability of duplicating records for the sake of decentralization of counseling should be carefully considered. Certain colleges have, for several years, employed clerks at periodical intervals to transfer information from central records to the records kept by faculty advisers, and from the records of faculty counselors to the central records. In one such institution studied by one of the authors where there was a group of 500 freshmen, and where clerks were paid at the rate of 50 cents per hour, it cost 27 cents per student to make these duplications at the end of the first semester.

Hand copying is laborious and always involves the possibility of errors. If it seems desirable in an institution to duplicate records (and there is always a certain amount of this that is absolutely necessary, if it is only the report of grades to students and transcripts of credits from one institution to another), we would recommend careful consideration of one of the new processes of duplicating records mechanically. One such process involves the purchase of a machine which costs about $1,400. With this machine, duplicates of records 10 by 11 inches can be made for 2 cents a copy, including labor cost and depreciation on the machine. From 5,000 to 6,000 records can be duplicated in 6 hours. The duplicating can be done overnight, so that records are not taken out of use during office hours. One institution, which is about to revise its record system and counseling plan, intends to set up a central office of records, make use of the new duplicating system, and send to each faculty counselor before registration a copy of whatever information has already been acquired about his advisees. The faculty counselor will make notes on his copy and return it at stated intervals to the central office, which will transfer significant information to the master record, sending the faculty counselor an up-to-date copy at periodical intervals. Thus this institution hopes to facilitate a system of centralized records, coordination of educational effort, and decentralized counseling.

There is always much discussion in personnel circles concerning cumulative student personnel records and their value for personal counseling. This is of vital importance, but it is also important for an institution to know something about its student body as a whole and by groups. It is now usually such a difficult task to attempt to find out how large a proportion of the student body has this or that characteristic that constructive curiosity in this direction lags out of sheer unwillingness to undertake the laborious and expensive counting involved. As a result, changes in educational policy are made on the basis of "hunches," he influencing most who persuades most eloquently.

An increasing number of colleges and universities are recognizing that it is worth while to make use of machinery such as the Hollerith in order to know at any time—and almost instantaneously—the combinations of qualities with which they have to deal in their student bodies. With recent revisions in coding for the Hollerith machine, it becomes a simpler matter than formerly to establish a system that will place at the fingertips of college administrators important facts about the student groups for whom educational programs have been set up.

Additional points to consider in setting up an adequate system of records are to be found in the discussion of office administration (Chap. XVII). It seems worth while to stress here again, however, the fact that it is important not to attempt to impose a new system of records, no matter how excellent, upon an unsuspecting campus. A wise administrator will utilize educational method just as carefully in enlisting the interest of the instructional and administrative staff in student personnel records as he would in the classroom. The project method, visual education, field work, pressure of competition, persuasion, and appreciation are all methods that have been known to work as well with faculty and office employees as they do with undergraduate students!

Having worked out a cumulative personnel record that seems really to meet the needs of one's institution, experience has proved that it is necessary to write a careful manual of directions for its use, so that lack of uniformity and lack of understanding need not prove a mounting obstacle to the utilization of a good record card and a good plan.

It is fairly well recognized now that, human nature being what it is, no one card, in precisely the same form, will ever adequately serve more than one situation. There is no easy road to an educational paradise via someone else's cumulative record system; there is even no royal road to salvation via one's own. But the knowledge of what one is trying to do, embodied in good cumulative personnel record forms that make possible control and evaluation of the process, will certainly aid materially rather than hinder the complicated process which we know as higher education.

BIBLIOGRAPHY

American College Personnel Association, "Report of Committee on Records and Research," *Proceedings of the Association*, 1934, pp. 20–25.

American Council on Education, "Central Committee on Personnel Methods Sub-committee on Personal Record Cards for Schools and Colleges," *Educational Record Supplement*, July 1928, no. 8, pp. 12–52.

American Council on Education, "Central Committee on Personnel Methods," in *Measurement and Guidance of College Students*, pp. 1–56, Williams & Wilkins Company, Baltimore, 1933, xi + 199 pp.

BENTLEY, JEROME H.: *The Adjustment Service*, American Association for Adult Education, New York, 1935, 64 pp.

CAMPBELL, S., and S. M. STURTEVANT: "Office Requirements of a High School Dean of Girls," *American School and University Yearbook* 4th annual ed., 1931–1932, pp. 91–92.

CLARK, MARY AUGUSTA: *Recording and Reporting for Child Guidance Clinics*, Commonwealth Fund, New York, 1930, 11 + 151 pp.

DOLLARD, JOHN: *Criteria for the Life History*, pp. 1–288, Yale University Press, New Haven, 1935.

Educational Records Bureau, "1935 Achievement Test Program in Independent Schools," *Educational Records Bureau Bulletin* 15: 5–57, 1935.

Educational Records Bureau, "Judging and Recording Pupil Characteristics," *Report of Second Conference of Educational Records Bureau*, 1933, pp. 68–89.

FLEMMING, C. W.: *Pupil Adjustment in the Modern School*, Teachers College, Bureau of Publications, Columbia University, New York, 1931, 94 pp.

GRAY, W. S. (Ed.): "Provision for the Individual in College Education," in *Proceedings of the Institute for Administrative Officers of Higher Institutions*, vol. IV, University of Chicago Press, Chicago, 1932, 262 pp.

LEESECKER, W., and F. C. SEWELL: "Legal and Regulatory Provisions Affecting Secondary Education," *U. S. Government Pamphlet* 39, 1933, 17 pp.

McCONN, MAX: "Educational Guidance is Now Possible," *Educational Record*, 14: 475–499, October, 1933.

MORT, PAUL R.: *Individual Pupil Programs*, Teachers College, Bureau of Publications, Columbia University, New York, 1929, 3 + 31 pp.

MURPHY, LOIS B.: "When School Records Display Insight," *Progressive Education*, 11: 467–473, December, 1934.

National Society for the Study of Education, "Educational Diagnosis: The Administration of a Program of Diagnosis and Remedial Instruction," *Thirty-fourth Yearbook of the National Society for the Study of Education*, 1935, pp. 501–523.

SCOTT, CLOTHIER, and MATHEWSON: *Personnel Management*, McGraw-Hill Book Company, Inc., New York, Chaps. 2, 3, 4, 5, 1931.

STEPHENS, WINSTON: *Educational Records Bureau Handbook for Independent Schools*, (mimeographed) Educational Records Bureau, New York, 1933, 148 pp.

STEVENSON, G. S., and S. SMITH: *Child Guidance Clinics*, pp. 106–107, 167, Commonwealth Fund, New York, 1934.

STURTEVANT, S., and H. HAYES (Ed.): *Deans at Work*, Chaps. 1, 2, 3, Harper & Brothers, New York, 1930.

WOOD, BEN D.: "Major Strategy of Guidance," *Educational Record*, 15: 419–444, October, 1934.

Chapter XVII

ADMINISTERING THE PERSONNEL OFFICE

Office Administration

While methods and procedures are important to good office administration, the establishment and maintenance of the right sort of personal and group relationships are also of basic importance. Whether the executive be the head of a large corporation or of the personnel division of a college or of one of the personnel services, his problems of administration are much the same and involve prominently problems in human relationships. Nor are there any tricks for insuring desirable relationships. These are conditioned directly by the sort of person who is in charge of the organization or office. But since relationships are amenable to cultivation and since the best administrators are always seeking to improve the effect they have upon the relationships in which they are involved, the following principles may be of some value. They were formulated by Professor Vladimir Karapetoff of the Engineering School of Cornell University and have had the enthusiastic approval of some successful business executives.

The good administrator believes in:

Accuracy.—Accuracy in all acts, statements, reasoning, workmanship, appointments, promises, in fact, in everything that is associated with him or the name of his organization.

Honesty.—Honesty toward associates, superiors, subordinates, clients, competitors, beggars, benefactors, and especially toward his own conscience.

Promises.—He believes in fulfilling his promises in spite of all obstacles, and even against his own advantage.

Initiative.—This usually means helping others without being told to do so and without being obnoxious.

System.—Order, and self-discipline for the sake of those with whom he is associated. He does not tax his memory beyond reason, recognizing that an omission or a mis-statement may mean injury to someone.

Harmony.—He believes in harmonizing views whenever possible and in foregoing the mention of a person, creed, or principle for the sake of friendship with those to whom the name may be offensive.

Breadth.—He believes in being open-minded, because he remembers many a case when he was afterward glad that things did not happen his way, and others when he was equally sorry that they did.

Appreciation.—He believes in giving full credit to others. Real worth cannot be hidden long, and a thief is not far-sighted.

Cooperation.—A lasting monument is usually the result of wise and unselfish cooperation wherein everyone works on the part for which he is best fitted and is so busy and interested he forgets to hew his name on his own stone.

Posting Superiors.—He believes in keeping his superiors posted on what he is doing. Having finished a task, he reports at once, or convinces his chief that when he does not report the job is progressing effectively.

Springing Surprises.—No surprises should be sprung on associates or subordinates in the form of an unexpected official act or letter. It is both wise and honorable to discuss a matter informally with those interested and find their attitude before taking a decisive step.

Persuasion.—He believes in persuasion rather than command for the same reason for which we prefer an electrically started auto. Incidentally, the most efficient organizations are those in which men understand what they are doing and believe in the method of procedure.

Mobilizing Resources.—He believes in mobilizing the resources of the organization when an important problem arises. He sees to it that those whose skill or knowledge exceeds his are drawn into the discussion and not kept out because of his selfishness.

Even more basic than a conscientious attempt to follow a set of principles, no matter how excellent, is the general adjustment of the administrator himself toward life. We have known some administrators who seemed to wish desperately to give appreciation where it was due, but who were still unable at crucial moments to give spontaneous, genuine appreciation to others, perhaps because of some lack of basic security within themselves. This same lack of basic emotional security makes others derive a temporary glow from repeating uncomplimentary information about an acquaintance or friend. A basic lack of confidence in others may make an administrator constantly interfere with the work of his subordinates in a way that cripples their growth. A lack of physical reserve, jittery nerves, personal problems of one sort or another may all complicate the relationships of an office to such an extent that no amount of good office routine can possibly compensate for it.

Assuming, then, that the administrator understands his own personal problems and is working at them successfully; that he has certain basic principles which guide his course so that the relationships between him and his assistants, between the various assistants themselves, and between his office and other offices are operating constructively; what else can the administrator of a personnel office do to insure the satisfactory operation of his office?

Certainly any administrator, if he is to be successful, must understand what the responsibilities of his office are. Many colleges and universities violate one of the basic principles of sound administration in being unwilling to clarify and keep clear the lines of administrative responsibility and the various functions of the respective administrative and personnel officers in the institution. It is easy to understand why this should be true where tenure of office is traditional and where age and length of service tend to an unusual extent to bring respect and power, but it is not to be condoned, because it is in opposition to the laws of sound administration. A wise personnel officer will help the chief executive of his institution patiently to work out a tentative plan of organization, which, after trial, may need to be modified and which will certainly need frequent review if the situation is not to revert to one of confusion and misunderstanding. Such a plan should evolve from painstaking consultation with all who are involved and must not, if it is to have any chance of success, be "sprung" on the group concerned.

Personnel offices, established originally to provide leadership, coordination, and counsel, often get cluttered up after a while by a myriad of routine duties that may eventually tend to defeat the main purposes for which the office was established. Directors of personnel and deans should review their activities regularly to find out to what extent their time is being devoted to "social traffic," *i.e.*, to such activities as inspection, supervision and listing of available lodgings, statistical information of scholarship averages of groupings of students, supervision of student elections, registration and regulation of social functions, ruling on individual exceptions to nonacademic regulations, and other activities, all of which are marginally rather than centrally important to the main purposes of a personnel office.

Good office administration involves consideration for the location of the office with reference to other offices, interior arrangement of the office, and its equipment and furnishing. It is well worth while, before deciding finally upon the location of the various administrative offices, to study the interoffice lines. The architectural structure of the building will also, of course, determine to some extent how the various offices must be located. The amount and kind of space assigned to each office should be determined by careful study and arbitration rather than by tradition and original possession. Frequently a "dog in the manger" can be persuaded to move to some other space quite peaceably if it can be shown that he can be as comfortably provided for and can, with the other changes that will take place simultaneously, operate his office more efficiently in the new location. Coercion and administrative fiat should always be the last resort; they are often an indication of failure or weakness on the part of the superior officers.

After the general location and amount of space have been decided upon, there should be serious consideration given to the utilization of that space. The various functions to be performed in the office, the kind and size of equipment, number of people to be located in the office, the light, heating, the number of doors desired, and ventilation of the various parts of the office will all condition the interior arrangements. It is helpful to draw a plan of the space to scale and experiment with similarly scaled furniture, trying to visualize lines of traffic and the most convenient arrangements.

Many offices in colleges and universities are ugly beyond description. It is frequently difficult to gain the cooperation of those who should feel a responsibility for doing something about the appearance because these officers usually have long since become accustomed to the look of the building and, in a sense, no longer are able to see it. Up-to-date business managers are beginning to realize that there are relatively inexpensive treatments for floors and woodwork which transform worn, drab wood into a semblance of beauty, and which subsequently cut down substantially on the cost of its care; that color carefully chosen can be even more satisfactory than the universal academic beige; that furniture can be refinished with charming results, that Venetian blinds frequently add a good deal to the appearance as well as comfort. If the head of each office would attempt to remain sensitive to the appearance of his office, we should not have the accumulations of junk piles in and on cupboards, on tables, and even on the floors of the offices. Offices would, instead of becoming more and more impossible, add attractive new touches year by year— a new rug, drapes, good pictures, interesting art objects, attractive vases to hold flowers. Principles of good administration now include consideration of aesthetic values just as surely as they do organization charts and office records.

The success of any administrator is probably in direct ratio to his ability to select, train, and hold good assistants.

A college administrator has one advantage in that he has an unusual amount of information about a large group of selected individuals, former students and graduating students of the college, who are on the whole more favorably disposed toward employment by their alma mater than would be any other equally superior group of nonalumni. The reqirements of a job in terms of maturity must be carefully gauged, but the employment of the cream of each graduating class for a one or two year period has, in many personnel offices, proved an excellent practice. There are, on the other hand, many fairly routine jobs which can more satisfactorily be performed by those who have had only high-school education with subsequent training in stenography and other office techniques. The use of tests, full credentials, and tryout periods are all worth while in the selection of employees.

Especially important is the choice of the person who receives those students and faculty who come to the office. The receptionist does a great deal to set the tone of the office in the minds of those who seek its services. The "most efficient" clerk is not always the most gracious, friendly, discreet person in human relations.

Even though one's selection of assistants has been fortunate, there still remains the importance of training. Not only must each employee learn new skills or adapt already learned skills to the needs of the office, but he must also learn faultlessly the policies of the office, realize that his discretion and trustworthiness must always be above reproach, and realize that character and personality qualities are equal in importance to special skills and abilities.

The employer-employee relationship demands a good deal of the employer as well as the employee. The employer always has a responsibility for looking after the welfare of his employees. Even though some employee may seem indispensable to him, if a greater opportunity opens for that individual and it seems to his best interests to take it, the employer has an obligation to encourage him not to hesitate. Questions of salary, advancement, vacations, considerate treatment in general, all usually rest upon the initiative of the employer. Good employer-employee relationships should not smack of paternalism; the employer should not in any way overprotect an employee from honest, hard effort, both for the sake of the job and for the sake of the employee's own development. But the employer must be on guard constantly to maintain balance of effort in a staff, must really know what is going on among his employees, how effectively each is working, and how well each is developing.

The relationship of employer effort to employee effort is always a delicate one and contains more than a little of the secret of good administration. Some employers are so zealous and full of their own responsibility that they, in effect, do all the work themselves. Feelings of guilt assail them at each effort to really delegate responsibility. There are others who expect their employees to do the work for them, but who supervise every detail closely, checking and rechecking to the desperation and confusion of those attempting to carry out their assignments. There are others who administer by giving orders, expecting them to be carried out, punishing for failure in execution. And, finally, there are those executives who know how to energize others to carry on in a program of cooperative effort. They are able to make others feel that they are responsible participants in each process. Only thus are tasks best accomplished, the power of the staff as a whole and as individuals enhanced, and the *esprit de corps* and morale of the staff built.

The question of the availability of the head of an office is another delicate matter. Some overconscientious personnel workers actually place themselves at the disposal of their clientele 24 hours a day. "Adhesions" develop, with serious results ultimately. Others lay themselves open to a state of siege only 8 hours a day. Still others have office hours only 4 hours a day, devoting themselves completely to the needs of students during those hours, but reserving the other working hours during each day to correspondence, research, planning, committee work, and executive sessions of one sort or another. This certainly seems by far the wisest course. There is a sense of being able to give oneself completely to students' problems during the hours set aside for them. Other considerations have no right to intrude. Similarly, other aspects of one's work can be attended to more satisfactorily if there is a minimum of interruption. One successful dean makes himself completely available during the 3 hours he gives to students each day. He has one of his desks in his outer office and stays there completely available to any student who comes in, unless someone comes with a problem that can better be discussed in his quieter inner office. It should not be necessary to urge that office hours be kept scrupulously. Students learn poor lessons when they must wait for a personnel officer who is late for his office hours or who fails to keep appointments.

It may be necessary to stress the wisdom of reserving some time in which to be a person. Some personnel officers, whether men or women, have maternal instincts developed not wisely but too well. They get tremendous unconscious satisfaction out of feeling indispensable and seem to use every effort to make students and staff feel dependent on them. The result is that, some years later, the lack of association with one's peers and starvation of the usual pleasures and experiences of normal mature adults will have rendered the personnel officer much less of a person than he would otherwise have been. He will have been denying in his own life the very principles he has probably been preaching to his counselees and will undoubtedly be paying a penalty for so doing.

Good office administration involves the use of records to aid in the maintenance of order, to insure accuracy, and to implement honesty. There are various classifications of records which a personnel officer should employ.

1. He should make use of those records which aid greatly the smooth operation of the office. Various sorts of interlocking calendars, each person's own calendar of his time commitments, a calendar of the social program as it evolves each year, calendars of various office commitments so that it is possible to tell far in advance in what ways and to what extent the time and energy resources of the total staff are promised; tickler files, wherein memoranda and reminders are filed ahead under future dates so that when those dates are reached there is automatic reminder of tasks to be done, considerations to be renewed, etc.; various other kinds of simple records—perhaps bound together in gummed tablets—can all greatly improve the routine and efficiency of the office.

2. He will institute a system so that it is easy for him to render an accurate accounting of his stewardship. He will have the office keep simple service cards so that it will be possible for him to state exactly what services his office has rendered and so that he can plan a future program based on their analysis. He will keep accurate accounts of all expenditures of money and will give receipts for money received. He will preserve and file various memoranda.

3. He will keep records that serve to clarify understanding and that lend legal protection. He will file letters received, carbons of letters that are sent from his office, various written agreements, parents' and students' requests.

4. He will analyze (preferably as a part of a total records survey throughout all administrative and personnel offices) the functions his office performs and how these may best be implemented by records. He may, for instance (implementing whatever functions pertain to his office), have any or all the following records: a cumulative personnel record for each student; a duplicate copy of the student's admission application; files of information concerning the housing of students—the rooms available, the kinds of rooms students wish, etc.; reports to be used by the health office reporting on the medical examination and treatment of students;

program cards for students; extracurricular activities records and reports both for groups and for individuals; absence slips; excuse slips; various social events reports; social calendar; application blanks for prospective heads of dormitories; files of vocational information; files of part-time job opportunities; files of students wanting part-time work; interview sheets; various kinds of form letters; scholarship application blanks, etc.

Certain general principles should be applied to all these records:

1. The making of even a simple form or record card is not a simple matter. Try out every new form a number of times on persons not familiar with it before it is printed, even tentatively.

2. All questions or statements should be clear and direct and no more than one interpretation should be possible for each item.

3. The information should be grouped, not only according to space requirements, but also by subject matter and, if possible, by chronology.

4. Every record form of every sort should have spaces prominently calling for date and signature of the person who takes the responsibility for recording the information. It is amazing in any survey of college administrative offices how much information on records and forms is quickly rendered unreliable because the date of recording is unknown or because the source of the information is no longer known. It must be remembered that the importance of any fact depends upon when it was known to be true as well as upon who thought it to be true or important enough to be recorded.

5. As many records as possible should be devised in such a way that students themselves can fill them out. This is a great economy of clerical time but frequently involves a sacrifice in legibility and completeness. To avoid this sacrifice, consider the use of items-to-be checked, or items-to-be-underlined to afford an answer. These minimize

writing, save much time, present the data in graphic form, make them readable at a glance and give results in a more uniform way. Consider also the desirability of furnishing students with supervision while they are filling out their various records. Frequently, if there is someone on the job while the students are filling in records, to call attention to an oversight or to answer a question, important omissions or errors may be avoided.

6. The appearance of a card is important. The purpose of a record somewhat determines its size and shape, but a record form that is too small usually results in a crowded card or in one providing insufficient information. A card that is unduly large is clumsy to handle, and frequently encourages too great detail. The use of margins, the type of printing used, the color of the printer's ink, the spacing, and the quality of paper are all important to the appearance of a card. It is also worth while to consider the use of a standard brand and color of ink for recording, a certain type of pen, and the possible use of rubber stamps, and whether or not the record should be made to fit into a typewriter.

7. Certain records are of strictly temporary usefulness, while others are more or less permanent in value. A cheap quality of paper may well be used for temporary records, but, for permanent records that are to have much handling, a good quality of paper or cardboard should be used. Certain kinds of cardboard bend or become dog eared in vertical files. Not all kinds of stock take ink well.

8. Consider the use of gummed pads for some records, the possible usefulness of having from 6 to 12 gummed pads mounted on one large board for convenience in recording and locating temporary memoranda.

9. Consider the use of colored paper and cards. Color is sometimes very convenient for quick location of information, but be sure that the colored stock will not fade.

10. Remember that highly glazed stock can be very wearing to look at for long periods as one may have to do in recording. A shade of buff is easier to work on than white.

11. Consider the use of colored marginal tabs for quick reference.
12. Have the name of the institution and the date and number of the record form printed inconspicuously on every one. This proves a convenience in identification of record forms, and in reordering new stocks of records.
13. Visit good office supply shops occasionally for new ideas.

Good administration dictates the compilation of an annual report, based on the daily service cards faithfully kept, and a résumé of calendars. The report should show clearly the purposes of the office as well as the extent to which these have been furthered during the year, all focused by constructive imagination. The writing of a report can be a very valuable experience for the head of any project. It requires the reexamination of purposes, and a frank facing of the extent to which these are being accomplished. It is conducive to the reformulation of purpose, and can prove a powerful impetus to better achievement.

A wise administrator will make use of councils to supplement his wisdom. Councils need have no authority other than that which is derived from the respect accorded to cooperatively derived wisdom. It is worth while to give careful thought to the composition of one's councils—the purpose which each should serve; the size of each; what, if any townspeople, students, and faculty should be included on each; how long a time each should serve; when and how often each should meet, etc.

Administration that conceives of itself as the hander-down-of-fiat, as the big stick, as the deliverer of wisdom and the law is outmoded and only briefly effective. The function of administration is to serve humbly in a cooperative endeavor, to stimulate the desire of a group to set its course, to watch the compass to be sure that the course is being followed, and to coordinate effort and maintain morale in order that the best progress be made.

Bibliography

BURKE, A. J.: "School Executive's Office," *School Executives*, 54: 181 ff., February, 1935.

CLARK, MARY A.: *Recording and Reporting for Child Clinics*, Commonwealth Fund, New York, 1930, 11 + 151 pp.

O'SHEA, HARRIET E.: "Development Organization and Administration of a Personnel Program," *Report of the Thirteenth Annual Meeting of the American College and Personnel Association*, 1936, pp. 11–16.

PARTRIDGE, F.: "Administrative Offices," *Journal of Higher Education*, 6: 367–370, October, 1935.

PIETENS, ALEIDA J.: "Administrative Duties," *National Association of Deans of Women, Twenty-third Yearbook*, 1936, pp. 149–150.

RICE, G. A., and FLEMING, P.: "Administration of Guidance," *University High School Journal*, 14: 3–8, June, 1935.

SCOTT, CLOTHIER, and MATHEWSON: *Personnel Management*, McGraw-Hill Book Company, Inc., New York, 1931, 546 pp.

STURTEVANT, SARAH M., and HARRIET HAYES (Ed.): *Deans At Work*, Harper & Brothers, New York, 1930, 290 pp.

WARD, MERLE SCOTT: *Philosophies of Administration Current in the Deanship of the Liberal Arts College*, Teachers College, Bureau of Publications, Columbia University, New York, 1934, no. 632, 128 pp.

WILLIAMSON, E. G.: "To Avoid Waste," *Journal of Higher Education*, 8: 64–70, February, 1937.

Chapter XVIII
STUDYING THE OBJECTIVES, PROCESSES, AND RESULTS OF THE PERSONNEL PROGRAM

Research and Evaluation

A successful business or industrial concern frequently and regularly takes an inventory of its assets and liabilities, resets its goals (whether they are in terms of earnings or services), and evaluates general policies. Long experience and the need to meet competition have taught business officials the usefulness of frequent evaluation upon the basis of facts. Education has not to any considerable extent felt this necessity, nor have the same factors emphasized the importance of taking stock as they have in business, but educators are more and more coming to see the desirability of knowing the results of their programs and the importance of facts and evaluation in education.

Research and evaluation have an important function in the type of personnel program advocated in this book. It is only through research and evaluation that the institution can determine whether its educational program is approximating its purposes, goals, and standards. Mere opinion as to whether the program is successful is not sufficient. Objective evidence is the groundwork upon which true evaluation is based. Research supplies objective facts, and these become instructive when viewed in the light of the purposes of the personnel program. Research and evaluation assist those in charge of the personnel program to discover what they have to work with; the type and capacities of the students; the nature and force of the influence exerted on them; the result of interacting forces; the type and nature of the equipment, space, and other facilities available and needed; trends and emphasis in their personnel efforts; and the results of their efforts. Research and evaluation may become the basis for changes in policies, for a more effective direction of efforts. Research and evaluation may also become the basis for further needed research and evaluation.

Unfortunately, research is a very high sounding word and much busywork can be glorified by this term without justification. Research, however, should not be undertaken without some worthy purpose, and the end must not be buried in the means to the end. Many of us know of instances where time and money were expended in research which gave results neither important nor significant. Research should discover relationships between what was purposed to be accomplished and what actually is accomplished. Only in this way can leverage be secured for altering purpose and method.

The research undertaken on a campus should not interfere with the ongoing activities of the students or of the offices studied. Services and functions must continue smoothly while research studies are being made, and, if the studies prevent this, they are not properly set up or directed.

Many personnel officers have suddenly discovered that they wished to evaluate a procedure or function only to find that the necessary and essential records were not available. If the purpose of the procedure or function is clearly understood, anticipation of a coming evaluation to determine whether the purpose is being served makes essential the keeping of the necessary records. All personnel records in a college or university are permanent sources of information convenient for research, but they cannot serve this purpose or other purposes unless they are thoughtfully conceived and efficiently and exactly kept. The many demands upon the personnel officer and his lack of time often prevent his keeping records regarding students and incidents which he hopes to be able to remember should the occasion demand. One can find a certain amount of sympathy for the overburdened personnel officer's attitude, but, at the same time, he may be renouncing valuable material needed in an evaluation or research program.

There is oftentimes an unfortunate division between research and the ongoing personnel process: research and evaluation are relegated to a separate and distinct research bureau or staff. A research bureau may have its place in the institutional scheme of things, but, at the same time, every respectable personnel process should make provision for its own continuing self-evaluation and self-criticism.

In recent years, there has been marked activity along research lines in the field of student personnel work. Strang mentions 582 investigations to be found in 10 educational and psychological journals over a period of 10 years,[1] while titles of 196 researches in the field of student personnel work underway in 1932 in collegiate institutions are listed in *The Partial List of Research Projects of the U.S. Office of Education*. Kitson reported in 1934 that the areas in which research is keenest are vocational guidance and placement; characteristics, needs, and backgrounds of students; factors associated with good scholarship; admission and orientation; and the construction and perfecting of instruments of measurement.[2] There is no doubt but that the philosophy of personnel work has reached the point where research can take on a more basic character than studies involving simple counting and classification.

Research in the field of student personnel work may be of two types, that of local significance and that of wider value. Research of local interest, *i.e.*, giving results important only to the institution concerned, may involve methods that are of general interest. Cowley describes methods and techniques of general value in "A Technique for Making a Student Personnel Survey."[3] This consists of an outline

[1] STRANG, RUTH M., "Development in Student Personnel Research," *Teachers College Record*, 35 (2): 120–134, November, 1933.

[2] KITSON, H. D., *American College Personnel Association, Eleventh Annual Report*, Cleveland, 1934, p. 21.

[3] COWLEY, W. H., "A Technique for Making a Student Personnel Survey," *Personnel Journal*, 10: 17–26, June, 1931.

for making an inventory of all the personnel agencies in any institution. Local surveys are of importance for gaining descriptive results of personnel services and functions. They are valuable in discovering what purposes are operating, and their relation to what the purposes of the program should be. Their results are usually, however, of only local significance.

A local survey may be undertaken by a personnel officer going into a new situation. He will wish to keep a careful record of all inquiries, requests, demands, and functions of his office. At the end of each week and month, these should be summarized under specific categories, such as counseling, housing, the social program, extracurricular activities, educational and vocational guidance, discipline, health, financial aid, etc. A careful study of these summaries over a period of 6 months or a year will give him a picture of the student and faculty attitudes toward the office, of student and faculty expectations of the office, what purposes the faculty and students think the office serves, and the number of contacts made by the office. The last may be broken down to show what institutional department and administrative divisions, what academic classes and sexes of students are using the office most frequently, as well as the number and nature of off-campus contacts. The results of this survey provide material enabling the personnel officer to ascertain the purposes his office is then serving and are a means for evaluating these purposes in the light of well-formulated goals which his office should serve. He may discover that other offices are functioning in areas in which his office also has responsibility, and thus he has the means to work out a program of coordination that will prevent duplication of effort. He may also learn the necessity for new emphases in the work of his own office in order that his program may become better directed and more inclusive of all personnel functions.

This type of survey and others may be carried a step farther into the administrative realm. After ascertaining purposes and functions, after their evaluation in terms of well-established purposes, after the redirection of his program (if that is necessary), the personnel officer will wish to control his program and to check accurately whether it is operating as he had planned. This will necessitate a continuous inventory kept in the same manner as that suggested in the initial survey: a continuous record of all inquiries, requests, demands, and services of his office.

The personnel office may wish to make other attacks upon specific problems of local interest. A survey of the number and nature of the penalties inflicted upon the students may lead to a modification of rules and regulations. A study of the number of men living in private homes off the campus and of the conditions under which they are living may result in the erection of a dormitory for men. Careful and accurate case studies of many of the students may provide a basis for a revision of the campus counseling program. Such studies and surveys will make it unnecessary to base changes in policy and procedures upon mere opinion. No doubt the personnel officers and staff will often have impressions that a certain condition or situation or relationship exists, but these impressions should desirably be supported by objective evidence before action regarding them is taken.

Every personnel staff should, in addition to carrying on research of local significance, contribute to personnel research of a more widespread interest, research that is more basic and fundamental for the entire field of student personnel work. The contributions of different institutions may well differ, some staff members may actively participate, carrying on parts or whole studies of national scope, while others may contribute only an active interest, knowledge of what is going on, and a knowledge of the importance of the results to them and to student personnel programs in general.

Development of new instruments for measuring aptitudes and for other diagnostic purposes is needed, as are studies of traits necessary for various occupations. In addition, a great deal of occupational information should be gathered and made available currently to college students. This information should emphasize particularly trends in occupational areas that are attractive to college graduates.

Qualitative rather than quantitative studies are needed in the field of student financial aid, since the vast sums expended in this field have become of national importance. Who should be helped and to what extent is a problem of growing concern, particularly with the entrance of the National Youth Administration into education. The establishment of degrees of need and other bases of selection must rest upon studies of student traits which will foretell contributions to both education and society.

Activities outside of the classroom are of major importance in the lives of students in colleges and universities. Sufficient data are not available regarding these activities, but such data should be collected and interpreted on a national scale. Nor are there sufficient data available concerning the outside-the-classroom relationships between faculty and students and the role these faculty contacts play in student development. Moreover, methods for making follow-up studies of graduates of colleges and universities need to be developed; at the present time it is only a matter of conjecture as to what effect college and university training has had upon the vocational and social adjustments of the thousands of college graduates.

There is relatively virgin territory in the area of sociological and sociopsychological research. We actually know little of the forms student relationships tend to take—and why; of student customs and mores, how they grow and how they variously affect individuals. Student personnel work is now at the stage where basic studies can and must be made if we in this field are not to be content to be merely counters and arrangers of the obvious. Basic research in the personnel field requires a broad, thorough knowledge of the underlying sciences, as well as sound training in statistics and methods of research other than statistics. We have been content too long with studies that involve little else than counting the obvious. We need studies of the nonintellectual aspects of personality, of the different levels of social maturation, of psychotherapy, of the derivation and modification of attitudes, and studies of methods themselves that are more adequate to the problems of the field. We need intensive, thorough case studies carried on over a long period of time in order to obtain a clearer, more effective understanding of how and why college students develop as they do and in order to obtain an adequate understanding of the unit situations that, taken altogether, comprise the college. One personnel officer at the present time, gifted in being able to relate himself understandingly to college students, is making protracted case studies of 25 college students. His purpose is, by getting at their "inner worlds," to obtain a picture of their actual environment in a way that can never be done by an objective study of the environment directly. He expects each case study to run several hundreds of pages in length, even after the elimination of a good deal of material. Another personnel worker, exceptionally gifted in working with groups, is undertaking a study of the dynamics of relationships that, taken altogether, constitute group situations. She is attempting not merely the sort of analysis that might be made of snapshot pictures of the groups; she is attempting to study the groups in motion in order not to distort and render lifeless the very forces which she is attempting to understand. The Adolescent Study of the Progressive Education Association is demonstrating a new and more productive approach to the study of adolescents. The Carnegie Foundation in its follow-up study of the Pennsylvania experiment is demonstrating the value of the time dimension in securing a useful understanding of college students and of situations. Methods being worked out in what is called "sociometry," methods evolved by Lois

Barclay Murphy in her study of the sympathetic reactions of young children, methods being developed by some of those associated with clinics and guidance laboratories, all hold promise of a more significant type of research when applied to the personnel field. We need no longer be under the necessity of dignifying the trivial with the term research.

There are personnel officers on a number of campuses who do not feel that research or evaluation is their concern. This may in part be due to the existence of separate and distinct bureaus of research in the institution. It is our point of view that it is a mistake to separate research and evaluation from the ongoing process. Personnel officers should be intimately concerned to ascertain facts regarding their own program and the various efforts made in connection with it. In instances where separate research agencies are responsible for conducting research and making evaluations of personnel practices, the personnel staff is prone to feel that they and their activities are going to be criticized by nonunderstanding "researchers" and their cooperation may not be so wholehearted as it would be if they themselves initiated and carried out the research. In much of the truly significant research that is yet to be done in this field, only those who are trained in personnel skills as well as research method will be qualified. A research bureau may have a place on the campus: it can become a source of research methods, of trained workers to assist with studies, of statistical experts; it can give advice and counsel in setting up studies. The personnel staff, however, should direct and stimulate its own researches and evaluations. This is a definite part of its responsibility.

In research and evaluation, the danger of bias cannot be stressed too greatly. Often, enthusiasm for a pet idea or for one's own work may prevent an accurate and objective procedure. Personnel workers must guard against this and be as unbiased and accurate in collecting and interpreting data as the most disinterested cold-blooded research expert in any other field.

In almost any institution of any size, there is need for a central clearinghouse for what is being done, for what has been done, and for what is being contemplated in the way of research. Separate personnel and administrative offices may undertake studies for their own enlightenment which are of value to other personnel and administrative units as well. A clearinghouse can prevent duplication, can disseminate information, and can coordinate the entire personnel research program of the institution. The director of personnel on the campus may wish his office to become this clearinghouse, either informally, or formally and officially. He will certainly need to be aware of the researches and evaluations of his own staff; of those of the registrar; of those of the health, the placement, and the financial-aid offices; of those undertaken by the different departments of the college or university, such as psychology, education, sociology, etc.; of those of the heads of residences and the heads of other housing units on the campus, etc.

The need for coordination of research and for knowing what is going on in this field has been felt nationally as well as in individual institutions. The American Council on Education, the American College Personnel Association, the National Occupational Conference, and the National Association of Deans of Women have all established committees to act as clearinghouses for research within these organizations. The American Council of Guidance and Personnel Associations is attempting to coordinate the committees on research of the separate personnel and guidance organizations. Coordination assists the focusing of research problems, prevents duplication and overlapping, and arouses widespread interest in what otherwise might have to remain a study with a small scope.

Whether each member of the personnel staff takes part actively in research or not, he should know what is going on in the general field of student personnel work. Somewhat comparable is the medical doctor who must keep up with all the latest treatments and experiments in his profession whether or not he is able to carry on research of his own. It is true that demands on the time of the personnel staff and the inaccessibility of technical journals play their part in the lack of research knowledge displayed by many personnel workers. Each individual will have to find his own remedy for the lack of time to read and discuss what is going on in his field, but inaccessibility of material is no longer an excuse. The American College Personnel Association has recently originated a news letter containing information about local and general studies and research in the field of student personnel work. Many personnel officers will wish to subscribe also to periodicals and abstracts which will keep them up to date in the field of research. The following is a suggested list for this purpose:

1. *Educational Abstracts*, published February, April, June, October, and December each year by Educational Abstracts, 230 Fifth Avenue, New York. $1.00 a copy, $4.00 yearly.
2. *The Educational Record*, published quarterly by The American Council on Education, 774 Jackson Place, Washington, D. C. $0.50 a copy, $2.00 yearly.
3. *Journal of Educational Research*, published monthly except June, July, and August by the Public School Publishing Company, Bloomington, Ill. $3.30 annual subscription.
4. *Journal of Higher Education*, published monthly by the Bureau of Educational Research, Ohio State University, Columbus, Ohio. $0.35 a copy, $3.00 yearly.
5. *Occupational Index*, published monthly by the National Occupational Conference, 551 Fifth Avenue, New York. $5.00 yearly.
6. *Occupations*, published monthly by the National Occupational Conference, 551 Fifth Avenue, New York. $0.50 a copy, $3.50 yearly.
7. *School and Society*, published weekly by The Science Press, Grand Central Terminal, New York. $0.15 a copy, $5.00 yearly.
8. *Teachers College Record*, published monthly by Teachers College, Bureau of Publications, Columbia University. $0.45 a copy, $3.00 yearly.
9. Publications of the American College Personnel Association, the National Vocational Guidance Association, the National Association of Deans of Women.

BIBLIOGRAPHY

Techniques of Research

ALEXANDER, CARTER: *How to Locate Educational Information and Data*, Teachers College, Bureau of Publications, Columbia University, New York, 1935, 101 pp.

ASHBAUGH, E. J.: "Bibliography of Research Articles Published in 1924," *Journal of Educational Research*, 11: 368–379, May, 1925.
GARRETT, HENRY E.: *Statistics in Psychology and Education*, Longmans, Green & Company, New York, 1926, 317 pp.
GOOD, CARTER V.: *How to do Research in Education*, Warwick & York, Inc., Baltimore, 1928, 298 pp.
———, A. S. BARR, DOUGLAS E. SCATES: *The Methodology of Educational Research*, Edwards Bros., Inc., Ann Arbor, Mich., 1935, 303 pp.
———, ———, ———: *The Methodology of Educational Research*, D. Appleton-Century Company, Inc., New York, 1936, xxi + 882 pp.
HOLZINGER, KARL J.: *Statistical Methods for Students in Education*, Ginn and Company, Boston, 1928, 372 pp.
KELLEY, TRUMAN LEE: *Scientific Method: Its Function in Research and in Education*, Ohio State University Press, Columbus, 1929, 233 pp.
MCCALL, WILLIAM A.: *How to Experiment in Education*, The Macmillan Company, New York, 1923, 281 pp.
MONROE, WALTER S.: "The Constant and Variable Errors of Educational Measurements," *University of Illinois, Bureau of Educational Research Bulletin* 15, 1923, 30 pp.
ODELL, CHARLES W.: "The Interpretation of the Probable Error and the Coefficient of Correlation," *University of Illinois, Bureau of Educational Research Bulletin* 32, 1926, 49 pp.
———: *Statistical Method in Education*, D. Appleton-Century Company, Inc., New York, 1935, 457 pp.
PEARSON, G. A.: "Some Conditions for Effective Research," *Science*, 60: 71–73, July 25, 1924.
PUPIN, M. I.: "Meaning of Scientific Research," *Science*, 61: 26–30, Jan. 9, 1925.
THURSTONE, L. L.: *The Fundamentals of Statistics*, The Macmillan Company, New York, 1925, 237 pp.
TROW, WILLIAM CLARK: *Scientific Method in Education*, Houghton Mifflin Company, Boston, 1925, 158 pp.

Research

American College Personnel Association "Developments in Student Personnel Research," *Proceedings of the Association*, 1934, 67–75.
American College Personnel Association, "Report of Records and Research," *Proceedings of the Association*, 1934, 20–25.
American College Personnel Association, *Ninth Annual Report*, Washington, D. C., 1932, 48–50; *Tenth Annual Report*, Minneapolis, Minn., 1933, 20–25; *Eleventh Annual Report*, Cleveland, Ohio, 1934, 16–21; *Twelfth Annual Report*, Atlantic City, N. J., 1935, 20–33.
American Council on Education, *Personnel Methods*, Educational Record Supplement, 9, 8: 1–68, July, 1928.
BROTEMARKLE, R. A.: "College Student Personnel Problems," Part I, *Journal of Applied Psychology*, 11: 415–436, December, 1927.

———: "College Student Personnel Problems," Part II, *Journal of Applied Psychology*, 12: 1–42, March, 1928.

COUNTS, GEORGE S.: "Procedures in Evaluating Extra-curricular Activities," *School Review*, 34: 412–421, June, 1926.

COWLEY, W. H.: "A Technique for Making a Student Personnel Survey," *Personnel Journal*, 10: 17–26, June, 1931.

———: *The Personnel Bibliographical Index*, Ohio State University, Columbus, 1932, v + 433 pp.

FRANKE, PAUL R., and ROBERT DAVIS: "Changing Tendencies in Educational Research," *Journal of Educational Research*, 23: 133–145, February, 1931.

HARTSON, L. D.: "The Validation of the Rating Scales Used with Candidates for Admission to Oberlin College," *School and Society*, 36: 413–416, Sept. 24, 1932.

HENDMARSH, ALBERT E.: "A Harvard Educational Plan," *Journal of Higher Education*, 3: 171–178, April, 1932.

HOPKINS, L. B.: "Personnel Procedure in Education," *Educational Record Supplement*, 3: 5, October, 1926.

JONES, LONZO: "Personnel Service and Freshman Scholarship," *Educational Record*, 12: 71–83, January, 1931.

KITSON, HARRY D., and EDGAR STOVER: "Measuring Vocational Guidance," *Personnel Journal*, 11: 150–159, 1933.

KNIGHT, FREDERICK B., and R. H. FRANZEN: "Pitfalls in Rating Schemes," *Journal of Educational Psychology*, 13: 204–213, April, 1922.

KORNHAUSER, A. W.: "A Comparison of Ratings on Different Traits," *Journal of Personnel Research*, 5: 440–446, 1927.

LASHLEY, KARL S. (Ed.): *Studies in the Dynamics of Behavior*, University of Chicago Press, Chicago, 1932, xiv + 332 pp.

LIBBY, P. A.: *Personnel Study of Junior College Students*, University of Southern California Press, Los Angeles, 1936, 66 pp.

MONROE, WALTER S.: "Ten Years of Educational Research, 1918–27," *University of Illinois Bulletin* 42, 1928, 367 pp.

ROSS, FRANK ALEXANDER: "Ecology and the Statistical Method," *American Journal of Sociology*, 38: 518, January, 1933.

STRANG, RUTH: "The Relation of the Dean of Women and Research," *Teachers College Record*, 31: 44–49, October, 1929.

———: "Trends in Educational Personnel Research," *Personnel Journal*, 10: 179–188, October, 1931.

———: "Developments in Student Personnel Research," *Teachers College Record*, 35: 120–134, November, 1933.

———: "Research Issues in Student Personnel Work," *Personnel Journal*, 13: 100–105, August, 1934.

SYMONDS, PERCIVAL M.: "Notes on Rating," *Journal of Applied Psychology*, 9: 188–195, June, 1925.

THEISEN, W. W.: "Recent Progress in Educational Research," *Journal of Educational Research*, 8: 301–314, November, 1923.

THURSTONE, L. L.: "What Is Personnel Research?" *Journal of Personnel Research*, 3: 52–56, 1924–1925.

———: "A Program of Research in Student Personnel," *Journal of Personnel Research*, 3: 421–448, April, 1925.

TRABUE, M. R.: "Educational Research in 1925," *Journal of Educational Research*, 13: 336–355, May, 1926.

WOODY, CLIFFORD: "Survey of Educational Research in 1923," *Journal of Educational Research*, 9: 357–381, May, 1924.

YOAKUM, C. S.: "Basic Experiments in Vocational Guidance," *Journal of Personnel Research*, 1: 18–34, 1922.

APPENDIX

The following is a selected list of tests for college students and adults classified according to their use:

INTELLIGENCE TESTS

Individual Test

New Stanford Revision of the Binet-Simon Test (Houghton Mifflin)

Group Tests—Adult Level

Army Alpha (Psychological Corp.)
Army Group Examination, Alpha (Kansas State Teachers College)
Brown University Psychological Examination (Lippincott)
Carnegie Mental Ability Test (Houghton Mifflin)
Detroit Advanced Intelligence Examination (Public School Publishing Co.)
George Washington University Mental Alertness Scale (Center for Psychological Service)
George Washington University Social Intelligence Test (Center for Psychological Service)
Henmon-Nelson Mental Ability Test (Houghton Mifflin)
Kuhlmann-Anderson Intelligence Tests (Educational Test Bureau)
Miller Mental Ability Test (World Book)
Morgan Mental Test (Clio Press)
Ohio State University Psychological Tests (Ohio State University)
O'Rourke General Classification Test (Psychological Corp.)
Otis Self-administering Test, Higher Form (World Book)
Pressey Senior Classification Test (Public School Publishing Co.)
Schubert Information Test (Transient Center)
Thorndike Intelligence Examination for High School Graduates (Teachers College, Bureau of Publications)
Thurstone Psychological Test IV (Stoelting)
Thurstone Psychological Examination for High School Graduates and College Freshmen (American Council on Education)

Nonlanguage and Nonverbal Tests

Army Beta Test (Psychological Corp.)
Cattell Group Intelligence Test (Harrap)
Porteus Mazes (Stoelting)

VISION TESTS

Betts: Telebinocular (Keystone View Co.)
Oculo-photometer: Test for Color Blindness, Visual Acuity and Astigmatism (Psychological Corp.)

Educational Achievement Tests

General Information and Background Tests

Cooperative Contemporary Affairs Test (Educational Records Bureau)
Cooperative General Culture Test (Educational Records Bureau)
George Washington Scholastic Aptitude Test (Center for Psychological Service)
Time's Current Affairs Test (Time, Inc.)

Mathematics

Cooperative General Mathematics Test (Educational Records Bureau)
Detroit Mathematics Examination (Board of Education, Detroit)
Iowa Placement Examination in Mathematical Aptitude (State University of Iowa)
Iowa Placement Examination in Mathematical Training (State University of Iowa)
Progressive Mathematics Tests (Southern California School Book Depository)
Rogers Test of Mathematical Ability (Teachers College, Bureau of Publications)
Schorling-Reeve Chapter Tests in General Mathematics (Ginn)

Algebra

Coleman Scale for Testing Ability in Algebra (University of Nebraska)
Columbia Research Bureau Algebra Test (World Book)
Comprehensive Objective Tests in Algebra (Harlow)
Cooperative Algebra Test (Educational Records Bureau)
Cooperative Intermediate Algebra (Educational Records Bureau)
Detroit Algebra Examination (Board of Education, Detroit)
Douglas Standard Diagnostic Tests for Elementary Algebra (University of Cincinnati)
Garman-Schrammel Algebra Test (Kansas State Teachers College)
Hotz First Year Algebra Scales (Teachers College, Bureau of Publications)
Illinois Algebra Scales (Public School Publishing Co.)
Institute of Educational Research Elementary Algebra Test (Teachers College, Bureau of Publications)
Iowa Every Pupil Test in Algebra (State University of Iowa)
Lee Test of Algebraic Ability (Public School Publishing Co.)
Multiple-purpose Objective Tests in Algebra (Webb-Duncan)
Nyberg Tests and Drills in First Year Algebra (American Book)
Orleans Algebra Prognosis Test (World Book)

Geometry

American Council Solid Geometry Test (World Book)
Becker-Schrammel Plane Geometry Test (Kansas State Teachers College)
Columbia Research Bureau Plane Geometry Test (World Book)
Comprehensive Objective Tests in Plane Geometry (Harlow)

APPENDIX

Comprehensive Objective Tests in Solid Geometry (Harlow)
Cooperative Geometry (Educational Records Bureau)
Cooperative Plane Geometry Test (Educational Records Bureau)
Cooperative Solid Geometry (Educational Records Bureau)
Detroit Geometry Examination (Board of Education, Detroit)
Greene Plane Geometry Tests (Turner E. Smith)
Iowa Every Pupil Test in Geometry (State University of Iowa)
Iowa Plane Geometry Test (State University of Iowa)
Lane-Knight-Ruch Geometry Rapid Drill Cards (Scott, Foresman)
Lee Geometric Aptitude Test (Southern California School Book Depository)
McMindes Achievement Test in Plane Geometry (Public School Publishing Co.)
Minnick Geometry Tests (Public School Publishing Co.)
Multiple-purpose Objective Test in Geometry (Webb-Duncan)
Orleans Geometry Prognosis Test (World Book)
Orleans Plane Geometry Achievement Test (World Book)
Seattle Geometry Test Series (Public School Publishing Co.)
Webb Geometry Tests (Public School Publishing Co.)
Welte-McKnight Geometry World Book (Scott, Foresman)

TRIGONOMETRY

American Council Trigonometry Test (World Book)
Cooperative Trigonometry Test (Educational Records Bureau)

READING TESTS

High-school and College Level

Buffalo Reading Test (University of Buffalo)
Chapman Unspeeded Reading Comprehension Test (Lippincott)
Haggerty Reading Test, Sigma 3 (World Book)
Institute of Educational Research Speed of Reading Test (Teachers College, Bureau of Pbulications)
Iowa Comprehension Tests (State University of Iowa)
Iowa Silent Reading Test, Revised Form (World Book)
Kansas Silent Reading Test III (State Normal School, Emporia, Kans.)
Knode XYZ College Freshman Reading Test (University of New Mexico)
Michigan Speed of Reading Tests (Psychological Corp.)
Minnesota Reading Examination for College Students (University of Minnesota)
Minnesota Speed of Reading Tests for College Students (University of Minnesota)
Monroe Standardized Silent Reading Tests, III (Public School Publishing Co.)
Mount Holyoke Reading Test (Mt. Holyoke College)
Nelson-Denny Reading Tests (Houghton Miffiin)
Ohio State Reading Comprehension Test (Ohio State University)
Ohio State Study Performance Test (Ohio State University)

O'Rourke Survey of Reading (Psychological Corporation)
Progressive Reading Test (Southern California School Book Depository)
Purdue Reading Test (Lafayette Printing Co.)
Shank Tests of Reading Comprehension III (C. A. Gregory)
Thorndike-McCall Reading Scale (Teachers College, Bureau of Publications)
Traxler Silent Reading Test (Public School Publishing Co.)
Whipple High School and College Reading Tests (Public School Publishing Co.)
Wrenn: Study Habits Inventory (Stanford University Press)

English Tests

High-school and College Level

Barrett-Ryan English Test (Kansas State Teachers College)
Charters Diagnostic Language Test (Public School Publishing Co.)
Charters Diagnostic Language and Grammar Test (Public School Publishing Co.)
Clapp's Test for Correct English (Houghton Mifflin)
Clapp-Young English Test (Houghton Mifflin)
Clark Letter Writing Test (Public School Publishing Co.)
Clatworthy Library Test for College Students (L. M. Clatworthy)
Cleveland English Composition and Grammar Test (Houghton Mifflin)
Columbia Research Bureau English Test (World Book)
Comprehensive Objective Tests in Correct English Usage (Harlow)
Comprehensive Objective Tests in Grammar and Composition (Harlow)
Cooperative English Test (Educational Records Bureau)
Cross English Test (World Book)
Davis Tests in English Fundamentals (Ginn)
George Washington University Language Aptitude Test (Center for Psychological Service)
Iowa English Organization Test (State University of Iowa)
Iowa Every Pupil Test in English Correctness (State University of Iowa)
Iowa Grammar Information Test (State University of Iowa)
Iowa Placement Examination in English Aptitude (State University of Iowa)
Iowa Placement Examination in English Training (State University of Iowa)
McClusky-Dolch Study Outline Test (Public School Publishing Co.)
Multiple Purpose Tests in Grammar and Composition (Webb-Duncan)
O'Rourke Achievement Test in English Usage (Educational and Personnel Publishing Co.)
Poley: Precis Test (Public School Publishing Co.)
Progressive Language Tests for High School and College Students (Southern California School Book Depository)
Purdue Diagnostic English Test (Lafayette Printing Co.)
Purdue English Test (Lafayette Printing Co.)
Purdue Placement Test in English (Houghton Mifflin)

APPENDIX

Rinsland-Beck Natural Test for English Usage (Public School Publishing Co.)
Scott-Reed-Weideman English Classification Test (Kansas State Teachers College)
Schutte Diction Test (Public School Publishing Co.)
Shepherd English Test (Houghton-Mifflin)
Starch Punctuation Scale (Public School Publishing Co.)
Trabue-Kelley Language Completion Exercises (Teachers College, Bureau of Publications)
Tressler: English Minimum Essentials Test (Public School Publishing Co.)
Wakefield Diagnostic English Test (C. A. Gregory)
Welling English Composition and Grammar Test (Houghton Mifflin)
Wilson Language Error Test (World Book)

Spelling and Vocabulary Scales

Armstrong-Danielson: Sentence Vocabulary Test (Southern California School Book Depository)
Ayres Spelling Scale (Russell Sage Foundation)
Buckingham Extension of the Ayres Scale (Public School Publishing Co.)
Davis-Schrammel: Spelling Test (Kansas State Teachers College)
Detroit Vocabulary Test (Board of Education, Detroit)
Guy Spelling Scale (Public School Publishing Co.)
Holley Sentence Vocabulary Test (Public School Publishing Co.)
Inglis Tests of English Vocabulary (Ginn)
Iowa Every Pupil Test in Vocabulary and Basic Study Skills (State University of Iowa)
Iowa Spelling Scales (State University of Iowa)
Kansas Every Pupil Test in Spelling (Kansas State Teachers College)
Kennon Test of Literary Vocabulary (Teachers College, Bureau of Publications)
Markham English Vocabulary Test (Public School Publishing Co.)
Minnesota College Aptitude Test (University of Minnesota Press)
Monroe Timed Spelling Test (Public School Publishing Co.)
Morrison-McCall Spelling Scale (World Book)
New York Spelling Tests (Board of Education, New York City)
O'Rourke Survey Test of Vocabulary (Psychological Inst.)
Philadelphia Index and Dictionary Test (Board of Education, Detroit)
Plymouth Educational Tests in Vocabulary (Plymouth Press)
Pressey Test of Technical Vocabularies (Public School Publishing Co.)
Thorndike Test of Word Knowledge (Teachers College, Bureau of Publications)
Turner-Miller: Cross Word Puzzle Speller (Public School Publishing Co.)
Van Wagenen Unit Scales of Attainment in Spelling (Educational Test Bureau)

Composition Scales

Cross Diagnostic English Composition Test (Little, Brown)
Detroit Composition Examination (Board of Education, Detroit)

Driggs-Mayhew National Scales for Measuring Composition (University Publishing Co.)
Hillegas Scale for Measuring English Composition (Teachers College, Bureau of Publications)
Hudelson Typical Composition Ability Scale (Public School Publishing Co.)
Lewis English Composition Scales (World Book)
Pressey-Bowers Diagnostic Tests in English Composition (Public School Publishing Co.)
Pressey-Conklin: Student's Guide to Correctness in Written Work (Public School Publishing Co.)
Seaton-Pressey Minimum Essential Test in English Composition (Public School Publishing Co.)
Van Wagenen English Composition Scales (World Book)

LITERATURE AND APPRECIATION OF LITERATURE TESTS

Abbott-Trabue Exercises in Judging Poetry (Teachers College, Bureau of Publications)
Analytical Scales of Attainment in Literature (Educational Test Bureau)
Carroll's Prose Appreciation Test (Educational Test Bureau)
Cavins Test in Poetry (Public School Publishing Co.)
Comprehensive Objective Tests in American Literature (Harlow)
Comprehensive Objective Tests in English Literature (Harlow)
Cooperative Literary Acquaintance Test (Educational Records Bureau)
Detroit Literature Appreciation Test (Board of Education, Detroit)
Gehlman American Literature Test (Harcourt, Brace)
George Washington University English Literature Tests (Center for Psychological Service)
Hahn: Tests on English Classics (Houghton Mifflin)
Inglis English Literature Tests (Harcourt, Brace)
Iowa Every Pupil Test in American Literature (State University of Iowa)
Iowa Every Pupil Test in English Literature (State University of Iowa)
Lagosa-Wright Literature Appreciation Test (Public School Publishing Co.)
Logan-Parks Literary Background Test (Heath)
Multiple-Purpose Objective Tests in American Literature (Webb-Duncan)
Multiple-Purpose Objective Tests in History of English Literature (Webb-Duncan)
Multiple-Purpose Objectives Tests in the Classics (Webb-Duncan)
New York English Survey Test in Literature Information (Public School Publishing Co.)
Odell Scale for Rating Pupils' Answers to Nine Types of Thought Questions in English Literature (University of Illinois)
Plymouth English Tests in Literature (Plymouth Press)
Stanford American Literature Test (C. A. Gregory)
Stanford English Literature Test (C. A. Gregory)
Stanford Tests in Comprehension of Literature (Stanford University Press)

Foreign Language Tests

General Tests in Foreign Language

    Handschin Language Predetermination Test (C. H. Handschin)
    Iowa Placement Examination in Foreign Language Aptitudes (State University of Iowa)
    Luria-Orleans Modern Language Prognosis Test (World Book)
    Symonds Foreign Language Prognosis Test (Teachers College, Bureau of Publications)
    Wilkins Prognosis Test in Modern Language (World Book)

French

    American Council Alpha French Test (World Book)
    American Council Beta French Test (World Book)
    American Council French Grammar Test (World Book)
    Broom-Brown: Silent Reading Test in French (Southern California School Book Depository)
    Columbia Research Bureau French Test (World Book)
    Comprehensive Objective Tests in French (Harlow)
    Cooperative French Test (Educational Records Bureau)
    Detroit French Examination (Board of Education, Detroit)
    Handschin Modern Language Test in French (World Book)
    Harvard French Vocabulary Test (Ginn)
    Henmon French Tests (World Book)
    Iowa Placement Examination in French Training (State University of Iowa)
    Miller-Davis: French Test (Kansas State Teachers College)
    Multiple-purpose Objective Tests in French (Webb-Duncan)
    Sammartino-Krause Standard French Test (Public School Publishing Co.)

German

    Aiken-Held First Year German Test (Kansas State Teachers College)
    American Council on Education German Reading Scale (Public School Publishing Co.)
    American Council Alpha German Test (World Book)
    Columbia Research Bureau German Test (World Book)
    Cooperative German Test (Educational Records Bureau)

Latin

    Comprehensive Objective Tests in Latin (Harlow)
    Cooperative Latin Test (Educational Records Bureau)
    Detroit Latin Examination (Board of Education, Detroit)
    Godsey Latin Composition Test (World Book)
    Henmon Latin Tests (World Book)
    Holtz Latin Tests (Kansas State Teachers College)
    Hutchinson Latin Grammar Scale (Public School Publishing Co.)
    Lohr-Latshaw Latin Form Test (University of North Carolina)

Multiple-purpose Objective Tests in Latin (Webb-Duncan)
New York Latin Achievement Test (World Book)
Orleans-Solomon Latin Prognosis Test (World Book)
Powers Diagnostic Latin Test (Public School Publishing Co.)
Pressey Test in Latin Syntax (Public School Publishing Co.)
Stevenson-Coxe Latin Derivative Test (Public School Publishing Co.)
Stevenson Latin Vocabulary Test (Public School Publishing Co.)
Tyler-Pressey Test in Latin Verbs (Public School Publishing Co.)
White Latin Test (World Book)

Spanish

American Council Spanish Test (World Book)
Columbia Research Bureau Spanish Test (World Book)
Comprehensive Objective Tests in Spanish (Harlow)
Cooperative Spanish Test (Educational Records Bureau)
Handschin Modern Language Test in Spanish (World Book)
Iowa Placement Examination in Spanish Training (State University of Iowa)
Multiple-purpose Objective Tests in Spanish (Webb-Duncan)
Wilkins Achievement Test in Spanish (Holt)

SCIENCE TESTS

Miscellaneous Science Tests

Comprehensive Objective Tests in General Science (Harlow)
Cooperative General Science Test (Educational Records Bureau)
Detroit Elementary Science Examination (Board of Education, Detroit)
Detroit Social Science Test (Board of Education, Detroit)
Downing: Range of Information Test in Science (University of Chicago Press)
Dvorak: General Science Scale (Public School Publishing Co.)
Giles-Thomas-Schmidt: General Science Examinations (State Department of Public Instruction, Madison, Wis.)
Iowa Every Pupil Test in General Science (State University of Iowa)
Multiple-purpose Objective Test in General Science (Webb-Duncan)
Odell Scales for Rating Pupils' Answers to Nine Types of Thought Questions in General Science (University of Illinois)
Powers General Science Test (Teachers College, Bureau of Publications)
Public School Achievement Test in Nature Study (Public School Publishing Co.)
Ruch-Popenoe General Science Tests (World Book)
Stanford Scientific Test (Stanford University Press)
Van Wagenen Reading Scales in General Science (Public School Publishing Co.)

Biology

Comprehensive Objective Tests in Biology (Harlow)
Cooperative Biology Test (Educational Records Bureau)

APPENDIX

Cooprider: Information Exercises in Biology (Public School Publishing Co.)
Davis: Biology Tests (Metzer-Bush)
Detroit Biology Examination (Board of Education, Detroit)
Hunter-Kitch Mastery Tests in Biology (American Book)
Multiple-purpose Objective Tests in Biology (Webb-Duncan)
Oakes and Powers: General Biology Test (Teachers College, Bureau of Publications)
Objective Unit Tests on Everyday Problems in Biology (Scott, Foresman)
Pressey Biology Test (World Book)
Ruch-Cossman Biology Test (World Book)
Van Wagenen Reading Scales in Biology (Educational Test Bureau)
Williams Biology Test (Kansas State Teachers College)

Chemistry

Columbia Research Bureau Chemistry Test (World Book)
Comprehensive Objective Tests in Chemistry (Harlow)
Cooperative Chemistry Test (Educational Records Bureau)
Detroit Chemistry Examination (Board of Education, Detroit)
Dull: Chemistry Tests (Holt)
George Washington University General Chemistry Test (Center for Psychological Service)
Glenn-Welton: Instructional Tests in Chemistry (World Book)
Iowa Placement Examination in Chemistry Aptitude (State University of Iowa)
Iowa Placement Examination in Chemistry Training (State University of Iowa)
Multiple-purpose Objective Test in Chemistry (Webb-Duncan)
Pershing Laboratory Chemistry Test (Public School Publishing Co.)
Powers General Chemistry Test (World Book)
Rich Chemistry Test (Public School Publishing Co.)
Rivett Chemistry Tests (Northwestern High School, Detroit, Mich.)

Physics

Columbia Research Bureau Physics Test (World Book)
Comprehensive Objective Tests in High School Physics (Harlow)
Cooperative Physics Test (Educational Records Bureau)
Detroit Physics Examination (Board of Education, Detroit)
Fulner-Schrammel Physics Test (Kansas State Teachers College)
Hughes: Physics Scale (Public School Publishing Co.)
Hurd Test in High School Physics (Teachers College, Bureau of Publications)
Iowa Achievement Examination in College Physics (State University of Iowa)
Iowa Placement Examination in Physics Aptitude (State University of Iowa)
Iowa Placement Examination in Physics Training (State University of Iowa)

Kilzer-Kirby: Physics Test (Public School Publishing Co.)
Michigan Instructional Tests in Physics (Public School Publishing Co.)
Multiple-purpose Objective Test in Physics (Webb-Duncan)

Botany

Cooperative Botany Test (Educational Records Bureau)

Zoology

Cooperative Zoology Test (Educational Records Bureau)

Agriculture

Auburn Test for Agricultural Information (Alabama Polytechnic Inst.)
Dickinson Test on Dairy Husbandry Information (University of Missouri)
National Agricultural Tests (Van Cleve Publishers)

Domestic Science and Home Economics Tests

Detroit Domestic Science Test (Board of Education, Detroit)
Detroit Household Mechanics Test (Board of Education, Detroit)
Engle-Stenquist Home Economics Test (World Book)
Frear-Coe Clothing Test (Public School Publishing Co.)
Illinois Information Test on Foods (Public School Publishing Co.)
Leary and Dry: Technical Information Test for Girls (Stoelting)
Multiple-purpose Objective Tests in Home Economics (Webb-Duncan)
Murdoch Analytic Sewing Scale for Measuring Separate Stitches (Teachers College, Bureau of Publications)
Murdoch Sewing Scale (Teachers College, Bureau of Publications)
Stevenson-Trilling Tests in Home Economics (Webb-Duncan)

Industrial Arts

Nash-Van Duzee Industrial Arts Test (Bruce)
Patrick Industrial Arts Test (Independent Press)

History

American

Barr-Dagett Information Test in American History (Educational Test Bureau)
Carman-Barrows-Wood Junior American History Test (World Book)
Clark Exercises in the Use of Historical Evidence (Scribner's)
Columbia Research Bureau American History Test (World Book)
Comprehensive Objective Tests in American History (Harlow)
Cooperative American History Test (Educational Records Bureau)
Denny-Nelson American History Test (World Book)
Detroit History Examination (Board of Education, Detroit)
Ely-King Interpretation Tests in American History (Southern California School Book Depository)
Ely-King Tests in American History (Southern California School Book Depository)

APPENDIX 301

Farley Test of Factual Relations in American History (Farley)
Harlan Information Tests in American History (Public School Publishing Co.)
Iowa Every Pupil Test in United States History (State University of Iowa)
Iowa General Information Test in American History (Webb-Duncan)
Multiple-purpose Objective Tests in American History (Webb-Duncan)
Odell Scales for Rating Pupils' Answers to Nine Types of Thought Questions in American History (University of Illinois)
Plymouth Educational Tests in History (Plymouth Press)
Pressey-Richards Tests in American History (Public School Publishing Co.)
Van Wagenen American History Scales (Teachers College, Bureau of Publications)

European

American Council European History Test (World Book)
Comprehensive Objective Tests in Modern European History (Harlow)
Cooperative Modern European History Test (Educational Records Bureau)
George Washington University Modern European History Test (Center for Psychological Service)
Multiple-purpose Objective Tests in Modern European History (Webb-Duncan)

English

Comprehensive Objective Tests in English History (Harlow)
Cooperative English History Test (Educational Records Bureau)

Ancient and Medieval

Comprehensive Objective Test in Ancient and Medieval History (Harlow)
Cooperative Ancient History Test (Educational Records Bureau)
Cooperative Medieval History Test (Educational Records Bureau)
Multiple-purpose Objective Tests in Ancient and Medieval History (Webb-Duncan)

World

Comprehensive Objective Tests in World History (Harlow)
Cooperative World History Test (Educational Records Bureau)
Iowa Every Pupil Test in World History (State University of Iowa)
Multiple-purpose Objective Test in World History (Webb-Duncan)

CIVICS AND GOVERNMENT TESTS

Almack Test of American Civics and Government (Gregory)
American Council Civics and Government Test (World Book)
Brown-Woody Civics Test (World Book)
Burton Civics Test (World Book)

Comprehensive Objective Tests in American Government and Civics (Harlow)
Comprehensive Objective Tests in Community Civics (Harlow)
Comprehensive Objective Tests in Democracy (Harlow)
Haley: American Government and Civics Test (Harlow)
Hill Test in Civic Attitudes (Public School Publishing Co.)
Hill Test in Civic Information (Public School Publishing Co.)
Hill-Wilson Civic Action Test (Public School Publishing Co.)
Iowa Every Pupil Test in American Government (State University of Iowa)
Magruder-Chamber-Clinton: American Civics and Government Test for High Schools (Public School Publishing Co.)
Mordy-Schrammel: Elementary Civics Test (Kansas State Teachers College)
Odell Scales for Rating Pupils' Answers to Nine Types of Thought Questions in Civics (University of Illinois)
Teeter Objective Tests in American Democracy (McGraw-Hill)

Economics Tests

American Council Economics Test (World Book)
Comprehensive Objective Tests in Economics (Harlow)
Iowa Every Pupil Test in Economics (State University of Iowa)

Geography Tests

Buckingham-Stevenson Geography Tests on the United States (Public School Publishing Co.)
Comprehensive Objective Tests in Physical, Industrial and Commercial Geography (Harlow)
Hill Tests in Physical Geography (Webster)
Multiple-purpose Objective Test in Industrial Geography (Webb-Duncan)
Multiple-purpose Objective Test in Physical Geography (Webb-Duncan)
Philadelphia Map Reading Test (Board of Education, Philadelphia)
Plymouth Educational Tests in Geography (Plymouth Press)
Posey-Van Wagenen Geography Test (Public School Publishing Co.)
Stevenson-Ridgley-Shipman Geography Test on Asia (Public School Publishing Co.)
Stevenson-Ridgley-Shipman Geography Test on Europe (Public School Publishing Co.)
Stevenson-Ridgley-Shipman Geography Test on South America (Public School Publishing Co.)
Wiederfeld-Walther: Geography Test (World Book)

Art Tests

Detroit Art Test (Board of Education, Detroit)
Detroit Lettering Test (Board of Education, Detroit)
Kline-Carey Measuring Scale in Drawing (Johns Hopkins Press)
Knauber Art Ability Test (University of Cincinnati)

APPENDIX 303

Lewerenz Tests in Fundamental Abilities of Visual Art (Southern California School Book Depository)
McAdory Art Test (Teachers College, Bureau of Publications)
Meier-Seashore Art Judgment Test (State University of Iowa)
Thorndike Drawing Scale (Teachers College, Bureau of Publications)

Music Tests

Beach Music Tests (Kansas State Teachers College)
Courtis Music Test (S. A. Courtis)
Drake Musical Memory Test (Public School Publishing Co.)
Gildersleeve Music Achievement Test (Teachers College, Bureau of Publications)
Hildbrand Sight Singing Test (World Book)
Hutchinson Music Tests (Public School Publishing Co.)
Kelsey Standardized Tests of Musical Accomplishment (C. A. Gregory)
Knuth Achievement Tests in Music (Educational Records Bureau)
Kwalwasser-Dykema Music Tests (Fischer Co.)
Kwalwasser-Ruch Test of Musical Accomplishment (State University of Iowa)
Kwalwasser Test of Music Information and Appreciation (State University of Iowa)
McCauley Examination in Public School Music (Joseph E. Avent)
Oregon Music Discrimination Tests (Stoelting)
Otterstein-Mosher Sight Singing Test (Stanford University Press)
Plymouth Educational Test in Music (Plymouth Press)
Providence Inventory Test in Music (World Book)
Seashore Music Talent Test (State University of Iowa)
Torgerson-Fahnestock Music Test (Public School Publishing Co.)

Laboratory Tests

Briggs Analogies Test (Teachers College, Bureau of Publications)
Burt Graded Reasoning Test—mimeographed copy (Guidance Laboratory)
Coordination Test (Association Press)
Directions Tests I, II, III, and IV (Stoelting)
Goddard Memory Picture Test (Stoelting)
Plymouth Educational Miscellaneous Laboratory Tests (Plymouth Press)
Ruggles Distraction Test (Association Press)
Speed Tests (Association Press)
Thurstone Substitution Test (Stoelting)
Whipple Analogies Test (Stoelting)

Mechanical Ability Tests

Badger: Mechanical Drawing Test (Public School Publishing Co.)
Detroit Mechanical Aptitude Tests—forms for girls and forms for boys (Public School Publishing Co.)
Institute of Educational Research Paper Cutting Test (Stoelting)

Kelley Construction Ability Test (Stoelting)
MacQuarrie Test for Mechanical Ability (Southern California School Book Depository)
Minnesota Paper Form Board Test (University of Minnesota)
Newkirk-Stoddard Home Mechanics Tests (State University of Iowa)
Stenquist Mechanical Aptitude Test (Stoelting)
Wright Achievement Test in Mechanical Drawing (Public School Publishing Co.)

Attitude and Opinion Scales

Attitudes S-A Test (Association Press)
Bruner-Linden: Tentative Check List for Determining the Positions Held by Students on Forty Crucial World Problems (Teachers College, Bureau of Publications)
Harper, H. R. Study of Opinions, Feelings and Attitudes Concerning International Problems (Association Press)
Harper, M. A Social Study (Teachers College, Bureau of Publications)
Hart: A Test of Social Attitudes and Interests (State University of Iowa)
Lentz: C-R Opinionnaire (Character Research Institute)
Maller-Tuttle: Social Orientation Test (Maller)
Neumann-Kulp-Davidson: Test of International Attitudes (Teachers College, Bureau of Publications)
Noll: What Do You Think? (Teachers College, Bureau of Publications)
Opinions on International Questions (Association Press)
Opinions on Race Relations (Association Press)
Palmer: What do you think about Orientals in the United States? (Friendship Press)
Pintner General Opinion Test—mimeographed (Pintner)
Raup: Teachers' Views on Some Problems in General Educational Theory (Teachers College, Bureau of Publications)
Sweet: Measurement of Personal Attitudes in Younger Boys (Association Press)
Thurstone: Measurement of Attitude toward the Bible (University of Chicago Press)
Thurstone: Measurement of Attitude toward Birth Control (University of Chicago Press)
Thurstone: Measurement of Attitude toward Church (University of Chicago Press)
Thurstone: Measurement of Attitude toward the Germans (University of Chicago Press)
Thurstone: Measurement of Attitude toward God (University of Chicago Press)
Thurstone: Measurement of Attitude toward the Negro (University of Chicago Press)
Thurstone: Measurement of Attitude toward Patriotism (University of Chicago Press)

APPENDIX

Thurstone: Measurement of Attitude toward War (University of Chicago Press)
Watson Test of Public Opinion (Teachers College, Bureau of Publications)

RELIGIOUS ATTITUDES AND INFORMATION TESTS

Case Test of Liberal Thought (Teachers College, Bureau of Publications)
Laycock Test of Biblical Information (Association Press)
Test of Religious Thinking, Advanced Form (Association Press)
Test of Religious Thinking, Elementary Form (Association Press)
Union Tests of Ethical Judgment (Union Theological Seminary)
Union Tests of Religious Ideas (Union Theological Seminary)

ENVIRONMENT MEASURES

Chapin: Measurement of Social Status (University of Minnesota)
McCormick Scale for Measuring Social Adequacy (Catholic University Press)
Sims Score Card for Socio Economic Status (Public School Publishing Co.)
Wallin Home Conditions, Personal and Family History Blank (Stoelting)
Whittier's Scale for Grading Neighborhood Conditions (California Bureau of Juvenile Research)

PERSONALITY TESTS

High School and College Level

Allport A-S Reaction Study—forms for men and forms for women (Houghton Mifflin)
Allport: A Study of Personality—a systematic questionnaire (Stoelting)
Allport-Vernon Study of Values (Houghton Mifflin)
Almack: Sense of Humor Test (Gregory)
American Council on Education Rating Scale, Revised Form B (American Council on Education)
Beckman: Revision of the A-S Reaction Study for Business Use (Houghton Mifflin)
Bell: Adjustment Inventory (Stanford University Press)
Bernreuter Personality Inventory (Stanford University Press)
Bregman Comprehensive Individual History Form (Psychological Corporation)
Brotemarkle: Comparison of Moral Concepts (Stoelting)
Cason: Annoyance Test—(mimeographed copy) (Guidance Laboratory)
Character Education Inquiry Interest Analysis Test (Association Press)
Chassell's Experience Variables Record (J. O. Chassell)
Colgate Emotional Outlet Tests (Hamilton Republican)
Davis: Personal Problems Test (Stoelting)
Detroit Scale of Behavior Factors (Case Record) (Macmillan)
Dougherty-O'Reilly Character Inventory Chart (Public School Publishing Co.)
Humm-Wadsworth Temperament Scale (Psychological Corp.)
Jones: Shall I Go to College (Public School Publishing Co.)
Kohs: Ethical Discrimination Test (Stoelting)

Lehman: Play Quiz (Association Press)
Loofbourow-Keys: Personal Index (Educational Test Bureau)
MacNitt: A Psychological Interview (Psychological Corp.)
Maller Case Inventory (Teachers College, Bureau of Publications)
Maller Character Sketches (Teachers College, Bureau of Publications)
Maller Controlled Association Test (Teachers College, Bureau of Publications)
Maller Personality Sketches (Teachers College, Bureau of Publications)
Maller Self-Marking Test (Teachers College, Bureau of Publications)
Minnesota Personality Traits Rating Scales (Stoelting)
Ohio State Personality Report Blank (Ohio State University)
Otis Suggestibility Test (Stoelting)
Pressey Interest-attitude Test (Psychological Corp.)
Pressey Sports Information Test (Stoelting)
Psychotic Questionnaire (Stoelting)
Root: Introversion-extroversion Test (Psychological Corp.)
Rorschach Psychodiagnostic Test (Bircher)
Shields: Moral Knowledge Test (F. J. Shields)
Smith: Self-comparison Inventory (University of Minnesota)
Strang: Test of Knowledge of Social Usage (Teachers College, Bureau of Publications)
Stephenson-Millet: Test on Social Usage (McKnight and McKnight)
Symonds: Adjustment Questionnaire (Psychological Corp.)
Symonds: Student Questionnaire (Teachers College, Bureau of Publications)
Thurstone Personality Schedule (University of Chicago Press)
Wechsler Self-administering Maze (Psychological Corp.)
Willoughby Emotional Maturity Scale (Stanford University Press)

Tests and Rating Scales in Education

For College Students, Teachers, Supervisors, and Principals

Almy-Sorenson Rating Scale for Teachers (Public School Publishing Co.)
Bathurst-Knight-Ruch-Telford: Aptitude Test for Elementary and High School Teachers (Bureau of Public Personnel Administration)
Bathurst-Knight-Ruch-Telford: Placement Test for Elementary Teachers (Bureau of Public Personnel Administration)
Brown: A Self-rating Scale for Supervisors, Supervisory-principals and Helping Teachers (Bruce)
Brueckner: Judgment Test of Teaching Skill (Educational Test Bureau)
Carrigan Score Card for Rating Teaching and the Teacher (World Book)
Cooperative Professional Education Test (Educational Records Bureau)
Coxe-Orleans Prognosis Test of Teaching Ability (World Book)
Edmond-Schorling: Practical Problems in Education (Public School Publishing Co.)
Frasier-Armentrout: An Introduction to Education (Scott, Foresman)
George Washington University Teaching Aptitude Test (Center for Psychological Service)

Geyer: Objective Examination on Intelligence Testing (Plymouth Press)
Howe-Kyte: Diagnostic Record of Teaching (Houghton Mifflin)
Johnson: Checking List and Standards for Supervision of High School Instruction (Teachers College, Bureau of Publications)
Jordan: Objective Tests on Educational Psychology (Holt)
Lewerenz-Steinmetz: Orientation Test Concerning Fundamental Aims of Education (Southern California School Book Depository)
Michigan Education Association Teacher Self-rating Scale for Self-improvement (Michigan Education Association)
Odell-Herriott: Standard Achievement Test in Principles of Teaching (Public School Publishing Co.)
Peik: Recitation Analysis and Survey Check List (Educational Test Bureau)
Potthoff-Corey: Tests in Educational Psychology (Public School Publishing Co.)
Schutte: Scale for Rating Teachers (World Book)
Stanford Educational Aptitude Test (Stanford University Press)
Van Hoesen: Comprehensive Examination in Education (Ann Arbor Press)
Van Wagenen Reading Scales in Educational Psychology (Educational Test Bureau)
Votaw-Grinnel: Standardized Examination on Principles of Secondary Education (Harlow)
Waples and Reavis: Classroom Procedure Test (University of Chicago Press)
Weber: Standard Achievement Test on Aims, Purposes, Objectives, Attributes and Functions in Secondary Education (Public School Publishing Co.)
Woodworth: Revised Standardized Examination in Psychology (Holt)

VOCATIONAL TESTS AND INTEREST SCALES

A-B-C Occupational Inventory (Publication Press)
Aids to Vocational Interview, Record Form B (Psychological Corp.)
Brainard Specific Inventories, Forms for Men, Women, Boys, and Girls (Psychological Corp.)
Comprehensive Objective Examination in Commercial Law (Harlow)
Crabbe-Slinker: Achievement Test for General Business Training (South-Western Publishing Co.)
Dillavou-Greiner: Business and Law Objective Test (McGraw-Hill)
Freyd: Occupational Interest Blank for Men (Stoelting)
George Washington University Aptitude Test for Nursing (Center for Psychological Service)
George Washington University Scholastic Aptitude Test for Medical Students (Center for Psychological Service)
George Washington University Test for Ability to Sell (Center for Psychological Service)
George Washington University Test for Automobile Drivers (Center for Psychological Service)

Hepner Vocational Interest Quotient Booklets (Psychological Corp.)
Hoppock Questionnaire for Studies of Job Satisfaction (Robert Hoppock)
Leahy-Fenlason Rating Scale for Social Case Workers (University of Minnesota Press)
Leonard Rating Scale for Predicting Success (Houghton Mifflin)
Lufburrow Vocational Interest Locator (Publication Press)
McHale Vocational Interest Test for College Women (American Association of University Women)
Manson Occupational Interest Blank for Women (Psychological Corp.)
Miner Analysis of Work Interests (Stoelting)
Minnesota Interest Analysis Blank (University of Minnesota)
Morris Trait Index (Public School Publishing Co.)
Ohio State Educational and Vocational Information Blank (Ohio State University)
Ohio State Educational Intentions Blank (Ohio State University)
Ohio State Vocational Information Blank (Ohio State University)
Otis General Intelligence Examination for Business Institutions (World Book)
Parke Commercial Law Test (Kansas State Teachers College)
Personnel Counseling Service Blanks (Cooperative Counseling Service)
Personnel Research Federation Personal History Record (Bureau of Personnel Research, Personnel Research Federation)
Prosser-Anderson: Practice Book on Getting a Job (McKnight and McKnight)
Public Personnel Administration Test for Automobile Mechanics (Bureau of Public Personnel Administration)
Record of Proficiency in Nursing Practice (University of Minnesota Press)
Sondquist Interest Finder (Association Press)
Steno-gauge Test (Psychological Corp.)
Strong Vocational Interest Blank for Men (Stanford University Press)
Strong Vocational Interest Blank for Women (Stanford University Press)
Stuart Objective Tests in Typewriting (Gregg)
Teeter Objective Tests in Guidance (McGraw-Hill)
Thurstone Vocational Guidance Test in Algebra (World Book)
Thurstone Vocational Guidance Test in Arithmetic (World Book)
Thurstone Vocational Guidance Test in Geometry (World Book)
Thurstone Vocational Guidance Test in Physics (World Book)
Thurstone Vocational Guidance Test in Technical Information (World Book)
Thurstone Vocational Interest Schedule (Psychological Corp.)
Westin Commercial Law Achievement Test (Southern California School Book Depository)

Clerical Ability

Graphic Rating Scale for Clerical Workers—mimeographed (Guidance Laboratory)
Linke and Koehne: Topical Filing Test (Stoelting)
Minnesota Vocational Test for Clerical Workers (Psychological Corp.)

O'Rourke Clerical Aptitude Test (Educational and Personnel Publishing Co.)
Scott Filing Test (Stoelting)
Thurstone Employment Test in Clerical Work (World Book)

BOOKKEEPING

Bowman Bookkeeping Achievement Test (American Book Co.)
Detroit Bookkeeping Examination (Board of Education, Detroit)
Ellwell-Fowlkes Bookkeeping Test (World Book)

STENOGRAPHY

Bisbee Shorthand Test (Public School Publishing Co.)
Blackstone Stenographic Proficiency Test (World Book)
Comprehensive Objective Examination in Gregg Shorthand (Harlow)
Detroit Shorthand Examination (Board of Education, Detroit)
Hoke: Prognostic Test of Stenographic Ability (Gregg)
Hoke: Tests in Gregg Shorthand (Gregg)
Rollinson Diagnostic Shorthand Tests (Psychological Corp.)

TYPEWRITING

Clem's Typewriting Test (Public School Publishing Co.)
Kauzer Typewriting Test (Kansas State Teachers College)
North's Objective Tests for Teachers of Typewriting (Gregg)
Stuart Objective Tests in Typewriting (Gregg)
Thurstone Employment Test in Typewriting (World Book)

PERFORMANCE TEST MATERIAL

Ferguson Form Boards (Stoelting)
I. E. R. Assembly Test for Girls (Stoelting)
Minnesota Assembly Boxes I and II (Stoelting)
Minnesota Assembly Test, A-B-C (Stoelting)
Minnesota Card Sorting Test (Stoelting)
Minnesota Packing Blocks Test (Stoelting)
Minnesota Spacial Relations Test (University of Minnesota)
Otis Test of Suggestibility—cards for test (Stoelting)
Passalong Test (J. and J. Cook)
Stenquist Mechanical Tests I, II, III (Stoelting)

ADDRESSES OF PUBLISHERS OF PSYCHOLOGICAL TESTS

Alabama Polytechnic Institute, Auburn, Ala.
American Association of University Women, 106 East 52 St., New York.
American Book Company, 88 Lexington Ave., New York.
American Council on Education, 744 Jackson Place, Washington, D. C.
Ann Arbor Press, Ann Arbor, Mich.
Association Press, 347 Madison Ave., New York.
Avent, Joseph E., Box 1455, Knoxville, Tenn.
Bircher, Ernst, Verlag, Bern und Leipzig, Germany.
Bruce Publishing Co., 40 East 34 St., New York.

Buffalo, University of, Buffalo, N. Y.
California Bureau of Juvenile Research, Whittier State School, Whittier, Calif.
Catholic University of America, Washington, D. C.
Center for Psychological Service, 2026 G Street, N. W., Washington, D. C.
Character Research Institute, Washington University, St. Louis, Mo.
Chassell, Dr. J. O., University of Rochester, Rochester, N. Y.
Chicago Press, University of, Chicago, Ill.
Cincinnati, University of, Cincinnati, Ohio.
Clatworthy, L. M., University of Denver, Denver, Colo.
Clio Press, Iowa City, Iowa.
Cook, J. and J., Paisley, and Glasgow, Scotland.
Cooperative Counseling Service, 715 South Hope St., Los Angeles, Calif.
Cooperative Test Bureau, 347 West 59 St., New York.
Curtis, Dr. S. A., 1807 East Grand Blvd., Detroit, Mich.
Detroit, Board of Education, Detroit, Mich.
Education and Personnel Publishing Co., Washington, D. C.
Educational Records Bureau, 437 West 59 St., New York.
Educational Test Bureau, 3416 Walnut St., Philadelphia, Pa.
Farley, Eugene S., Director of Research, Newark, N. J.
Fischer Company, 56 Cooper Sq., New York.
Friendship Press, 150 Fifth Ave., New York.
Ginn and Company, 15 Ashburton Pl., Boston, Mass.
Gregg Publishing Company, 270 Madison Ave., New York.
Gregory Co., C. A., 347 Calhoun Street, Cincinnati, Ohio.
Guidance Laboratory, Teachers College, Columbia University, New York.
Hamilton Republican, Hamilton, N. Y.
Handschin, C. H., Miami University, Oxford, Ohio.
Harcourt, Brace & Company, 383 Madison Ave., New York.
Harlow Publishing Co., 217 North Harvey, Oklahoma City, Okla.
Harrap & Company, Ltd., George G., 39–41 Parker St., Kingsway, London, W. C. 2, England.
Heath & Company, D. C., 285 Columbus Ave., Boston, Mass.
Henry Holt & Company, 1 Park Ave., New York.
Houghton Mifflin Company, 2 Park St., Boston, Mass.
Illinois, University of, Urbana, Ill.
Independent Press, Mexico, N. Y.
Iowa, State University of, Bureau of Educational Research and Service, Iowa City, Iowa.
Johns Hopkins Press, Baltimore, Md.
Kansas State Teachers College, Bureau of Educational Measurements, Emporia, Kans.
Keystone View Company, Meadville, Pa.
Lafayette Printing Company, Lafayette, Indiana.
Lippincott & Company, J. B., 227 South 6th St., Philadelphia, Pa.
Little, Brown & Company, 34 Beacon St., Boston, Mass.
McGraw-Hill Book Company, Inc., 330 West 42 Street, New York.
McKnight and McKnight, Bloomington, Ill.

APPENDIX

Macmillan Company, The, 60 Fifth Ave., New York.
Maller, Dr. Julius B., Teachers College, Columbia University, New York.
Mentzer, Bush and Company, 55 Fifth Ave., New York.
Michigan Education Association, Lansing, Mich.
Minnesota Press, University of, Minneapolis, Minn.
Missouri, University of, Columbia, Mo.
Mount Holyoke College, South Hadley, Mass.
Nebraska, University of, Extension Division, Lincoln, Neb.
New Mexico, University of, Albuquerque, N. M.
North Carolina, University of, Chapel Hill, N. C.
Northwestern High School, Detroit, Mich.
Oculo-Photometer, Educational Laboratories, Brownwood, Tex.
Ohio State University, Columbus, Ohio.
Personnel Research Federation, 29 West 39 St., New York.
Philadelphia, Board of Education, Philadelphia, Pa.
Pintner, Dr. R., Teachers College, Columbia University, New York.
Plymouth Press, 6749 Wentworth Ave., Chicago, Ill.
Psychological Corporation, 522 Fifth Ave., New York.
Psychological Institute, 3506 Patterson Street, N. W., Washington, D. C.
Public Personnel Administration, Bureau of, Box 226, Trenton, N. J.
Public School Publishing Company, Bloomington, Ill.
Publication Press, 1511 Guilford Ave., Baltimore, Md.
Russell Sage Foundation, 130 East 22 St., New York.
Scott, Foresman & Company, 114 East 23 St., New York.
Scribner's Sons, Charles, 597 Fifth Ave., New York.
Shields, F. J., 1594 Whitefield Rd., Pasadena, Calif.
Smith and Company, Turner E., 424 West Peachtree Street, N. W., Atlanta, Ga.
Southern California School Book Depository, 1927 North Highland Ave., Hollywood, Calif.
Stanford University Press, Stanford University, Calif.
State University of Iowa, Ames, Iowa.
Stoelting Co., C. H., 424 North Homan Ave., Chicago, Ill.
Teachers College, Bureau of Publications, Columbia University, New York.
Time, Inc., 135 East 42 St., New York.
Transient Center, 159 Swan St., Buffalo, N. Y.
Union Theological Seminary, 3041 Broadway, New York.
Van Cleve Publishers, State College, Pa.
Webb-Duncan Company, 311 North Harvey, Oklahoma City, Okla.
World Book Company, Yonkers-on-Hudson, New York.

INDEX

A

Administration, functions of, 276
    human relations important in, 265–267
    principles of good, 265–266
Administrator, of financial aid, qualifications, duties and responsibilities of, 150–151
    a good, qualifications of, 267
Admissions and selection, 51–69
    a good system of, 65
Admissions plan of Ohio State College Association, 62, 63
Adolescent Study of Progressive Education Association, 284
Aiken Commission of the Progressive Education Association, 252
Allport, F. H., 133
American Association of University Women, 220
American College Personnel Association, 286
American Council on Education, 256, 286
    cumulative personnel record folder, 256
American Council of Guidance and Personnel Associations, 286
Amos, Thyrsa, 178
Angell, R. C., 186, 221
Aspects of student personnel program, 21
Assistants in personnel office, selection and training of, 270
Athletics, 170

B

Badgley, Herbert, 151
Bennett, Mary, 63

Bennington College, 199
Black Mountain College, 206
Bogardus, Emory S., 167
Boring, M. M., 240
Bower, William Clayton, 220
Brewer, John M., 139, 165
Brogdon, Mary C., 205
Business administration, coordination between instructional program, student personnel program and, 22
Business officers, cooperation between personnel office and, 193
Business program, functions or services of, 23

C

Calendar of preparations for freshman week, 87–88
Campus community, coordination of administration, faculty and students in, 177
Carnegie Foundation, 284
Carrell, Alexis, 99
Case studies, 282
Chambers, M. M., 147
Chapel, 228–229
Chapin, Stuart F., 175, 176
Cheek, Mary Ashby, 199
Choice of vocations, factors that contribute to, 142
Cleavage lines in higher education, 7–11
Clinical method in study of individual, 131–134, 141–142
Collective opinion, importance of, in disciplinary program, 124–126
Committees, desirable size of, 186
Control of social environment, 95–100

313

Coordination, between business administration, instructional program and student personnel program, 22
  of participants in student personnel program, 44
  of program for educational and vocational guidance, 142
  of research, 286
Coordinator, duties of, 44–47
Cooperation of students, faculty and administration in campus community, 177
Cornell University, 136, 213
Councils, 276
Counseling, 102–118
  fourteen points pertinent to, 110–116
  importance of, with respect to vocational interests, 103, 104
  overintellectualization of, 110–116
  specialists in, 108–110
  typical organizations of, 104–106
  value of cumulative personnel records in, 261
  various levels of, 107–108
Counseling programs, reasons for increasing frequency of, 102
  typical organizations of, 104–106
  use of psychiatrists in, 109–110
Counselors, approaches possible for, 106–108
  curriculum at Northwestern University for sophomore, 77–86
  designation of special, 44
  difficulties that are faced by, 112
  faculty, 76, 87
  in personnel programs, 44
  in religious program, 230–231
  sophomore, 76–77, 86–87
  student, 76–77, 86–87
  and student personnel records, 257
Cowley, W. H., 18, 26, 102, 165, 280
Cumulative personnel records, 249–251, 256, 261–263
  use of, manual of instructions for, 262
  in selective admissions, 54

Cumulative personnel records, values of, for personal counseling, 261
Curriculum, place of extracurricular division in, 166
  for sophomore counselors at Northwestern University, 77–86
  use of, in vocational program, 136

D

Darley, J. D., 140
Denominationalism, role of, in religious program, 225–226
Development of student personnel program, determining factors in, 36
Development of value concepts, 95–100
Dewey, John, 122
Diagrammatic representation, of relationship between business program, instructional program, and student personnel program, 22
  of student personnel program, 21
Dining room, and the social program, 203
  table assignments in, 202–203
  well-run, goals of, 202
Director of admissions, qualifications and duties of, 66, 67
Disciplinary officer, qualifications, responsibilities and duties of, 127–128
Disciplinary program, aspects of prevalent, 121–124
  assumptions underlying the, 120–121
  importance of collective opinion in the, 124–126
  influences of faculty in, 123
  responsibility of personnel workers in, 123–124
  use of advisory council in, 127–128
Discipline, 119–128
  in dormitories, 195
  various philosophies of, 119

Disciplined individuals, the development of, 119–120
    influences in, 123–124
Dormitories, administration of, 191–208
    assigning of students to rooms in, 196
    dining facilities in, 202
    distribution of students in, 195–196
    financing the social program of, 200
    functions of night employees in, 197–198
    health program in, 200–201
    importance of building traditions in, 194
    as an influence in the scholastic success of students, 204
    origin and present operation, 191
    recreational facilities in, 201
    rules and regulations in, 194
    social and recreational program of, 198
    use of record systems in, 197
Duffus, R. L., 5
Duties of coordinator, 44–47

E

Educational guidance, 129–134
    close relationship of vocational guidance to, 133–134
    coordination of, 142
    definition of, 131
    important considerations in, 143
    personnel point of view in, 131
    personnel techniques useful in, 141–142
    purpose of, 130
    typical organizational plans for, 135–137
Edwards, R. H., 165, 181, 233
Eliot, Charles W., 6
Employer-employee relationships, 270–271
Extracurricular activities, 165–189
    annual reports of, 175

Extracurricular activities, correlation between social adjustments and, 186
    developing of leaders by, 168
    disadvantages of, 167
    effect on scholastic standing, 176–177
    faculty-student committee in, 173
    guidance for nonparticipating students in, 176
    importance to undergraduates, 165
    opportunities offered by, 186
    a part of curriculum, 165–166
    percentage of students participating in, 175
    point system in, 171
    relation of personnel officer to, 185–186
    stimulating participation in, 170–171
    student government as a form of, 169–177
    survey of, 174
    various forms of, 169–170

F

Faculty, as counselors, 76, 87
    influences of, as individuals, 123
    participation in religious program, 228, 230
    use of, in reorganizing system of records, 251–253
Fellowships and scholarships, restriction by donors, 159
    study of, 151–152
"Fifth wheel" of higher education, 14
Financial aid, 147–164
    application blank for, 152
    centralization of, 151
    for emergency situations, 156
    need for a definite philosophy of, 150
    philosophy of, 147
    proposed remedy for existing situation, 150

Financial aid, at public expense, 147–148
  recommendations for, 160–161
  suggested form card for, 160–161
  survey of, 149
  typical system of, 149–150
  various types of, 148
Financing the social program in the dormitories, 200
Findex system, use of, 241
Flexner, Abraham, 4
Fosdick, Harry Emerson, 221
Fraternities and sororities, 169
  arguments in favor of, 182–183
  constructive use of, 184
  objections to, 183
Freshman adjustments, 70–74
Freshman week, 74–77
  calendar of preparations for, 87–88
  its purpose with respect to vocational guidance, 138
Frequency of personnel titles, 29–34
Functions and services, of business program, 23
  of instructional program, 23
  of student personnel program, 23–25

G

Gauss, Christian, 224
Gray, George W., 221, 223
Group adviser, duty of, 185–186

H

Harmon Foundation, 154–155
Harvard University, 199
Hawkes, H. E., 250
Hayes, Harriet, 201, 202, 206
Head of residence, qualifications and duties of, 192–198, 201, 211–212
  records for, 197
Health, the concept of, 209
  as a major objective of education, 209
Health adviser, 215

Health council, 211–212
Health program, 209–219
  coordination of social and recreational program with, 212
  director of, 213, 217–218
  the objectives of, 210
  physical education and the, 212
  physical examinations in, 212
  the psychiatrist in, 214
  records for, 215
  responsibility of personnel staff in, 211–213, 215, 218
  supervision of, 210
  tie-up between program of admissions and, 212
  value of physiology and hygiene classes in, 216–217
Health reports, 216
Health service, 212–213
  community hospital and the, 212, 214
  financial arrangements for, 214–215
Helping students, to belong in college, 70–91
  to learn social wisdom and skill, 92–100
Higher education, assumptions underlying the disciplinary program of an institution of, 120–121
  confliction of ideas in, 3, 4
  objectives of, 12, 13
  philosophy of, 3, 5, 7–11
  progression of patterns in, 5
  relation of student personnel program to, 3–15
  religion in, 220
Hollerith machine, 241, 262
House government, student participation in, 193
House manager, responsibility of, 192, 193
Housemothers, cooperation between personnel staff and, 205
  desirable traits of, 205
  organization of, 205

INDEX

Housing, 190–208
 various plans of, 199
Hughes, William Leonard, 210
Hutchins, Robert Maynard, 4

I

Individual, study of, 131–134, 141–142
Individualized education, modern theory of, 5, 6
Infirmary, 212
Instructional program, coordination between business administration, student personnel program and, 22
 functions or services of, 23
Interdenominationalism, role of, in religious program, 225–226
Interest in student personnel program, 26–27

J

Jessup, Walter Albert, 35
Johnstone, Edgar G., 171
Jones, Arthur J., 134

K

Katz, Daniel, 133
Kent, Raymond A., 13, 19
Kitson, Harry D., 136, 280
Kurani, Habib Amin, 60

L

Leaders, use of extracurricular activities in developing, 168
Leadership, definition of, 167
Leadership traits, study of, in college women, 167–168
Lemaître, Abbé, 222
Levels of admission practices, 52–61
Levine, Albert J., 116
Lloyd-Jones, Esther, 18, 21, 26–27, 95, 256

Loan funds, administration of, 154
 increase of, during depression, 152–153
 sources of, 160
 study of, 155
 types of, 155
Loans to students, bases for, 153
 security for, 155–156
Locke, John, 5
Lowell, A. Lawrence, 4
Lyford, Carrie Alberta, 203

M

McCalister, W. H., 180–181
McKnight, N. D., 156
Middlebury College, 172
Minrow, Maude E., 205
Money-raising drives, problem of, 184
Moon, George R., 148
Moore, L. H., 167–168
Murphy, Lois Barclay, 284–285

N

National Association of Deans of Women, 286
National Occupational Conference, 286
National Youth Administration, 149, 158–159, 283

O

Objectives of higher education, 12, 13
Occupational class in vocational guidance program, 136, 137
Occupational conference, 138
Occupational Index, 138–139
Occupational information, need for research on, 283
Off-campus houses, 204–206
Office administration, 265–277
Ogan, R. W., 62
Ohio experiment in selection and admission of students, 56–57, 62–63

Onthank, Karl, 156
Oregon plan for recruiting of students, 63–65
Organization of personnel work, 27–28
  best plan for, 36–40
  typical examples of, 41–43
Orientation, 70–91
Oxford University, 199

P

Part-time work, administration of, 157–158
  coordination of, 157
  disadvantages and dangers of, 156–157
  need for careful records in program of, 157
Pennsylvania Study, 54–55
Periodicals and abstracts useful to personnel workers, 287
Persing, Alma Stack, 77
Personnel director, availability of, 271–272
  and the religious program, 224–228, 232
Personnel office, cooperation between business office and, 193
  equipment and furnishings, 269
  location of, 268–269
  organization of, 268–269
Personnel officer, 282, 284–285
  relation to extracurricular activities, 185–186
  and research, 279
  routine duties of, 268
Personnel program, housing units as subpersonnel divisions of, 190–192
Personnel programs, designation of special counselors in, 44
  typical examples of organization of, 41–43
Personnel records, 247–264
  best method for introducing a system of cumulative, 249–254

Personnel records, control of, 257–259
  four difficulties in introducing adequate, 248–249
  general types of, 247
  suggested plan for a system of, 251–253
  who should use, 257–259
Personnel research, 280–285
Personnel services, wide variability of, 35
Personnel staff, cooperation between housemothers and, 205
  responsibility in health program, 211–213, 215, 218
Personnel techniques, use of in educational and vocational guidance, 141–142
Personnel titles, frequency of, 29–34
Personnel workers, disciplinary responsibility of, 123–124
Philosophy and organization, 36–48
Physical examinations of students, 212
Pitkin, Walter B., 133
Placement, 235–246
  coordination of efforts at, 243
  counseling in, 239–240
  cultivating opportunities for, 242
  decentralized, 243
  follow-up program, 242–243
  of graduates, 240
  obtaining information concerning opportunities for, 240–241
  types of students who are preferred for, 241
  vocational guidance in 239–240
  vocational guidance program related to, 142
Placement office, discreet use of records in, 208
  expense of operating, 244
  functions of, 236–241, 244
  purpose of, 235–236
Placement officer, 237–238, 240, 242, 244
  information for the use of, 237–238, 240–241
  qualifications of, 244

INDEX

Point system, 171
Price, Louise, 166
Progressive Education Association, Aiken Commission of, 252
   its project for improving secondary education, 58–59
Psychiatrists, use of, in counseling program, 109–110
Publications, criteria for evaluating, 181
   how the school may be served by, 181
   how the students may be served by, 181
   voluntary employment of students in, 181–182

R

Record area, model for, 253
Record files, 259–260
Record system, centralization of, 253–255
   decentralization of, 254–255
   enlisting interest in, 262
Records, classification of, 272–274
   desirability of duplicating, 260
   ethical use of, 256
   general principles for making, 274–276
   organization of a central system of, 260
   system for duplicating, 261
Recruiting of students, methods used for, 61–65
   Oregon plan for, 63–65
   plan of Commission on College Entrance of Ohio College Association for, 62–63
Religion, 220–234
   courses in, 231
   definitions of, 220–221
   factors which contribute to students attitude toward, 221–222
   in higher education, 220
   indifference of students to organized, 221–222
   intercollegiate conferences on, 225
   neglect of, 222
   programs for men and women in, 226–227
   science and, 222
   some attitudes of students toward, 223–224
   value of student leadership in, 227
Religious education, need for, 220, 222–223
   value of chapel program in, 228–229
Religious organization, 232
   standards of, 225
   student participation in, 230
Religious program, community churches in, 231–232
   controversial social questions and the, 226
   coordinator of, 232
   counselors in, 230–231
   criteria for success of, 233
   difficulties in organization of, 227
   director of personnel and the, 224–228, 232
   elements in a good, 227
   faculty participation in, 228, 230
   the role of denominationalism in, 225–226
   week-end conferences in, 230
Report, annual, 276
Research and evaluation, 278–290
   central clearinghouse for, 286
   criticism of, 283
   dangers of bias in, 285
   function of, in personnel program, 278–279
   importance of efficient record keeping in, 279
   need for coordination of, 286
   sociological and sociopsychological, 283–285
   student personnel work and, 280–282
   suggested list of periodicals and abstracts for, 287

Residence halls, study of cooperative, 206
Reynolds, R. G., 238

S

Sarah Lawrence College, 166
Scholarships, effect on freshmen, 148
  sources of funds for, 159
Scope and organization of student personnel program, 26–48
Scott, William E., 175
Secondary education, Progressive Education Association's project for improving, 58–59
Selection and admission of students, 51–69
  bases of, 51–52
  levels of, 52–61
  Ohio experiment in, 56–57
  Pennsylvania Study in relation to, 54–55
  use of cumulative record in, 54
Services of student personnel program, 20, 23–25
Smith, Margaret Ruth, 149, 155
Social adjustments, use of extracurricular activities in, 186
Social clubs, 169
Social connections, factors in determining, 93–94
Social education, program of, 92–100
Social environment, control of, 95–100
Social program, 92–100
  and the dining room, 203
Social wisdom, helping students to acquire, 92–100
Sociological and sociopsychological research, 283–285
Sociometrical methods in research, 284–285
Sophomore counselors, 76–77, 86–87
Sororities and fraternities, 169
  arguments in favor of, 182–183
  constructive use of, 184
  denominational, 230

Sororities and fraternities, objections to, 183
South, E. B., 186
Sports program, 170
Stephens College, 166
Stevens Institute of Technology, 137
Strang, Ruth, 26, 35, 52, 280
Student activities, democracy in, 168–169
  desirable characteristics of, 168–169
  good results from, 167
  limiting participation in, 170–172
  relation of personnel director to, 185
  at Sarah Lawrence College, 166–167
  stimulating participation in, 170–172
Student affairs, reports of, 173
  responsibility of personnel officer for, 173–175
Student counselors, 76–77, 86–87
Student employment, correlation with academic work, 158
Student government, coordination of faculty and students in, 177
  a form of extracurricular activity, 169–177
  role of, in disciplinary program, 127–128, 178
  women students in, 179
Student handbook, use of, 170
Student organizations, filing of records for, 175
  financial accounts of, 172
  meeting places of, 172
Student participation in government, 169–177
Student personnel program, 16–25
  aspects of, 18–22
  coordination of participants in, 44
  determining factors in development of, 36
  diagram, of aspects of, 21
  of coordination of business administration, instructional program and, 22

INDEX

Student personnel program, financial aid a part of, 161–162
  functions and services of, 23–25
  good organizational plan of, 36–40
  interest in, 26–27
  organization of, 27–28
  services included within, 20
  scope and organization of, 26–48
Student personnel records, 247–264
Student publications, 169
Student residents, responsibility of, 194
Students, methods used for recruiting of, 61–65
  orientation of, 70–91
  physical examinations of, 212
  selecting and admitting of, 51–69
  selection and admission of, 51–52
Students' organization, 177
  funds for, 180
  objectives of, 178
  officers and constitution of, 178–179
  program of, 180
Study of the individual, 131–134, 141–142
Summer jobs, value for vocational planning, 139
Surveys, their use in evaluation, 281
  types of, 280–285
Syracuse University, 133
System of admission, 65

T

Teachers College, Columbia University, 149
Terminology, confusion in, 16–17
Testing program, personnel workers in the, 141
Tests, addresses of publishers of, 309–311
  attitude and opinion, 304–305
  of clerical ability, 308–309
  educational achievement, 292–302
  of environment, 305
  general information and background, 292

Tests, group, 291
  individual, 291
  intelligence, 291
  laboratory, 303
  mechanical ability, 303
  music, 303
  nonlanguage and nonverbal, 291
  performance, 309
  of personality, 305
  purposes of, 139
  use of in vocational guidance, 139–141
  vision, 291
  vocational and interest, 307
Titles, frequency of personnel, 29–34
Typical examples of organization of personnel programs, 41–43

U

University of Chicago, 135, 175
University of Michigan, 186, 221
University of Minnesota, 137, 142, 175
University of Oregon, 156

V

Value concepts, development of, 95–100
Variability of personnel services, 35
Vocational guidance, close relationship of educational guidance to, 133–134
  coordination of, 142
  definition of, 129
  during freshman week, 138
  importance of curriculum in, 136
  importance of extracurricular activities in, 136
  important considerations in, 143
  the need for, 133
  occupational classes for, 136–137
  occupational conferences for, 138
  personnel point of view in, 131
  personnel techniques useful in, 141–142
  purpose of, 130
  relationship of other aspects of guidance to, 134

Vocational guidance, responsibility of colleges for, 7–9, 236
   typical organization plans of, 135–137
   use of summer tryout in, 139
   use of tests in, 139–141
Vocational interests, importance of counseling with respect to, 103–104

W

Walker, Ernest Timothy, 204
Waller, Willard, 165

Warren, Constance, 167
Wells, George C., 180–181
Whitney, R. E., 241
Williamson, E. G., 129, 135, 137, 140
Woellner, R. C., 152–153
Wood, Ben D., 139
Wriston, Henry Merritt, 4

Y

Yale University, 199
Y.M.C.A., 232
Y.W.C.A., 232